The Campus History Series

The Webb School of Bell Buckle

On the Cover: Early Tennis Team. Tennis, played at Webb at least as early as the 1890s, was offered to both male and female students. Pictured is the 1897–1898 tennis team, with the home of John M. Webb in the background. There are several Webb family members in this photograph. From left to right are (first row) Emma Webb (daughter of William R. "Sawney" Webb), Cornelia Webb (daughter of John), Sarah Webb (daughter of John), and Matt McFerrin; (second row) Irving Clary (nephew of Sawney's wife), Susan Webb (daughter of Sawney), Mary Webb (daughter of John), Maud Rankin, and Sam Berg; (third row) Steve Noland, Alfred Lund, John Childress, Frank Carr, and James House. The dog, Spica, was the pet of the John M. Webb family.

Cover Background: All-school Photograph in Culleoka. This building was the first structure built especially for The Webb School. Before this, the Webb brothers used the basement of a local church. According to the Maury County Historical Society, "when Sawney claimed his school was the first 'strictly preparatory school' west of the Alleghanies, all others, he said . . . 'were denominated colleges.' " Sawney was likely happy to move his nearly 100 students from the church basement to their own building in 1876.

The Campus History Series

THE WEBB SCHOOL OF BELL BUCKLE

SUSAN COOP HOWELL AND HANNAH BYRD LITTLE

ARCADIA PUBLISHING

ISBN 978-1-4671-0341-1

Published by Arcadia Publishing
Charleston, South Carolina

Printed in the United States of America

Library of Congress Control Number: 2019930774

For all general information, please contact Arcadia Publishing:
Telephone 843-853-2070
Fax 843-853-0044
E-mail sales@arcadiapublishing.com
For customer service and orders:
Toll-Free 1-888-313-2665

Visit us on the Internet at www.arcadiapublishing.com

*To The Webb School, a great place to work,
and to our families, the Coops, Howells, Byrds, and Littles.*

Contents

Acknowledgments

This work would not have been possible without the love and support of our families; thank you to Mark, Macy, and Cooper Howell and Blaine, Betsy, and Amanda Little.

We appreciate all of the logistical support from members of our alumni and development department, including Gayle McClanahan, Rita Mitchell, Alyce Allen, and especially, Dorothy Elkins.

We are indebted to the writers and editors of the student publications the *Oracle* newspaper and the *Sawney* yearbook throughout the years. We have relied on the alumni publications from the past 150 years, including the *Webb Magazine* and the *Alumni Bulletin*. Thanks to all of the editors and writers of these publications.

We would like to acknowledge those who helped to pass down the oral history of the school. Specifically, we would like to thank the members of the Webb family: Julie Webb, Thompson Webb III, Margaret Webb Reagan, and Susie Webb Ries, as well as faculty members, historians, and graduates like Glenn Holliman, Terry Barkley, Cecil Irvin, Ralph Jones, Maddie Rose Taff, and L.R. Smith.

We would like to show our appreciation for librarians, archivists, and record keepers who helped to preserve the substantial archives held by The Webb School Library and Archives; to Alla Webb and David McQuiddy, who preserved the mementos and information from the earliest days of our school; and to those who came later and realized the importance of preserving our history, including Lynn Holliman, Sandy Sanders, Penny Frere, Kimi Abernathy, and Marilyn Morgan.

Finally, to our students—we love you like our own children and hope, in the words of Sawney, that you "go out and lead a large life!"

All images in this book are courtesy of The Webb School Library and Archives. This book is just a sample of the extensive photograph and letter collection housed in our library and archives. We hope that this will merely whet your appetite to see more of our story at The Webb School of Bell Buckle.

INTRODUCTION

Webb's future is intimately connected to the values of its original visionaries.

The school was first located in Culleoka, Tennessee. It was founded in 1870 in the midst of Reconstruction by noted scholar and disabled Civil War veteran William R. "Sawney" Webb. The Webb School of Bell Buckle is the South's oldest continuously operating boarding school. In 1869, while teaching at the Horner School on the outskirts of Oxford, North Carolina, Sawney spoke at length with a fellow teacher about his dream of an "educational utopia." The very next year, W. H. Wilkes, the town father of Culleoka, wrote in a letter, "the school is yours."

The school, first known as Culleoka Institute, was housed in the basement of the Culleoka Methodist Church. The fall session began on August 8, 1870; the tuition for the preparatory school was between $10 and $15, and boarding was an additional $13–$15. According to files found at the Maury County Historical Society, Webb introduced teaching methods that were unconventional for the time. When not reciting lessons, students were free to come and go as they pleased to study and talk outside under the trees, as long as they did not disturb other students. When the residents questioned Sawney's methods, his response was "before I would imprison innocent children, I would quit the profession of teaching."

The first couple of years were a struggle, and in 1872, a local newspaper, the *Columbia Herald*, reported that Webb was afflicted with a mild form of smallpox. The school was dismissed between April 26 and May 13, 1872. In 1873, Sawney wrote his younger brother John M. Webb, asking him to join him at Culleoka. John too had been deeply affected by Reconstruction, in that his education was interrupted because of unrest and infighting at his university. He was eager to join his brother's new venture. Sawney was quite proud of his accomplished younger brother and placed an announcement of his arrival in the *Columbia Herald*. In the late 1870s, the school's name was changed to Webb Brothers' School. Although the brothers were offered professorships at Vanderbilt in 1875, they remained the school principals until their respective deaths: John Webb in 1916 and Sawney Webb in 1926.

Sawney married Emma Clary of Unionville, Tennessee, in the spring of 1873. She gave birth to their first son, William R. Webb Jr., in the spring of 1874. Sawney and Emma opened their own home to eight boarders in the 1874–1875 school year.

In the mid-1880s, problems arose when the town of Culleoka became incorporated and the local saloon owners began trying to sell liquor to Webb students. Sawney was a prohibitionist and impressed these standards on his students, so he soon began looking for somewhere to move the school. His wife's brother lived in Bell Buckle. Sawney made a connection with the townspeople, and in 1886, Bell Buckle became the school's new home.

Emma and Sawney's son William R. Webb Jr., called "Son Will," graduated from the University of North Carolina (UNC) in 1896. He joined the UNC faculty as an English professor the following year. After a year of teaching at UNC, he returned to Bell Buckle to teach at the school. In 1908, Son Will was made co-principal with his father and uncle, and the active management of the school was in his hands until 1953. When Son Will became one of the principals, the name of the school was again changed, this time becoming simply Webb School. In 1920, the alumni started the movement to raise funds for an endowment to provide for better equipment, expressing the "hope that they may perpetuate the fine instruction of the school when the present principals are gone." A board of trustees was elected and a charter secured. Son Will was beyond erudite and had a laser focus on several projects for research including Native Americans, World War I, and Tennessee highways. The Webb School Library and Archives is home to his extensive collection.

The Webb School of Bell Buckle has an unusual mission statement. The current mission of the school is an ideal that was penciled in the hand of one of the principals in 1875. In the 1970s, the statement was slightly revised to be gender neutral: "to turn out young people who are tireless workers and who know how to work effectively; who are accurate scholars, who know the finer points of morals and practice them in their daily living; who are always courteous." Besides the mission statement, other speeches by both Sawney and John revealed their pursuit of an educational ideal. In an address to the Southern Education Association in 1905, Sawney made a case for private schools. He assured his audience "public high school and the private high school are in no sense rivals, in no sense antagonistic and in no sense duplicates of the same advantages, they are supplementary." He spoke of progress and encouraged the private school to be an "experiment station for the children where authority in the use of tools and methods is not compulsory."

Beginning in 1946, the school became a single-sex school for a short period. This trend continued throughout the 1950s and 1960s under the leadership of Son Will, G.W. Follin Sr., John Lewis Morgan, Henry O. Whiteside, and Kenneth F. Stuckey. With the exception of these decades, the school had a number of female graduates over the years, and these students went on to do amazing things, including start schools of their own. Even when in Culleoka, Webb was a coeducational institution, and local girls, including many in the Webb family, attended as day students. Some of the female students from the 1870s until the late 1940s became university professors, college deans, nurses, teachers, and librarians. Female students returned to Webb in the 1970s. From then forward, they have enjoyed more equality in careers and have become naval officers, award-winning authors, doctors, lawyers, and business owners.

Not only did Webb welcome female students in the 1970s, it also welcomed these students into the residential program. Not long after the return of female students, the school began accepting more international students as well. In 1975, four students from The Gambia graduated from The Webb School. Before this era, international students were limited to the Americas, with possibly a few from Europe. Today, students and alumni from Webb represent more than 50 countries.

Traditions that tie the generations together include the mastery of content and skills. In the early days of Webb, graduation was based on whether or not one had sufficiently mastered the skills necessary to move on to college. Dating to the founders, The Webb School has placed great importance on its public-speaking curriculum, especially regarding declamations and chapel talks. The *Columbia Herald* on June 13, 1873, summarized the commencement ceremonies and makes mention of the speaking program: "The declamations were good, the selections were in the main unexceptionable." The most traditional assignment is the declamation, a memorized piece of literature with an original introduction written by the performer. Today, each sixth- through ninth-grade student presents a declamation to the student body during chapel. In 2012, the Emerging Voices program developed a progressive form for the subsequent years of high school students to build on the foundation of their declamation performance with an oration in 10th grade, a creative public performance in 11th grade, and a capstone presentation of their original research in their senior year.

Above all other traditions of The Webb School is the focus on honor and integrity. Students sign honor books at the beginning of each year, they write an honor pledge on every major assessment, and there is a student-elected honor council that presides over disciplinary matters related to honor offenses. The school's motto is a Latin phrase that translates to English as "Do Nothing on the Sly." Two students from the class of 1889 took this honor system with them to college and helped to create the honor code and council at Princeton University.

In the spirit of the founders' drive for innovation and in the words of Sawney himself, "Progress is made only by experiment manipulated by individual initiative." The 2020 strategic plan for the future of Webb affirms that the school still emphasizes independent thinking, creative initiative, personal integrity, and civic responsibility. Along with these priorities, Webb provides a challenging academic curriculum and a full extracurricular program in order to prepare graduates for college and life.

One

The Webb Brothers, Sawney and John 1870–1926

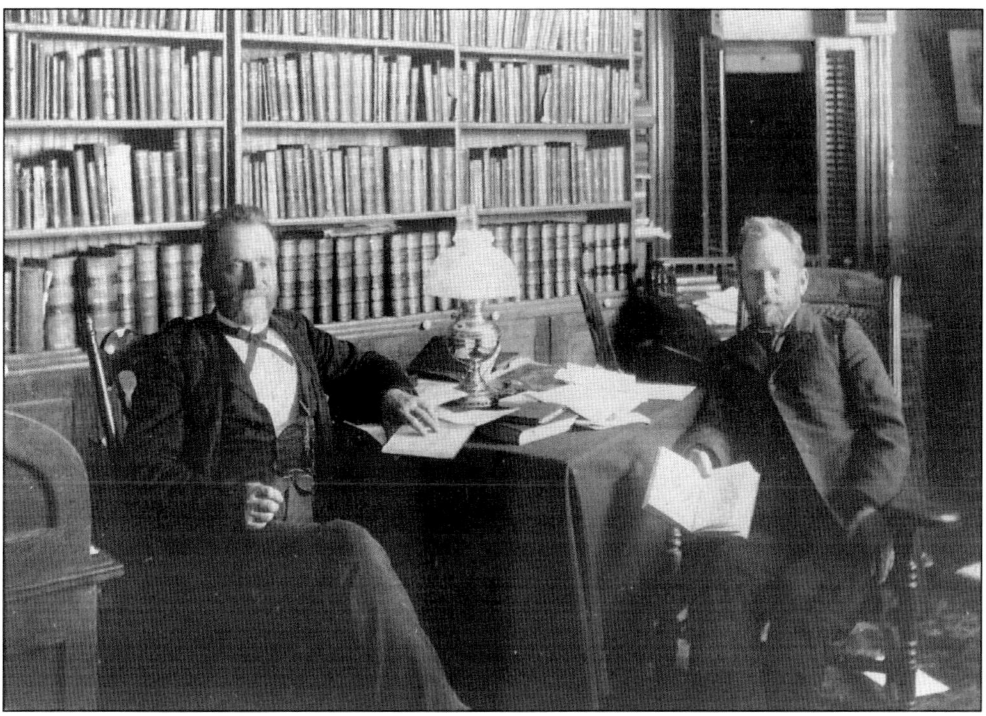

Sawney and John Webb. Brothers Sawney (left) and John Webb are pictured sitting together in 1897 in what appears to be a personal library. According to John Andrew Rice, "The two had made the school together, disciplinarian and scholar."

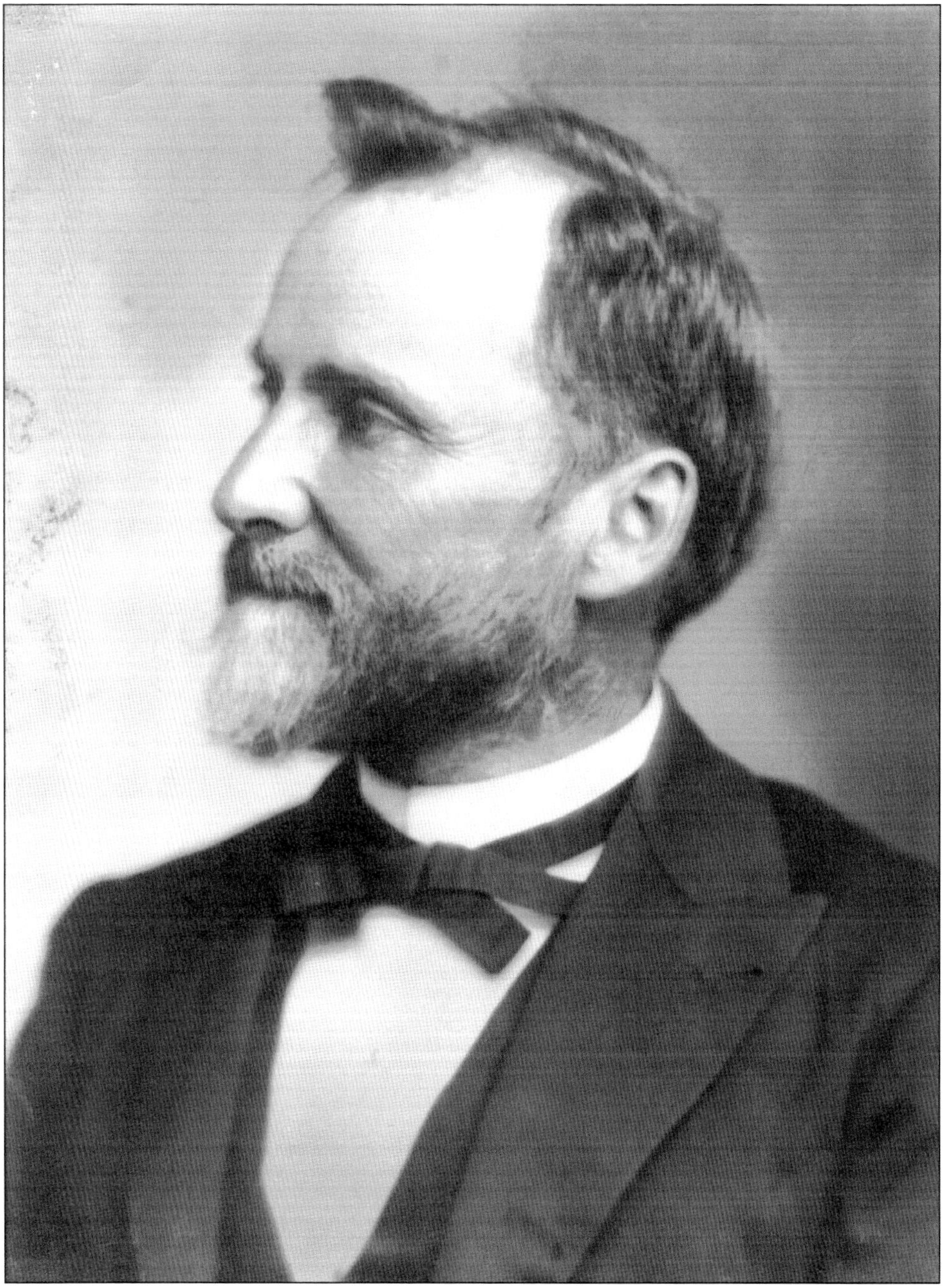

WILLIAM ROBERT "SAWNEY" WEBB SR., C. 1899. Born in Mount Tirzah, North Carolina, on November 11, 1842, Sawney was one of twelve children. He served in the Civil War from 1861 to 1865. Sawney attended the University of North Carolina and was awarded an AB in 1867 and then his AM in 1868. In 1869, he taught at Horner's School, and he and a fellow teacher spoke at length about the dream of an educational utopia. He became the principal of the Culleoka Institute in 1870. He was married April 23, 1873, to Martha Emma Clary in Unionville, Tennessee. They had eight children: William Robert "Son Will" Jr., Alla, John Stanford, Adeline, Daniel Clary, Susan, Emma, and Richard Thompson.

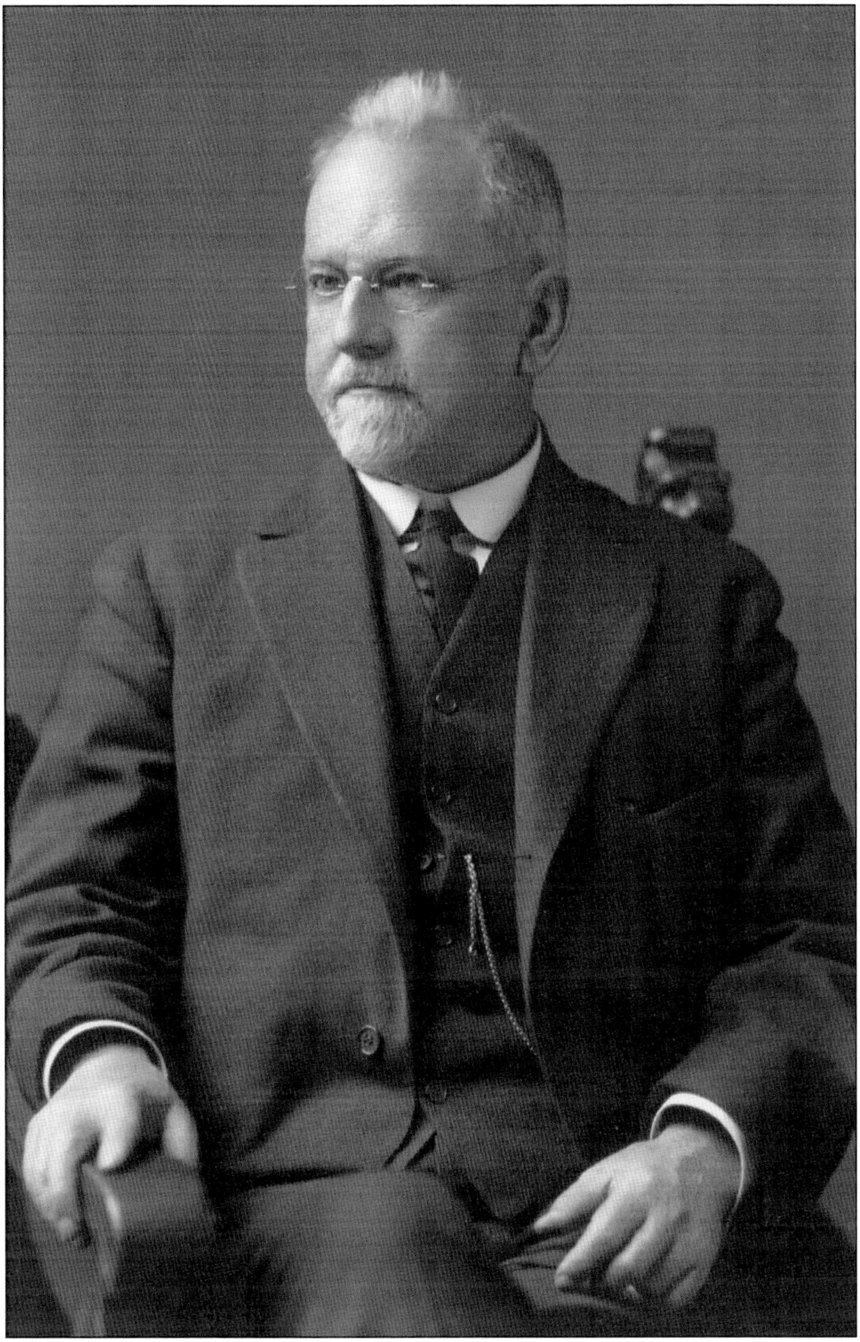

John Maurice Webb. Born on November 29, 1847, in North Carolina, John Webb joined his brother in 1873, becoming co-founder and co-principal with Sawney at The Webb School. John was scholarly and intellectual but also very quiet. He was the complement to Sawney, the disciplinarian, providing balance. John married Harriet Elizabeth "Lily" Shipp on December 7, 1876, and they had five children: Sarah, Mary Gillespie, Hazel Alexander, Albert Micajah, and Cornelia. John M. Webb died on April 5, 1916. A humble man, he asked to be buried in an unmarked grave.

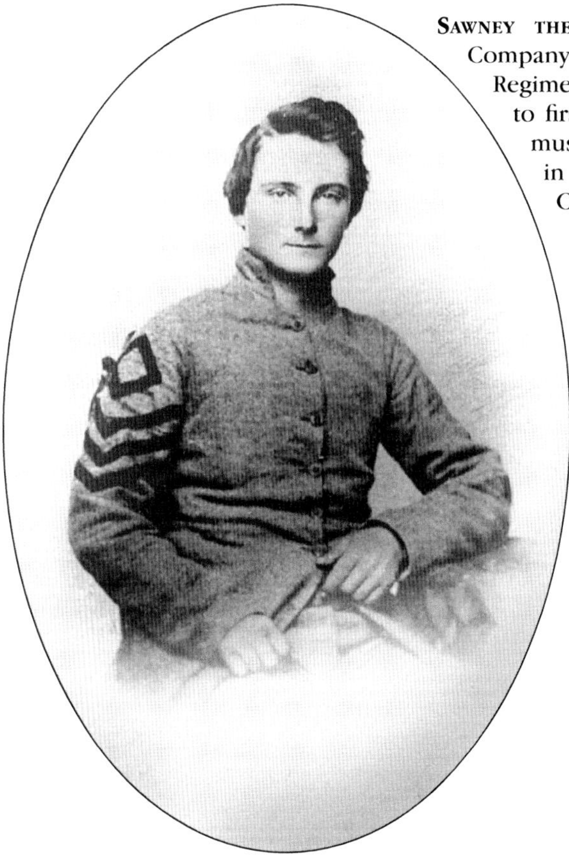

SAWNEY THE SOLDIER. Sawney was enlisted in Company H, North Carolina 15th Infantry Regiment, on May 21, 1861. He was promoted to first lieutenant on March 17, 1863, and mustered out on June 27, 1863. He enlisted in Company K, North Carolina 2nd Cavalry Regiment, on March 5, 1864.

SAWNEY LETTERS HOME. William Robert "Sawney" Webb Sr. enlisted in the military when he was 18 years old and fought in the Civil War from 1861 to 1865. He was captured and imprisoned at Hart's Island in New York Harbor but later escaped. This envelope stored his prisoner of war card.

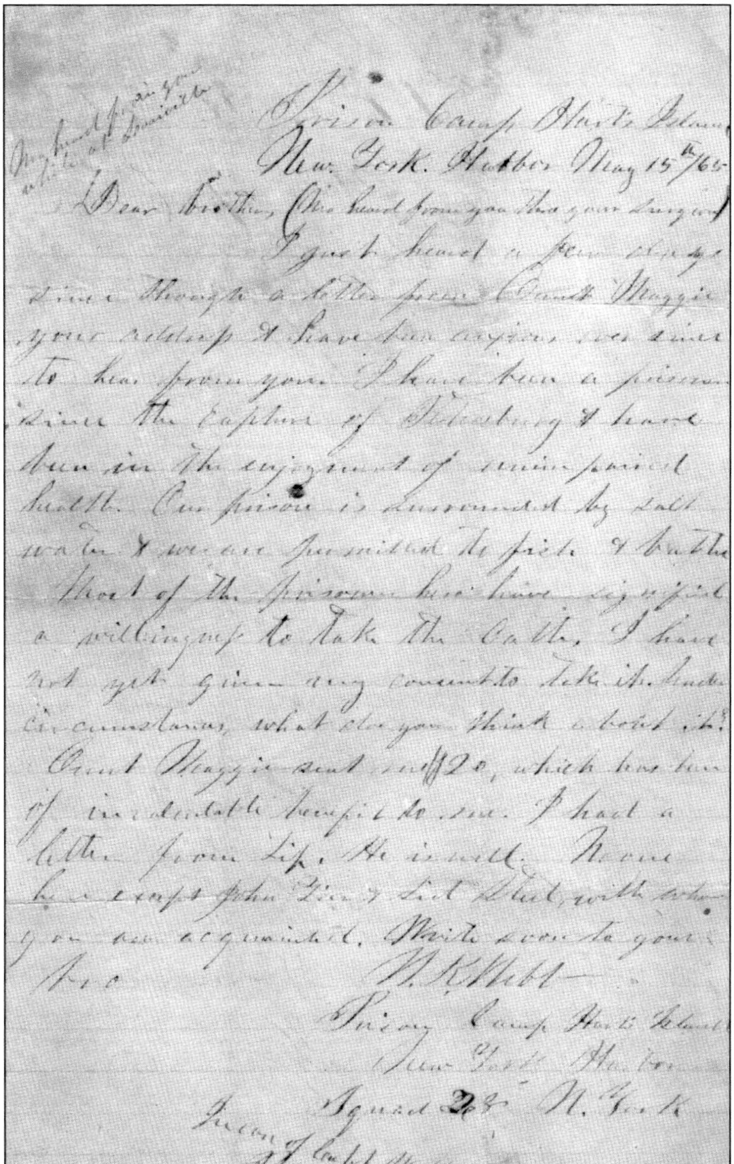

Sawney as Prisoner. The following is a translation of a letter from the Hart's Island camp: "Ma heard from you while at Louisville Prison Camp Hart's Island, New York Harbor May 15th/65. Dear brother, (Ma heard from you thru your surgeon) I just heard a few days since through a letter from Aunt Maggie your address & have been anxious ever since to hear from you. I have been a prisoner since the capture of Petersburg & have been in the enjoyment of unimpaired health. Our prison is surrounded by salt water & we are permitted to fish & bathe. Most of the prisoners here have signified a willingness to take the oath. I have not yet given my consent to take it. Under circumstances, what do you think about it? Aunt Maggie sent me $20, which has been of incalculable benefit to me. I had a letter from Tip. He is well. No one here except John [?] & [?] [?], with whom you are acquainted. Write soon to your bro. W. R. Webb, Prison Camp Hart's Island, New York Harbor, Squad 28 N. York, In care of Capt. Walker."

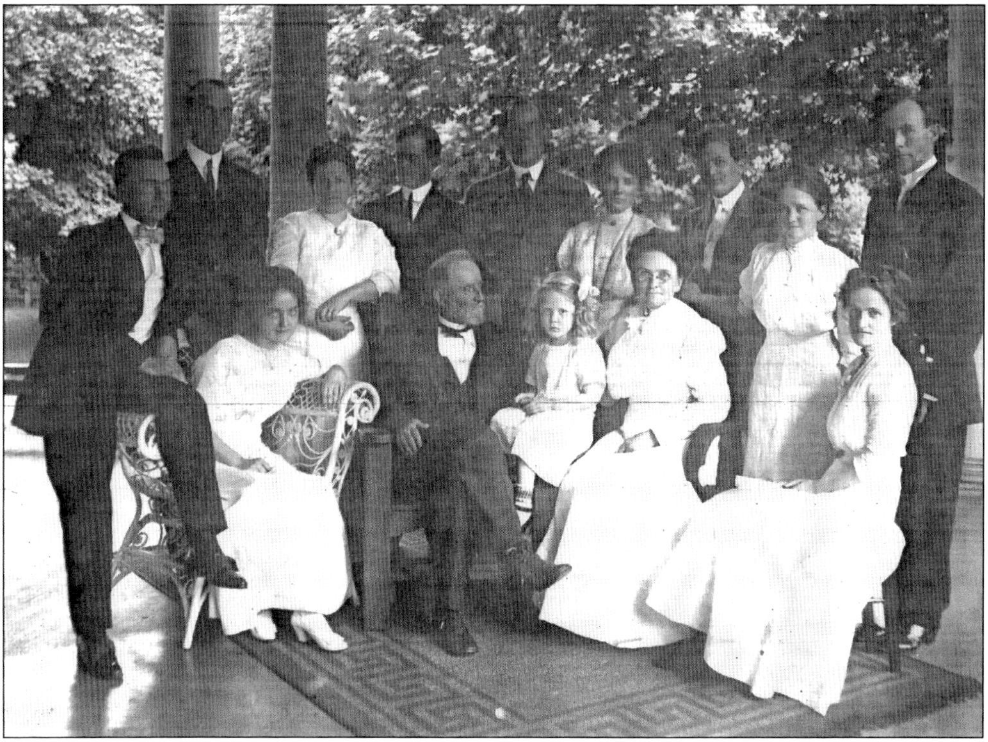

Sawney Webb Family Photograph. William Robert "Sawney" Webb Sr. is seen here with his wife, sons and daughters, and only grandchild around 1911. Sawney and Emma had eight children: five boys, and three girls. Pictured from left to right are (first row) Richard Thompson Webb, Emma Webb, Sawney, Emma Bowen Webb (granddaughter), Martha Emma Clary Webb, and Susan Webb Price (daughter); (second row) Daniel Clary Webb, Louise Manning Webb, William Robert "Son Will" Webb Jr., John Stanford Webb, Adeline Webb Sibley (daughter), Josiah Sibley, Alla Webb, and Ed T. Price Sr.

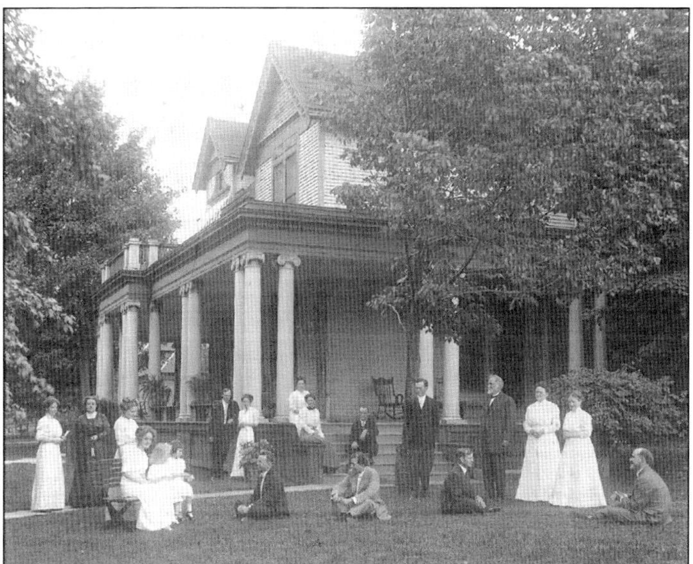

Wedding of Susan Webb and Ed Price. Sawney Webb's daughter Susan married Ed T. Price Sr. on June 20, 1911. Ed was a 1900 Webb School graduate, and Susan was a 1901 graduate. Ed taught at Webb School in Bell Buckle and also at Webb School in California. They are at back left, standing in front of the columns. Ed Price was the cofounder and headmaster of the Price-Webb School in Lewisburg, Tennessee, from 1913 to 1925.

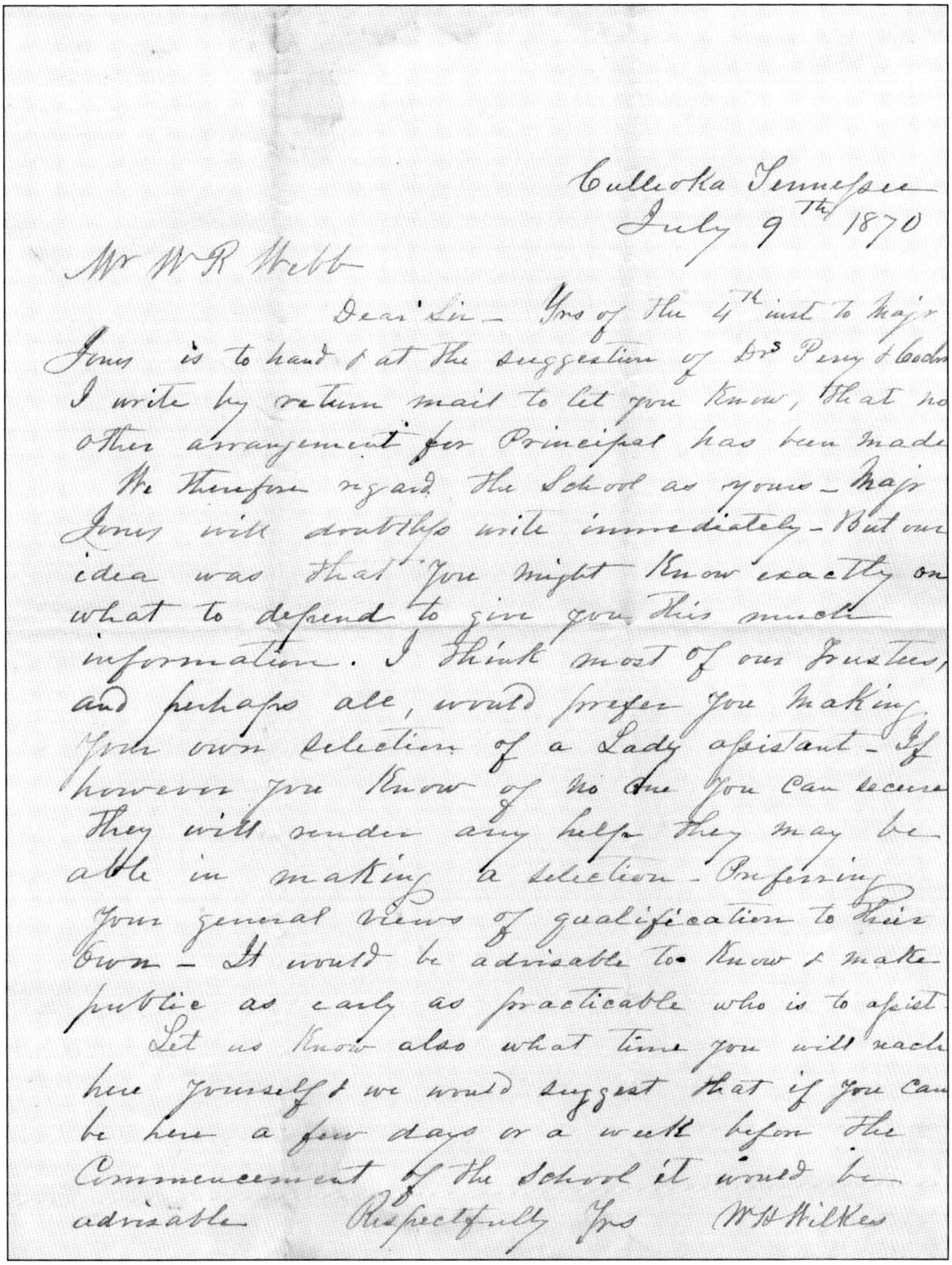

Culleoka Tennessee
July 9th 1870

Mr W R Webb

Dear Sir — Yrs of the 4th inst to Major Jones is to hand & at the suggestion of Drs Perry & Cod[illegible] I write by return mail to let you know, that no other arrangement for Principal has been made. We therefore regard the School as yours — Major Jones will doubtless write immediately — But our idea was that you might know exactly on what to depend to give you this much information. I think most of our Trustees, and perhaps all, would prefer you making your own selection of a Lady assistant — If however you know of no one you can secure they will render any help they may be able in making a selection — Preferring your general views of qualification to their own — It would be advisable to know & make public as early as practicable who is to assist.

Let us know also what time you will reach here yourself & we would suggest that if you can be here a few days or a week before the Commencement of the School it would be advisable.

Respectfully Yrs
W H Wilkes

Culleoka Letter to Sawney. On July 9, 1870, W.H. Wilkes, also known as the "Father of Culleoka," sent Sawney a letter informing him that no arrangement for principal had been made for the institute yet. He then informed him that he could have the school.

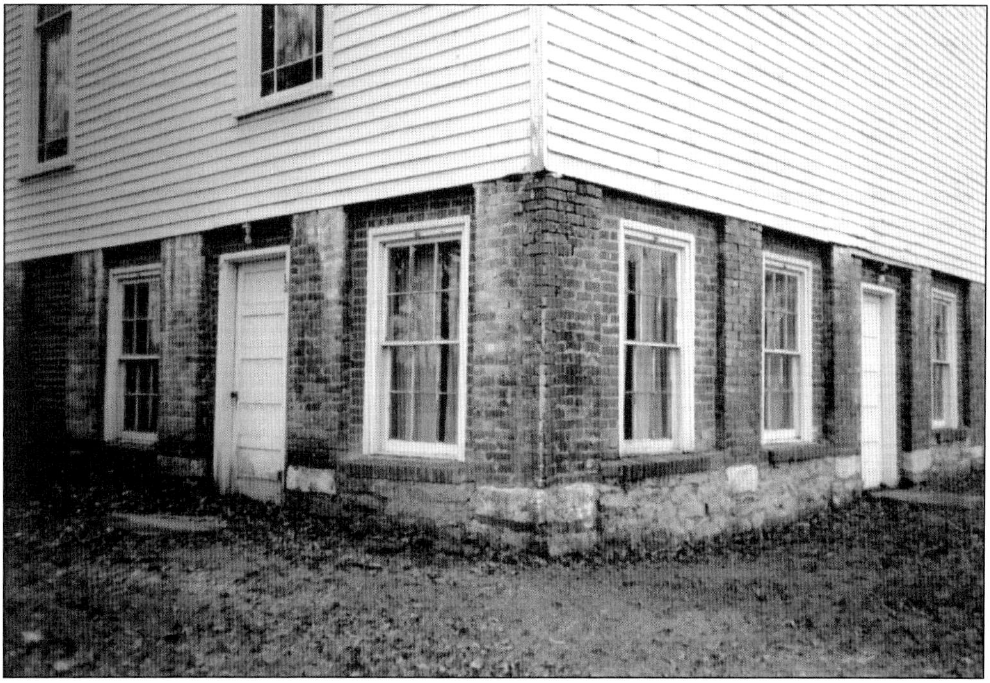

Culleoka Basement. The basement of the Methodist church was where Sawney first began teaching students at Culleoka in 1870. This broken-down building was all there was when Sawney took over the principalship. In a few short years, the school had grown so much that this building quickly became too small.

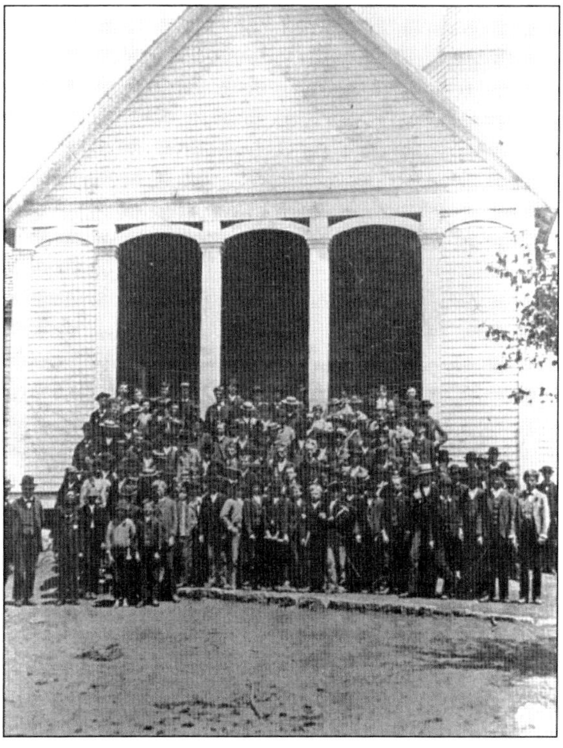

Culleoka "Big Room." Webb School at Culleoka students are pictured in front of the Big Room in the late 1870s.

CULLEOKA INSTITUTE,

W. R. WEBB, A. M., J. M. WEBB, A. M., Principals.

NEXT SESSION BEGINS AUGUST 9th, 1875.

Rev. Jacob Ditzler, D. D., of Kentucky Conference, says: "I attended their exercises (meaning the daily class-room work,) and witnessed their great pains in disciplining the mind to the closest habits of thought; the unusual success in starting their pupils in the languages—never saw pupils surpass, if equal them."

From the Rev. A. T. Goodloe, in the Western Methodist: "It (the Culleoka Institute) is regarded by many as the foremost preparatory school in the South, and some think it will be one of the most prolific feeders of the Vanderbilt. Such is my opinion. The religious tone of the community in which it is situated cannot be excelled."

From Rev. J. A. Orman, in Christian Advocate: "The Webb Bros. have an excellent school here, as you know, worthy of the patronage of all who desire to lay the foundation of a first-class education."

From the Pulaski Citizen: "Professors Webb, two of the best teachers in the State. We commend them and their school to the favorable consideration of our readers."

CULLEOKA INSTITUTE.

The Commencement exercises of the Culleoka Institute took place May 26, 27. A number of the *literati* of Tennessee were present, and witnessed the proceedings with much interest. The exercises were well attended, and the pupils acquitted themselves with credit. It was clearly evinced at every recitation that constant labor and much painstaking had been undergone by both pupils and teachers during the session. The committee are prepared to say with all candor, that they never witnessed a more thorough and impartial examination. It was rigid, we are tempted to say, to a fault. Every chapter, verse, paragraph, and problem, discussed, was designated by some spectator, without any reference to the proficiency of the pupil, or the intricacy of the subject. This Institute has already made an enviable reputation as a high school, in which language, its science, its development, and its use, is thoroughly taught. In addition to this, an accurate knowledge of mathematics, and the ordinary branches of an English education, including book-keeping, is insisted upon. The object of the teachers seems to be to form character, by developing in fair proportions the moral, intellectual, and physical man, by instilling into the youthful mind a love of truth, and reverence for whatever is noble and virtuous, by teaching the pupil that the facts are only valuable as furnishing material for thought, and by encouraging him to engage in those athletic sports which give strength and vigor to the physical organism. The rare merits of this Institute have been acknowledged by a number of the principal colleges of the South. Pupils are prepared in it have, on entering Lebanon University, Emory and Henry, and Stewart Colleges, taken the highest honors in the Sophomore and Junior classes. During the last session there have been six young men attending this school who are preparing for the ministry; they are all young men of good promise, and exert a fine influence in the community, and have done much to assist the principals in toning the moral *status* of the Institute. The Brothers Webb have displayed a very liberal and magnanimous spirit in giving so much assistance to the young men who desire to preach. Any community might well feel proud of such liberal-spirited, enterprising, Christian gentlemen as the Messrs. Webb. The thoroughness of the instruction, the high tone of morality contended for, and the gentility of deportment required of the pupils, by the principals, together with the cheapness of board and tuition, the healthfulness of the country, and the eligible locality, go to make the Institute all that parents and guardians could desire of a first-class high school. And we take great pleasure in recommending this school to all persons who wish to patronize a male school. It is well conducted, and in every respect worthy the confidence and patronage of the public at large.

A. G. DINWIDDIE,
W. MOONEY,
R. K. HARGROVE.

MAY 31, 1875.

Culleoka Institute grows in usefulness and in favor with the public. The patronage which it receives from teachers and other educated persons is certainly very complimentary. The Messrs. Webb are not only instructors of experience, but gentlemen of varied culture, and of spotless character. If the Institute has any superior as a high school for boys, the writer is free to confess that he has no knowledge of it.—[Rev. W. Mooney, in Columbia District Directory.

Dr. Summers in Christian Advocate: "Culleoka Institute advertises in this issue. The Webbs do capital work at Culleoka. We thank them for a kind invitation to the semi-annual examination, Dec. 22-24. But Conference and Christmas both are in the way. There are six students there preparing for the ministry, and the Institute is looking for some Mexican youths."

CULLEOKA INSITUTE.

The Columbia Journal says: "This institution, under the management of Prof's W. R. and J. M. Webb, located in Culleoka, ten miles South of Columbia, has gained deserved reputation as a preparatory school, having young men in it from nearly every State in the South. There are about 90 pupils in this school, 50 of whom are from a distance. The examination will be held the 25th, 26th and 27th insts. Bishop Marvin, of the Methodist Church, will preach a sermon to the school on Wednesday night."

Dr. Summers in Christian Advocate says: "The Culleoka Institute advertises in this issue. The Messrs. Webb are the accomplished Principals. They have a large experience in teaching, and know how to do it. They are eminently successful in their profession. We hope their halls will be crowded with students the next session. Culleoka is a capital location for a school. The society is good, and board in respectable families is very reasonable."

CULLEOKA INSTITUTE.

MR. EDITOR:—It was our privilege to be present at the recent semi-annual examination of the pupils of the Culleoka Institute. The examination was conducted with perfect fairness and impartiality. It seemed to us to be as thorough a test of scholarship as possible. It proved to us the following facts:

1. That the country affords no better instructors than the Messrs. Webb; that their learning is both extensive and thorough; and that their pupils are equal to any of their class.
2. We are convinced that no better preparatory school can be found.
3. The discipline, from all that we could see, was just such as develop the highest moral character.

In view of all, then, we are prepared to give the Culleoka Institute our indorsement, as worthy the patronage of all that have sons to be educated.

R. H. RIVERS,
F. C. WILKES.

The Columbia Herald says: "In another column will be found an advertisement of Culleoka Institute, which begins its new session on the 9th of August. About six years ago Prof. W. R. Webb left his home in North Carolina and took charge of the Culleoka Institute. A few years thereafter his brother, Prof. John M. Webb joined him. They have worked with great industry, and patience, and skill, and have established a character for their school that is far more valuable than money. What Bingham's school is to North Carolina Webb's school is to Tennessee. Educators everywhere speak well of it, and many of its pupils are sons of eminent teachers, preachers, scholars and jurists. This fact alone is positive assurance of its real excellence. No one can attend their examinations without coming away strongly convinced of the thoroughness of the school. We recently received a letter from a young man who had been a pupil in Culleoka Institute; he paid a glowing tribute to the Messrs. Webb, as men of thorough scholarship and as rigid disciplinarians, but kind and lovable in disposition. He spoke in high terms of their character as Christian men, and of the great influence which they exert for Christianity. We recommend it as a good school in every respect, and Culleoka as an excellent place for children to be educated at. It is a healthy place; board can be had much cheaper than in larger towns, and the moral tone of society is good."

CULLEOKA INSTITUTE NEWSLETTER. This is an 1875 newsletter from the school in Culleoka. When Sawney first began teaching, the school was called the Culleoka Institute before being eventually named for the Webb family. This newsletter contained comments from various people and newspapers endorsing Sawney and his brother John on the quality of education that they offered at Culleoka Institute.

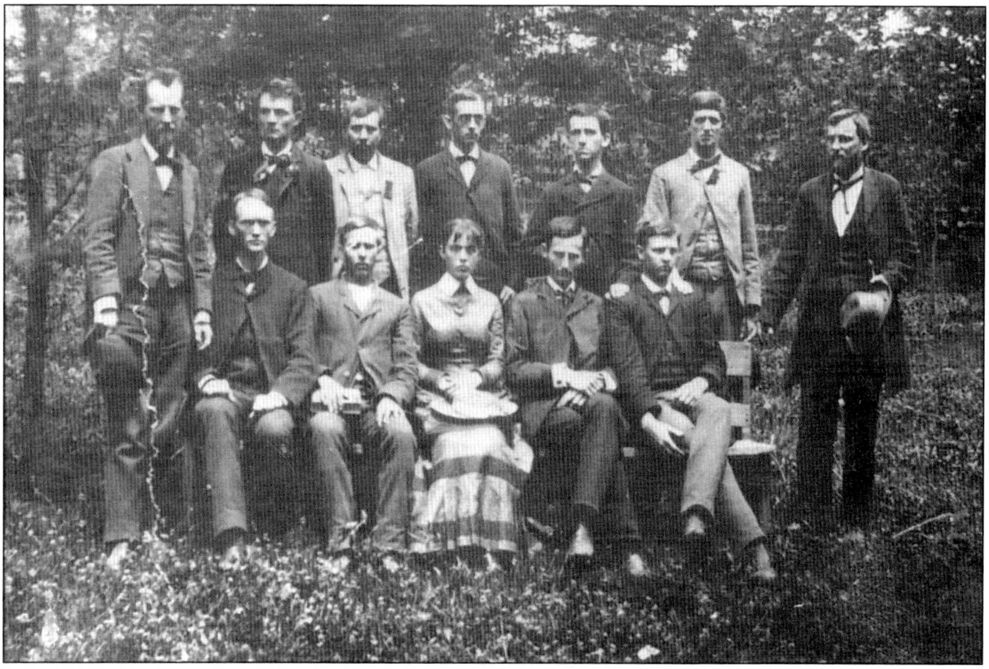

Culleoka Students, c. 1883. The students pictured here are from the Culleoka days of Webb School and are most likely the senior class. Standing at far left in the second row is John M. Webb, and at far right is William Robert "Sawney" Webb Sr.

The transfer of the property which is now the WebbSchool campus is recorded in Deed Book XXX page 223

Transferred from Alfred D. Fugitt

To

Board of Trustees of Webb School

namely-

Dr. W. F. Clary
L. J. Whitaker
Madison H. Webb
T. F. Smalling
A. D. Fugitt
Tom J. Peacock
Tom J. Ogilive
Z. T. Crouch, Sr.
J. H. Freeman

On February 16, 1886 valued at $1200

Old Big Room cost approximately $1500 to construct

Moving to Bell Buckle. Pictured is a land transfer document found in a letter from Dr. William F. Clary to Sawney about the purchase of land in Bell Buckle. This document shows the transfer of land from Alfred D. Fugitt to the board of trustees of The Webb School. Once purchased, Sawney was able to make plans to move his family and students to Bell Buckle and continue educating young people. He would soon begin building the Big Room, Junior Room, Senior Room, and his family's house.

Debating Society Invitation. This Debating Society invitation from Culleoka was produced in the 1880s. Debates between the societies were grand affairs. The question of the May 19, 1880, debate was "Resolved, that Napoleon Bonaparte was not justifiably banished." The Hamilton society argued the affirmative and the Platonic society argued the negative.

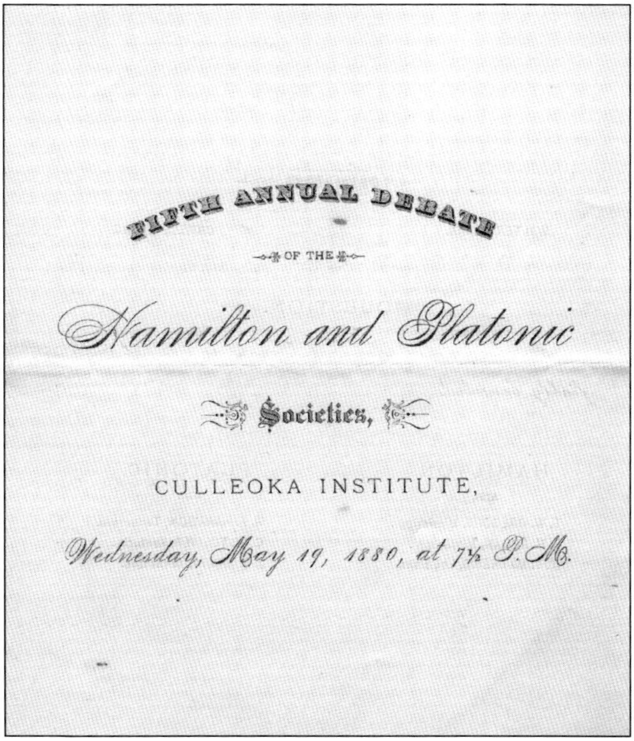

Fifth Annual Debate
of the
Hamilton and Platonic
Societies,
CULLEOKA INSTITUTE,
Wednesday, May 19, 1880, at 7½ P.M.

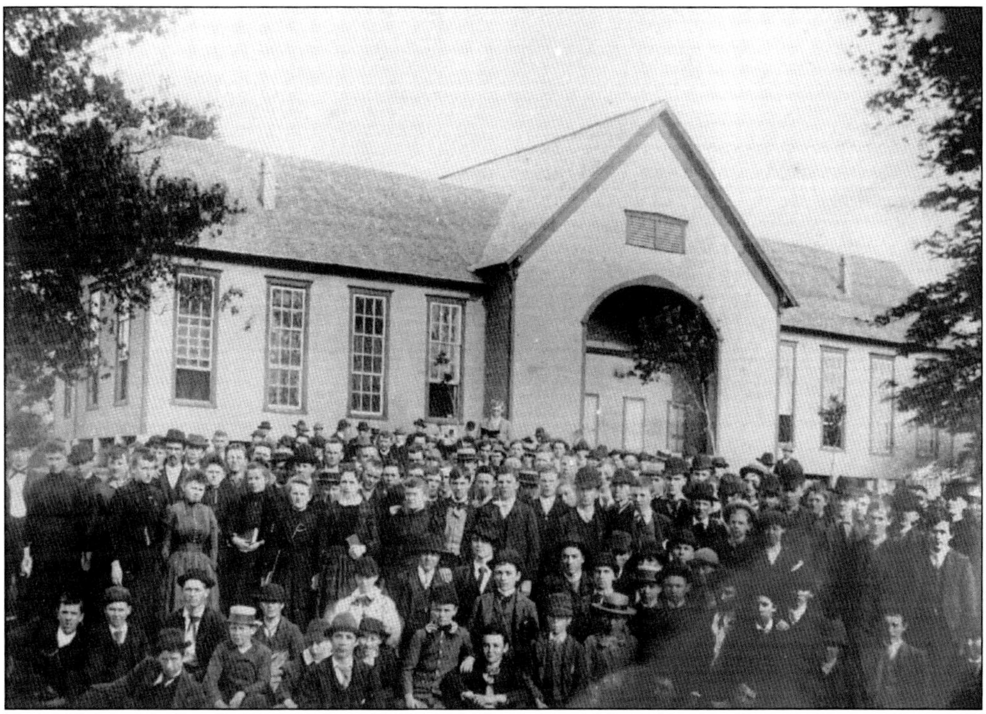

Early Big Room. Students stand in front of the new schoolhouse in Bell Buckle, also referred to as the Big Room. It consisted of two large school rooms and an auditorium. There is still a very large academic building on the Bell Buckle campus called the Big Room.

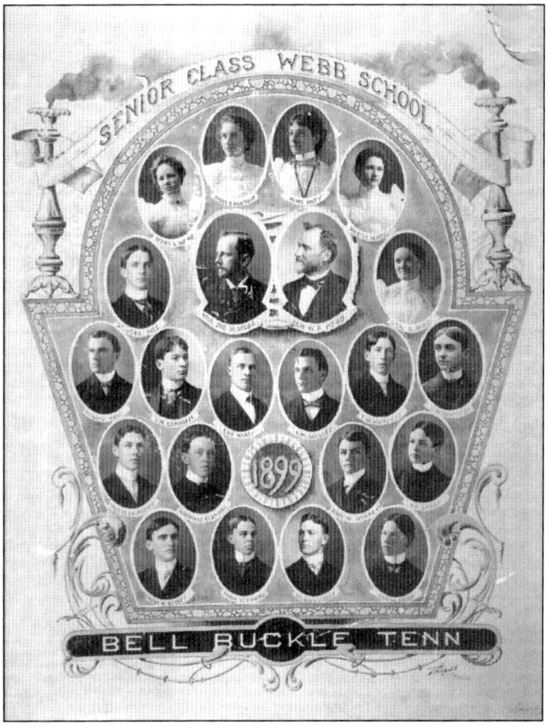

Class of 1899. This image of the 1899 senior class includes both Sawney and John Webb. Sawney's son D.C. Webb, or Daniel Clary Webb, is pictured along with John's daughter Mary G. Webb. Also pictured is F.M. Massey, the well-known founder of the Massey School in Pulaski, Tennessee, also later known as Massey Military School.

Early Webb Faculty. Pictured here are early faculty of The Webb School around 1905. From left to right are (first row) William L. Clark(e) (class of 1896), Ed Thomas Price Sr. (1900), and Sawney; (second row) William Robert "Son Will" Webb Jr. and John M. Webb.

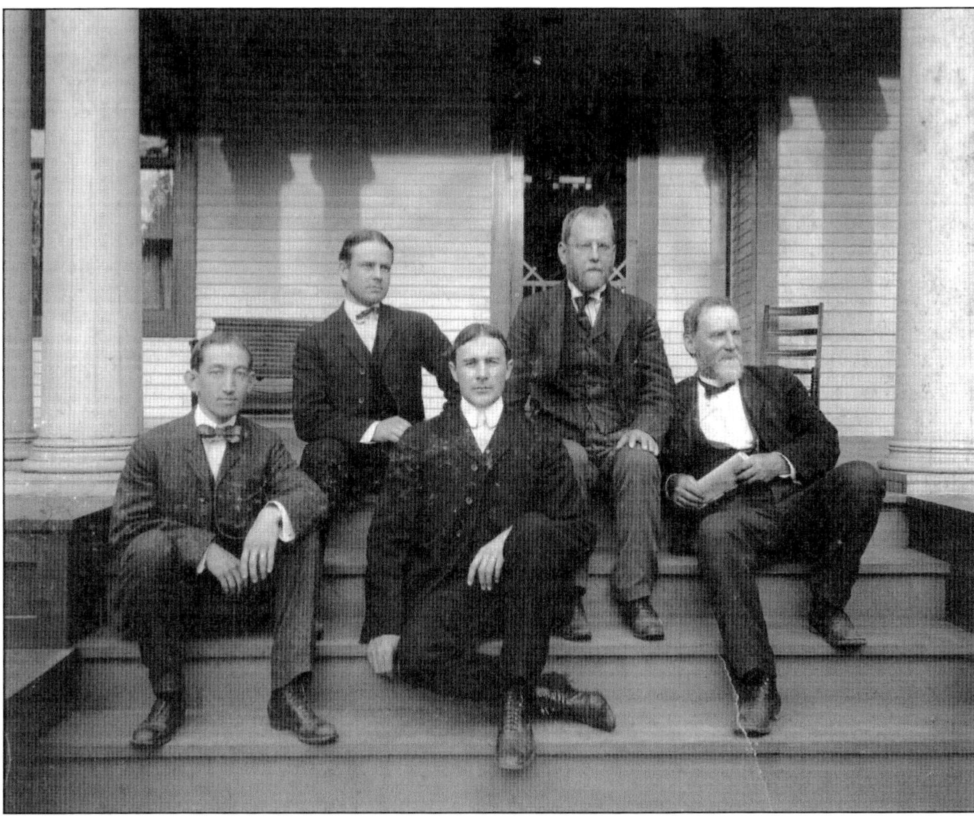

WEBB BASEBALL. Pictured here is Addie Webb's and Myrtle Skeen's intramural baseball team and sponsors sometime around 1894 or 1895. Webb's athletics were primarily intramural until the mid-20th century, when they began participating in interscholastic sports.

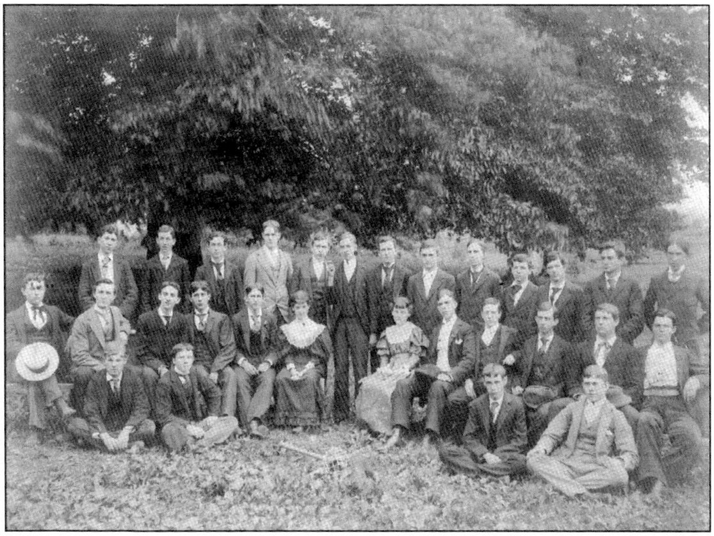

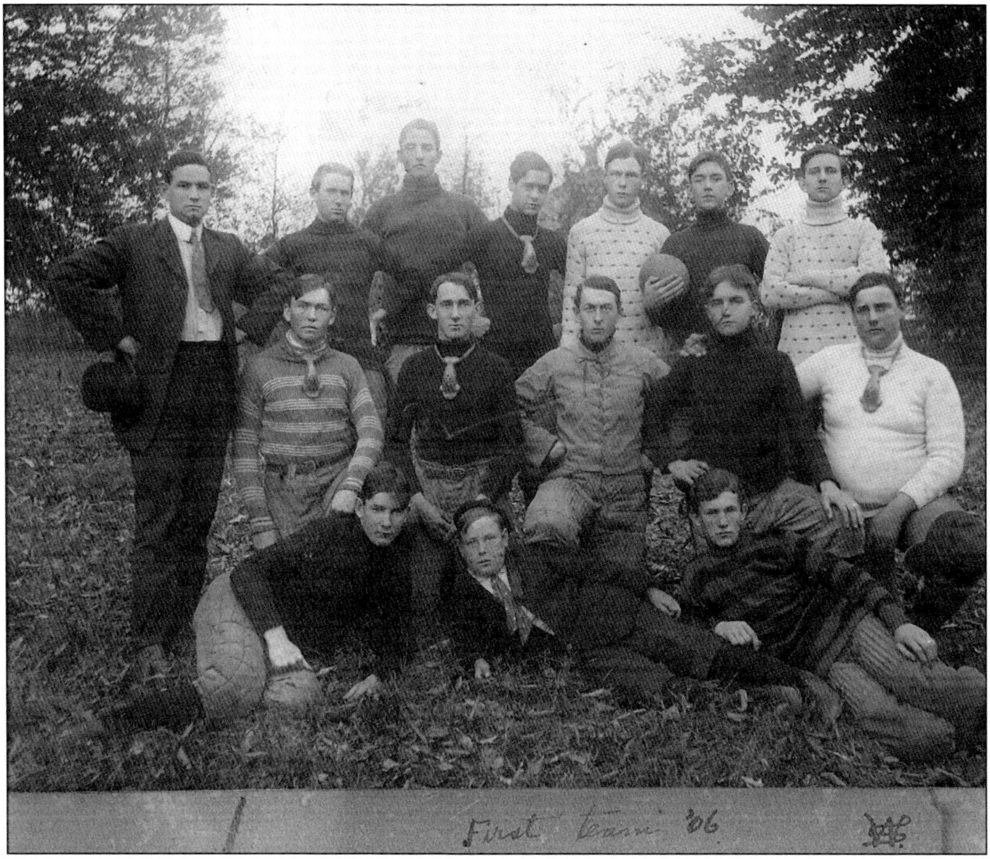

WEBB FOOTBALL. Tennis, baseball, basketball, and football were among the first documented sports at Webb. There are photographs of football from the late 1890s, but pictured here is the football team of 1906. Football was popular among students and graduates—in fact, Tennessee's first Rhodes scholar graduated from Webb and played both football and basketball at Vanderbilt.

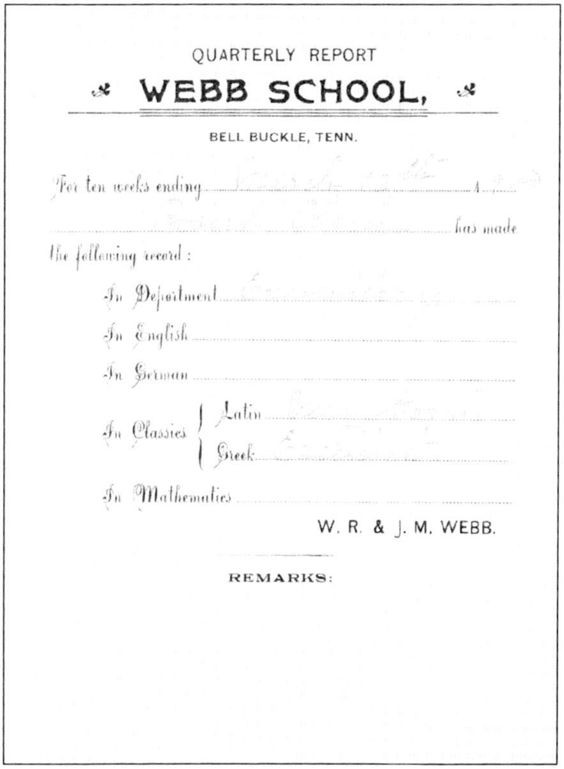

QUARTERLY REPORT

WEBB SCHOOL,

BELL BUCKLE, TENN.

For ten weeks ending ....

.... has made

the following record:

In Department ....

In English ....

In German ....

In Classics { Latin .... / Greek .... }

In Mathematics ....

W. R. & J. M. WEBB.

REMARKS:

EARLY WEBB SCHOOL REPORT CARD. This is a progress report card from the turn of the 20th century. The quarterly report reflects high marks for Robert Clark on March 16, 1900.

MERRY COEDS. These girls attending Webb School in 1897 are pictured with Sawney; the Big Room is in the background.

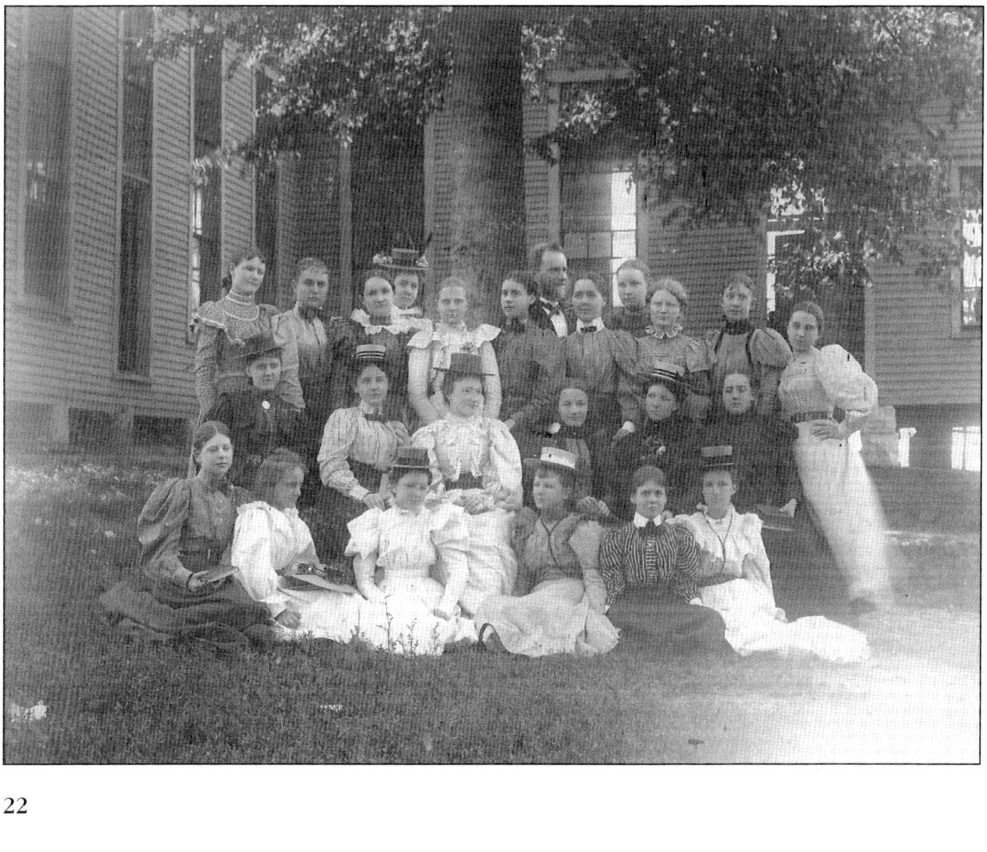

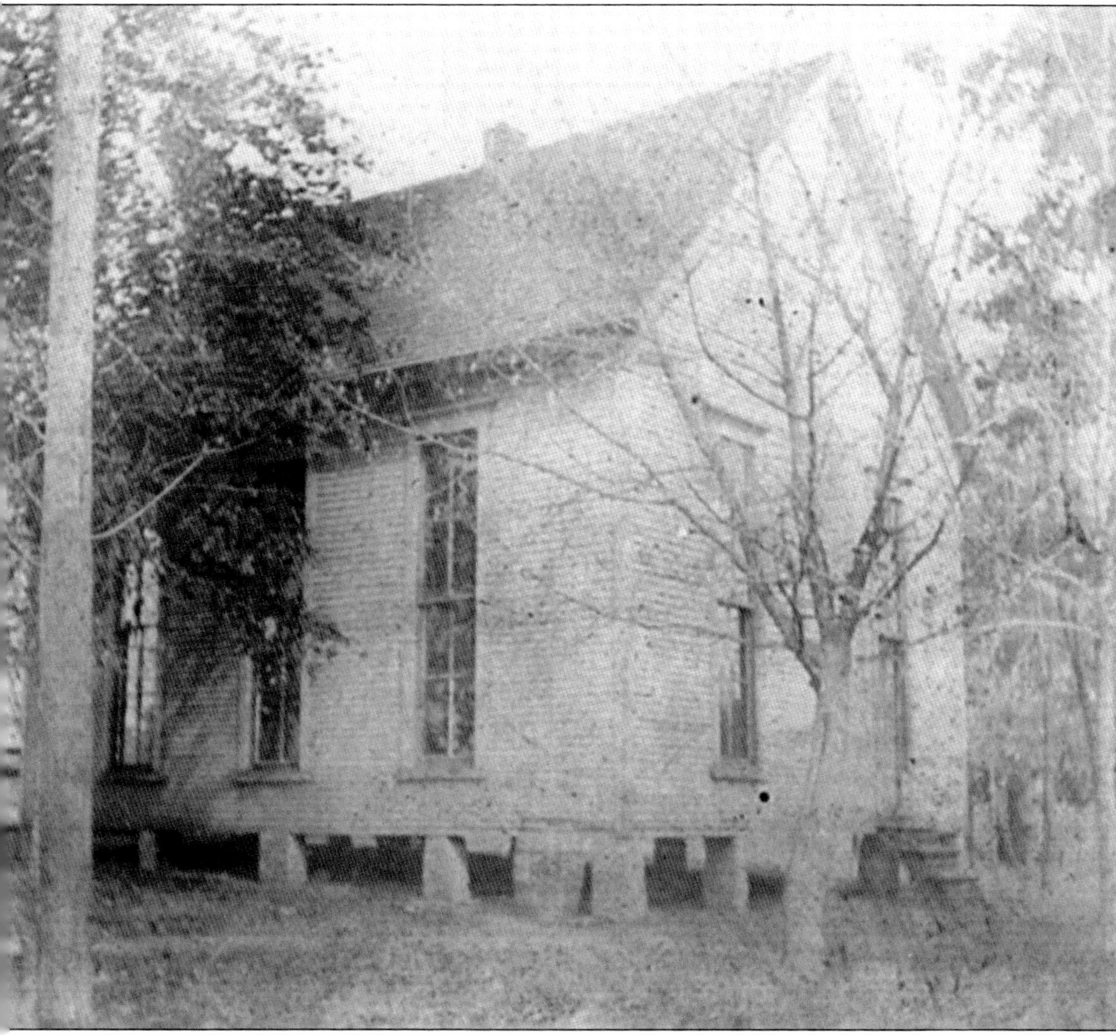

SENIOR ROOM AND FIRST LIBRARY. This building was one of the three first structures erected when Webb School moved to Bell Buckle. It was called the Senior Room because it was where the seniors were taught by John M. Webb. It was also where the first library book collection was housed. The Senior Room stood on campus until it was torn down in 1927.

1 Old Muse home, later Will Anderson Home
2 Epps House
3 Bingham House, Liberty Pike
4 Miss Sally Hoover
5 Peacock House
6 Dalby House
7 Hinkle House
8 Tom Lynn Bingham Home
9 Sawney Webb House
10 Sturdivant's House
11 Mrs. John Sutton's House
12 Side Yard at Mrs. Garner's
13 W. J. Davis Home
14 "Son Will's" House
15 Z. T.Crouch House
16 Dr. White Home; John Finley Whiteside
17 Z. R. Pickens; Mrs. Hinkle
18 Mrs. Garner's House; (Old Batch Remodeled)
19 Hutton House
20 J. W. Paty; J. W. Paty, Jr., Jack Crouch
21 Long Home; later Eph Woods
22 Miller House
23 Follin House
25 Bingham Sisters
26 Paty House
27 Albert Gill
28 Miss Kate Carney; Mrs. Carney

BOARDINGHOUSES KEY. In 1968, many of the earliest boardinghouses were cataloged. Pictured is a key to the boardinghouses pictured on the following pages.

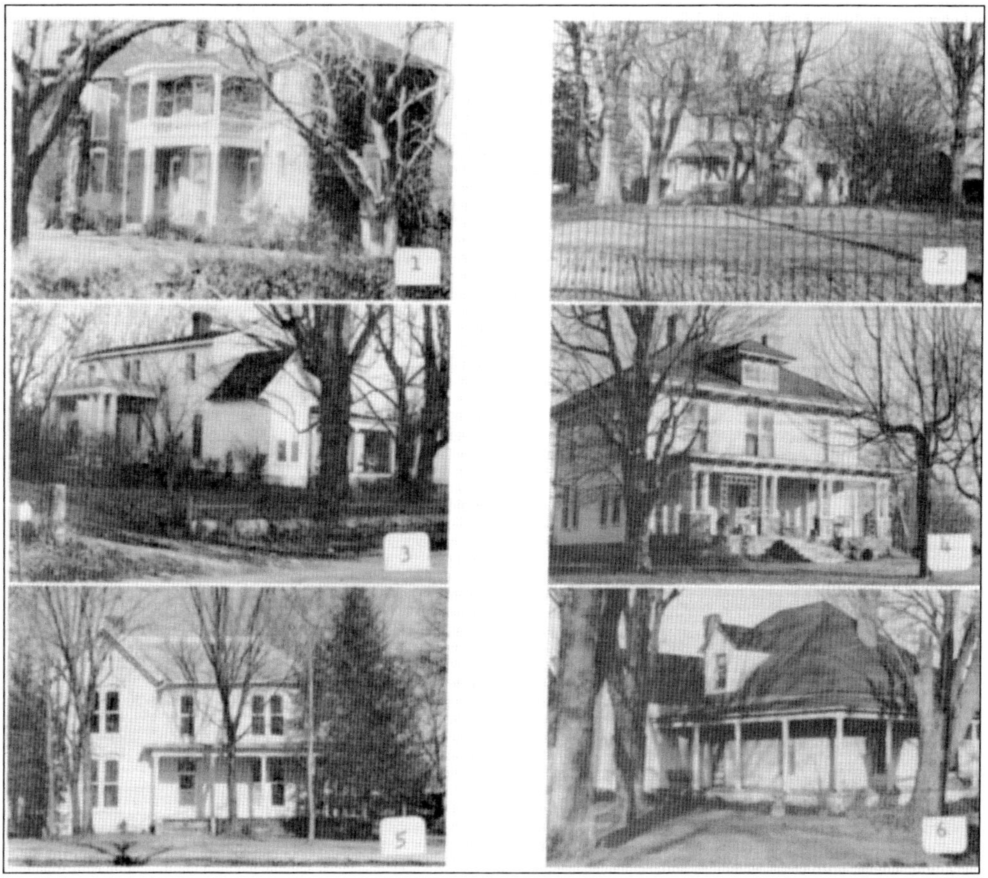

BOARDINGHOUSES 1–6. Upon moving Webb School to Bell Buckle, there were no dormitories for students. Students boarded with many of the townspeople, sometimes several in just one house.

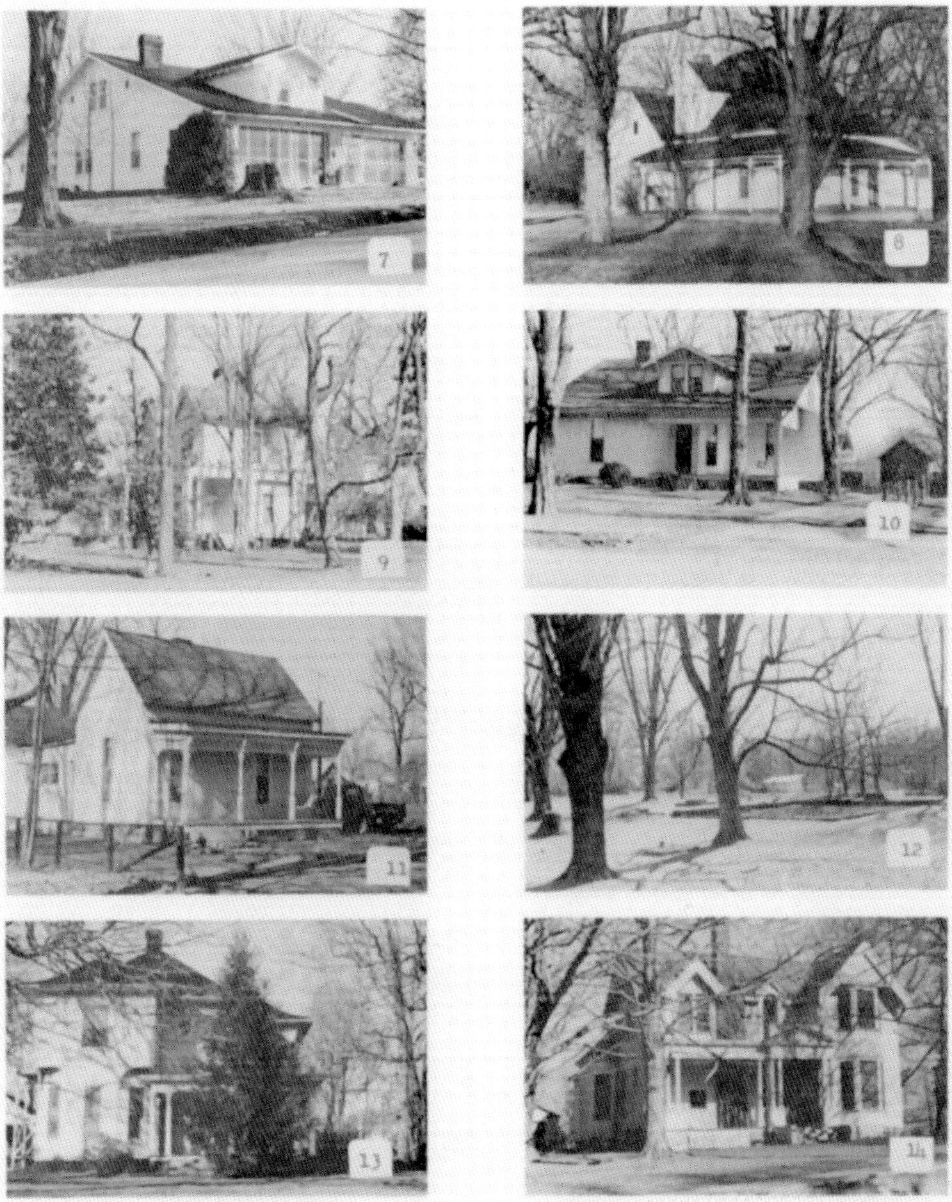

BOARDINGHOUSES 7–14. This collection of photographs was compiled in 1968 by Henry Whiteside Jr., a 1960 graduate. Many of the Bell Buckle boardinghouses still stand today.

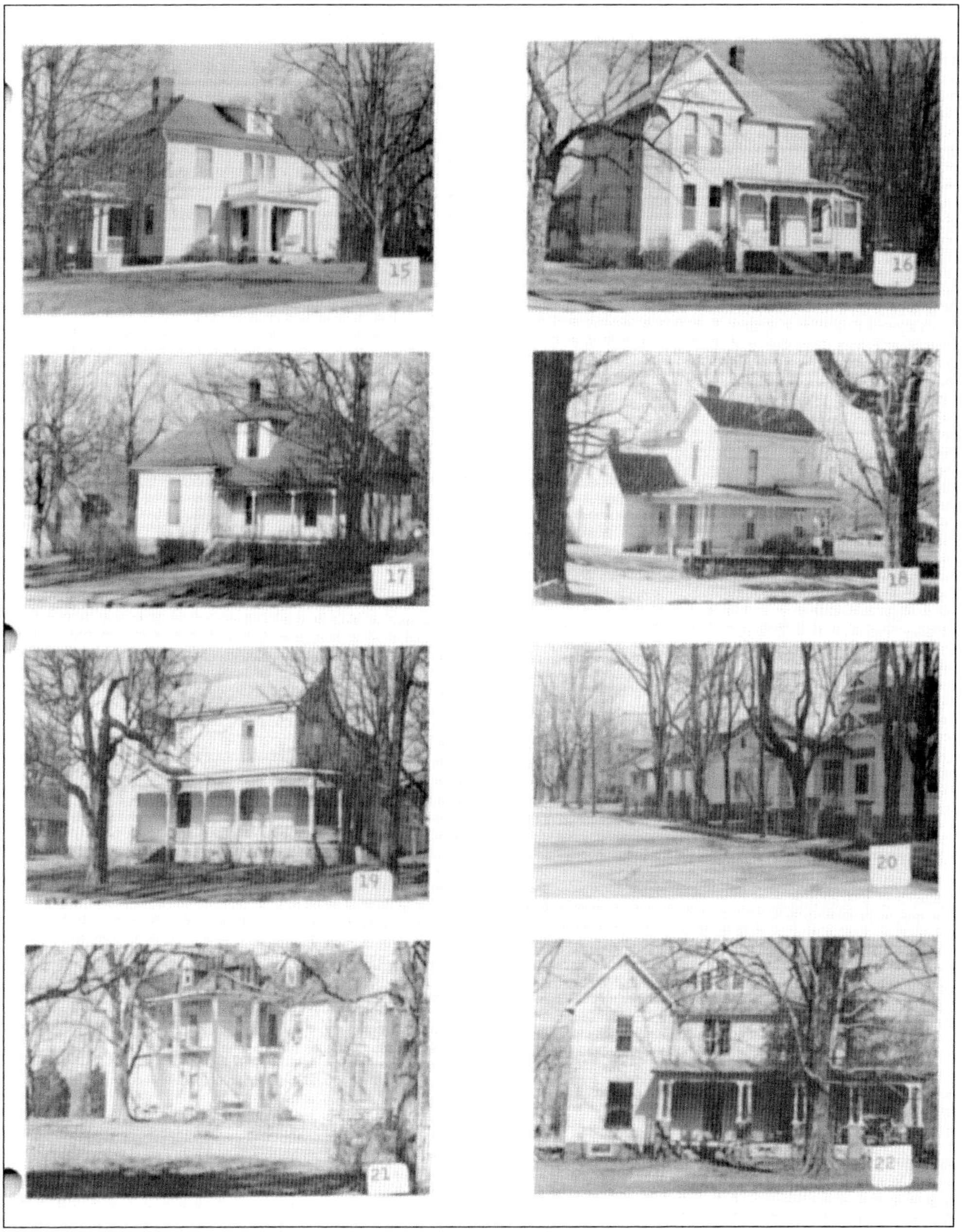

Boardinghouses 15–22. No. 16, the Dr. White Home, is today a bed and breakfast called the Walker Inn, which is owned and operated by a Webb School family. No. 20 was the J.W. Paty House.

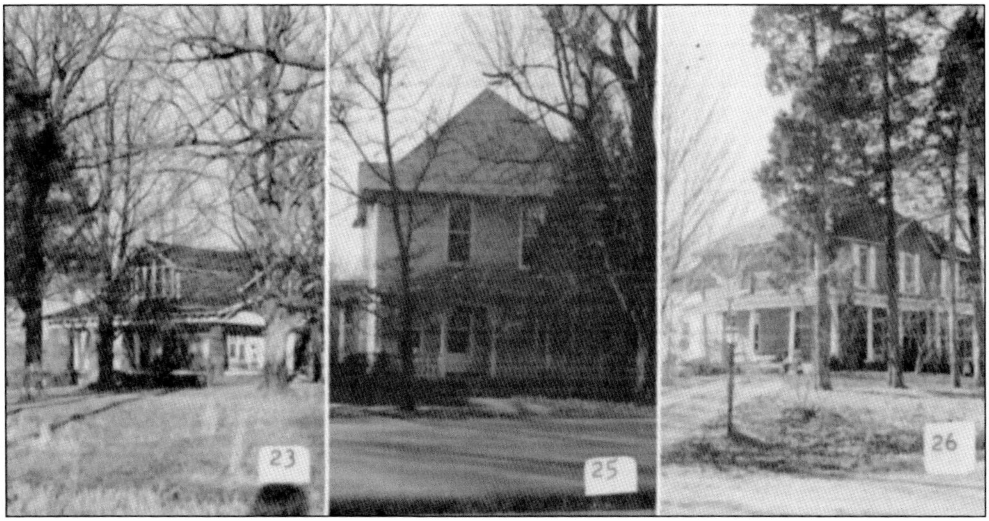

Boardinghouses 23–26 and 27–28. The No. 23 house belonged to G.W. Follin Sr., a 1908 graduate of The Webb School. Follin later returned to teach at Webb and eventually became headmaster, holding that position from 1953 to 1959. His son G.W. Follin Jr. and grandson G.W. Follin III also graduated from Webb. Follin Sr. also directed the Webb Camp for many years. No. 26 is the Paty House, which was owned by Judge Robert M. Paty. Some of his children graduated from The Webb School, and some also returned to teach at Webb. The building still stands today and is owned by the parents of two Webb School graduates.

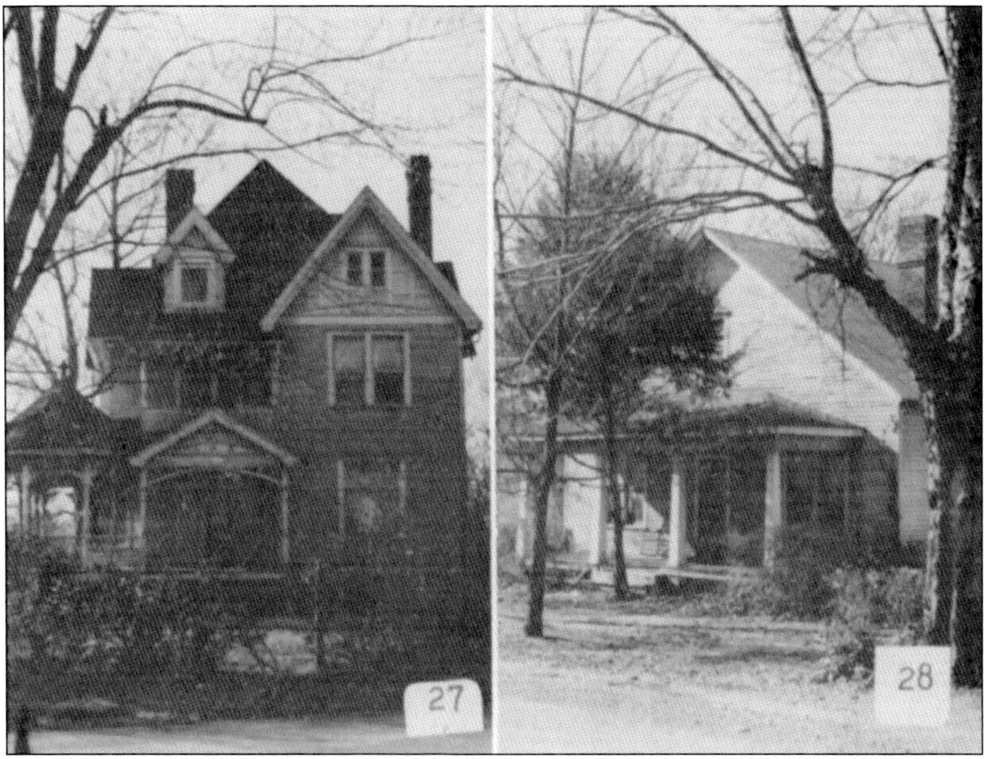

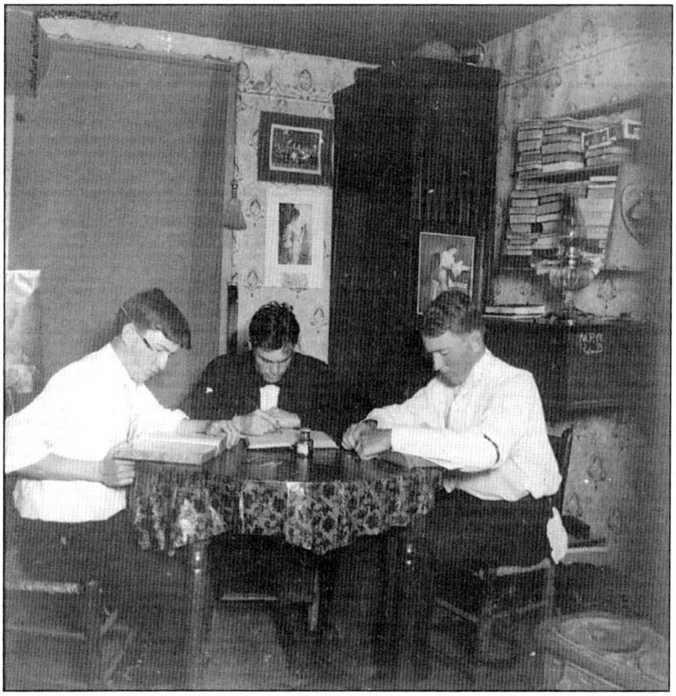

Night Studying at Mary F. Hoover's House. In 1908, students study at their boardinghouse. From left to right are Maston Williams, John Story, and Roy Beadles (class of 1909). (Courtesy of Roy Beadles.)

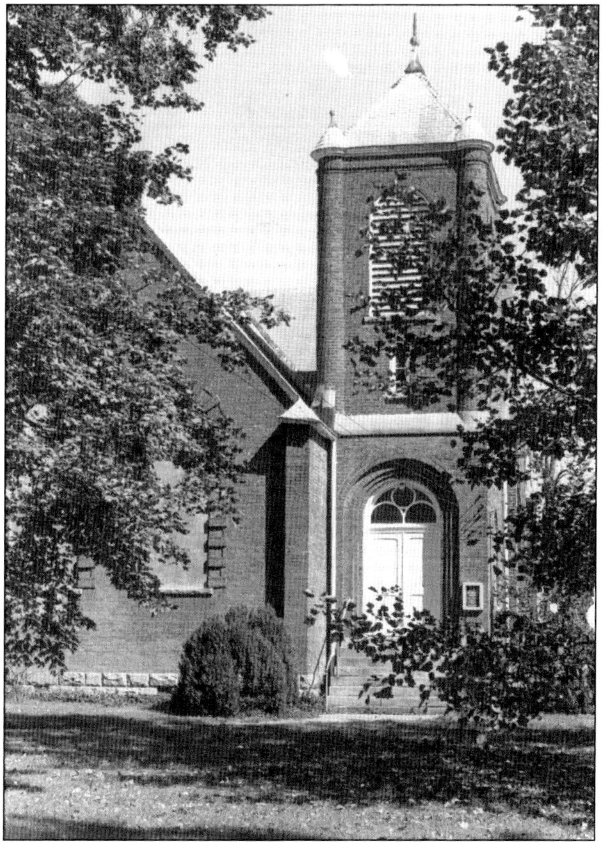

Bell Buckle United Methodist Church. The current Bell Buckle United Methodist Church building (pictured) was erected in 1893. Around the 1940s, one of the pastors organized a Sunday school for Webb students. During certain periods of the school's history, students were required to attend church on Sunday, either at the Methodist church or the Baptist church.

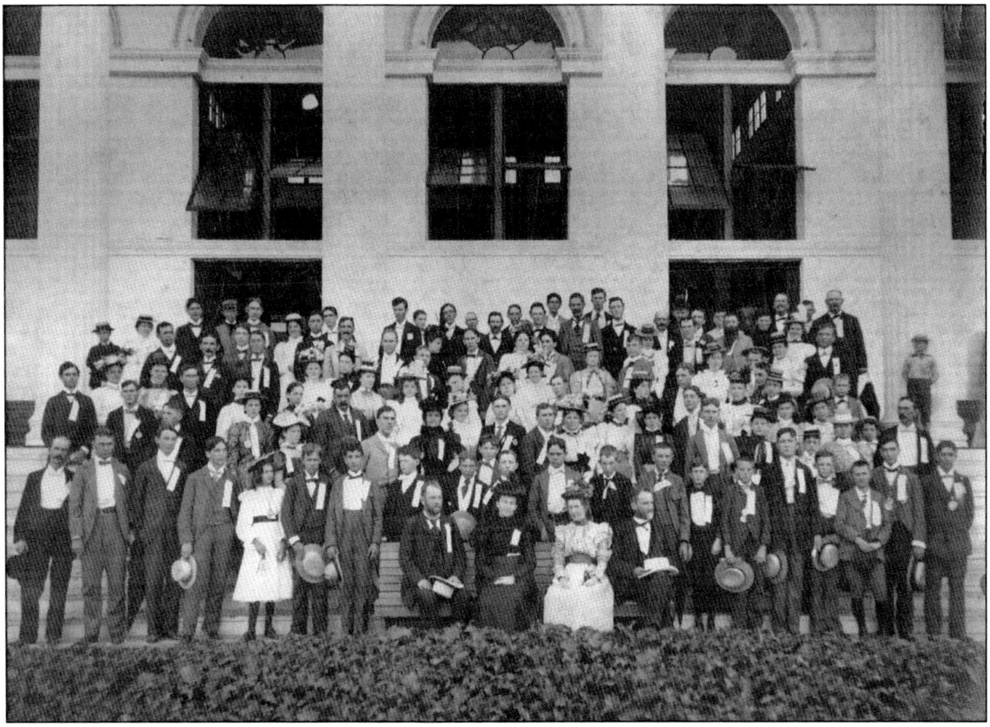

The Tennessee Centennial Exposition. The Tennessee Centennial Exposition took place in Nashville, Tennessee, in August 1897. It was a six-month-long celebration of the 100th anniversary of Tennessee's statehood. The celebration was from May 1 to October 30, 1897. Several groups and organizations were assigned a specific day. August 17, 1897, was designated as Webb's day. Many current and former students and teachers came that day for the celebration.

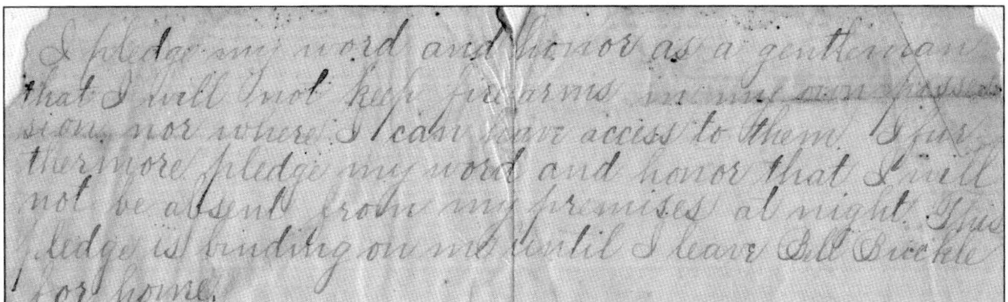

I pledge my word and honor as a gentleman
that I will not keep firearms in my own posses-
sion nor where I can have access to them. I fur-
thermore pledge my word and honor that I will
not be absent from my premises at night. This
pledge is binding on me until I leave Bell Buckle
for home.

Honor Code. Students at Webb sign the honor pledge at the beginning of each school term: "I pledge my word of honor as a Webb gentleman or lady that I will not lie, cheat, or steal." A second pledge that all students sign is the premise pledge: "I will be on my proper premise when the curfew bell tolls at night." This premise pledge from 1888 addresses a different concern: "I pledge my word and honor as a gentleman that I will not keep firearms in my own possession nor where I can access them. I furthermore pledge my word and honor that I will not be absent from my premises at night. This pledge is binding on me until I leave Bell Buckle for home." An additional pledge signed on all tests, papers, and other assignments states, "I pledge my word of honor as a Webb Lady/Gentleman that I have neither given nor received any help on this assignment."

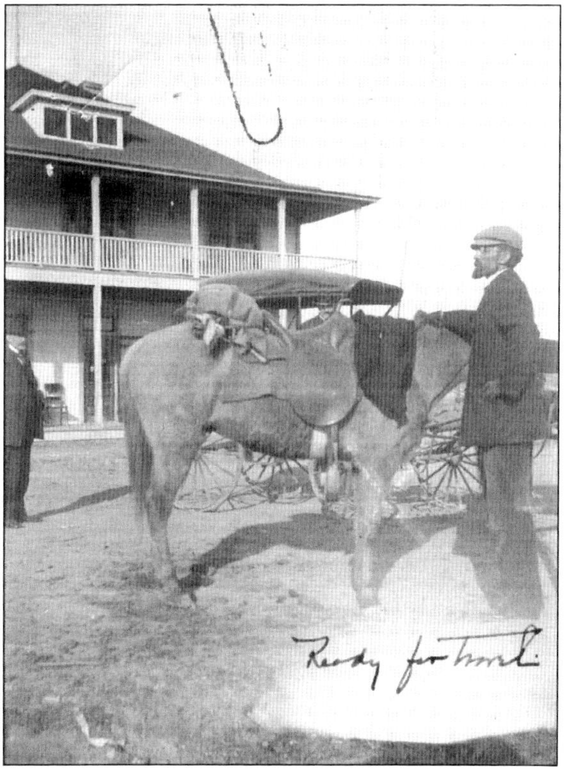

Charles Ottley. Ottley was an 1889 graduate of The Webb School and an 1893 graduate of Princeton University. After Princeton, he went on to study medicine at Johns Hopkins University. He became a medical missionary, then a hospital administrator, and a professor of biology. In 1906, Ottley returned to the United States to begin work in Atlanta, Georgia. However, the doctor died in 1907 in his early thirties. The infirmary at Oglethorpe University was named in his memory. While at Princeton, he and James Maclin Brodnax, another Webb School graduate, initiated the process, with the involvement of other students, of forming the Princeton Honor Code.

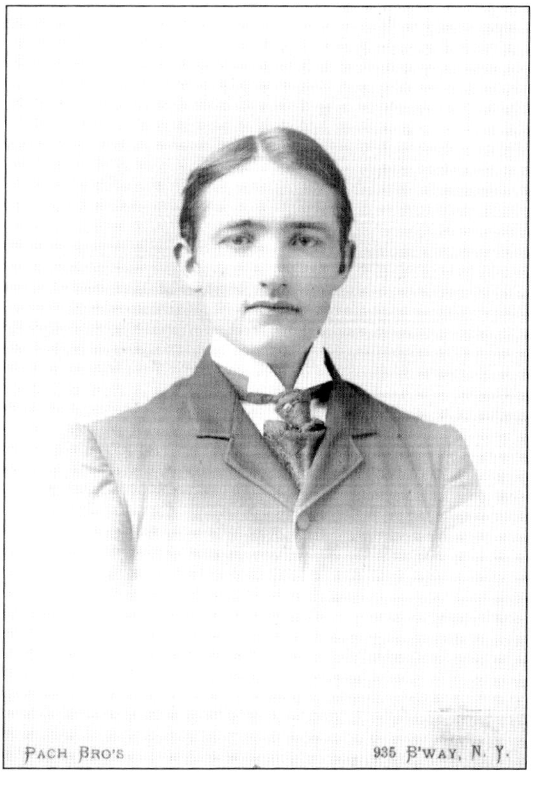

James Maclin Brodnax. Brodnax was an 1889 graduate of The Webb School and an 1894 graduate of Princeton University. He worked with Charles Ottley and other students to develop the Princeton Honor Code. (Courtesy of Princeton University Archives.)

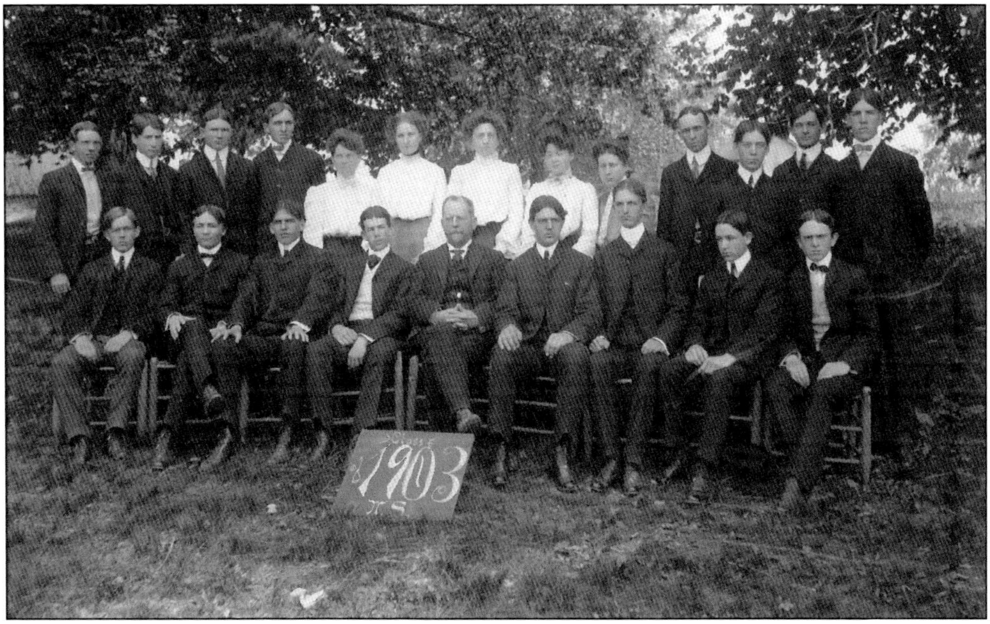

Senior Class of 1903. John M. Webb is pictured here with the senior class of 1903, sitting in the first row directly behind the sign. Since he taught the seniors, he was usually the one staff member pictured in the senior class photograph.

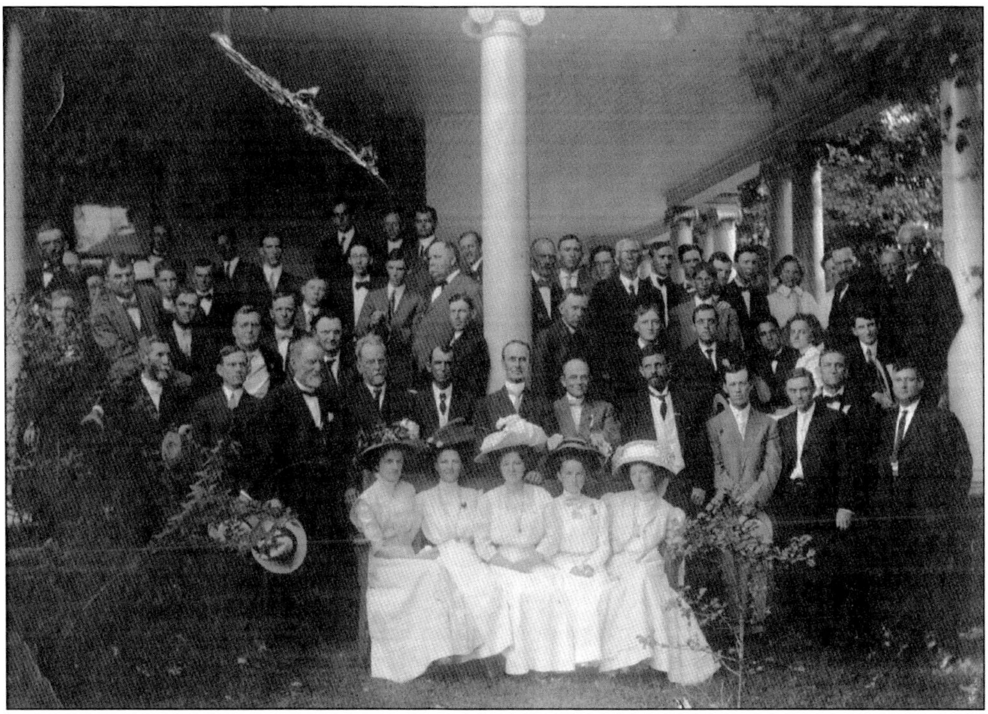

Commencement, 1909. Commencement exercises at Webb School usually lasted throughout the week. This photograph is from a gathering at the time of the 1909 commencement. There are former students, friends, family, and 1909 graduates in this picture. Several of the women in the first row are daughters of Sawney and John Webb.

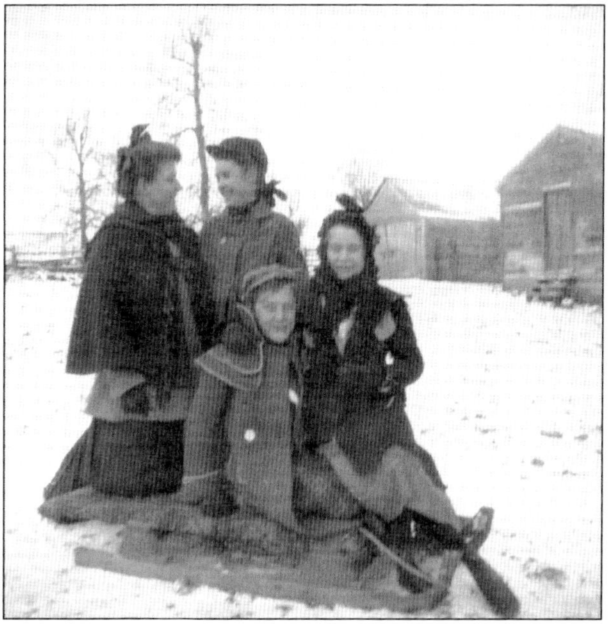

Sledding, 1906. This photograph, donated to the archives by Thompson Webb III, Sawney's great-grandson, is from an album of pictures taken around 1906 in Bell Buckle.

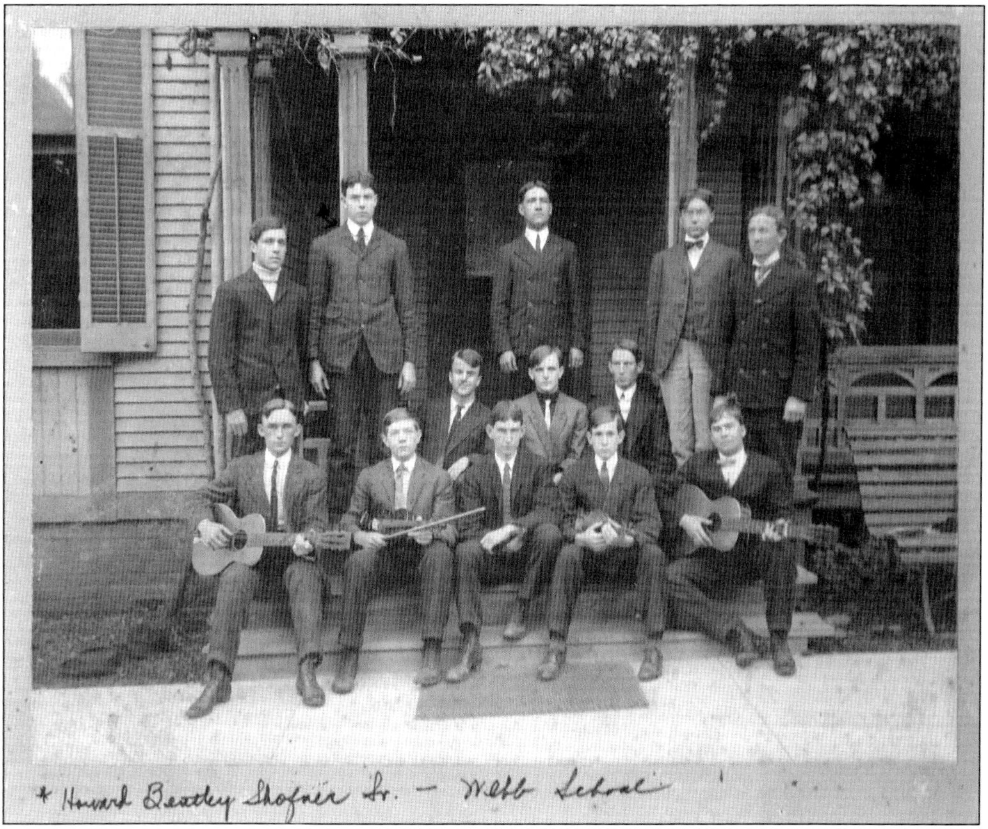

Orchestra, c. 1907. Orchestra was another activity in which students participated. Sawney's son, Richard Thompson Webb, stands in the third row, second from the right. This group is pictured in front of the John M. Webb home.

PRINCETON UNIVERSITY
PRINCETON, N. J.

PRESIDENT'S ROOM

22 November, 1905.

My dear Mr. Webb:-

I am planning to leave Nashville for Bell Buckle at 9:30 next Monday morning, the 27th, and shall hope to remain there until the train which returns to Nashville at 5 oclock in the afternoon.

I hope that these hours will prove suitable to your convenience and I shall look forward to the occasion with the greatest pleasure.

Cordially and sincerely yours,

Woodrow Wilson

Mr. W. R. Webb,

Bell Buckle, Tenn.

WOODROW WILSON VISITS BELL BUCKLE. Princeton's president Woodrow Wilson visited Bell Buckle on November 27, 1905. In the *Time* magazine issue from September 16, 1946, Wilson is quoted: "The Webbs defy all the accepted laws of pedagogy, but their boys were the best prepared that we got." He sent Sawney a letter to inform him of when he would be coming to Bell Buckle to visit. One of his engagements was to speak to the students.

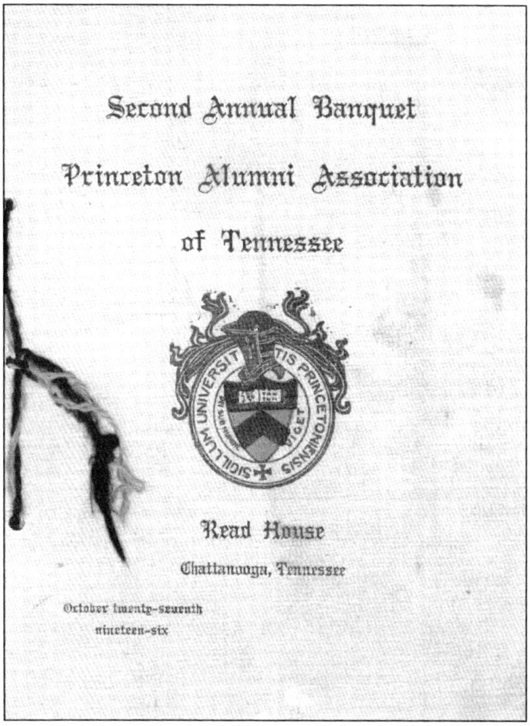

PRINCETON ALUMNI ASSOCIATION BANQUET. Sawney had many speaking engagements throughout his life as an educator. Pictured is the invitation for the Princeton Alumni Association Banquet that took place on October 27, 1906, in Chattanooga, Tennessee.

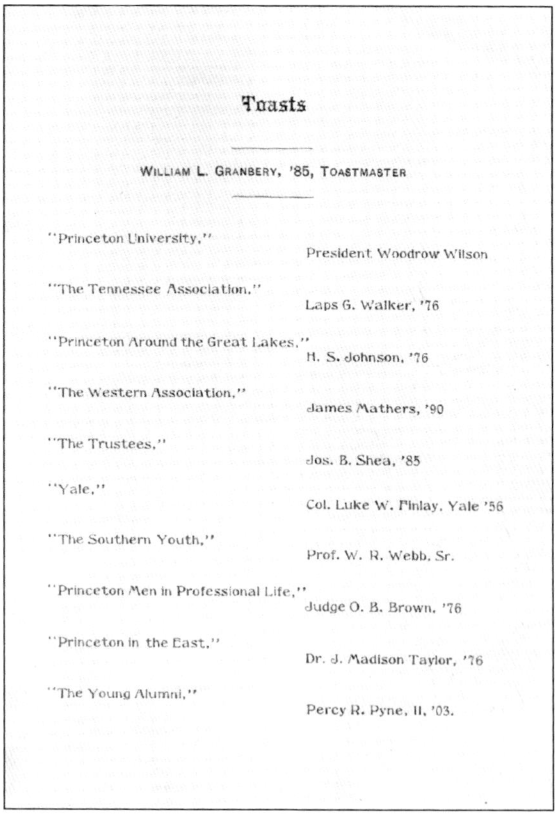

Toasts

WILLIAM L. GRANBERY, '85, TOASTMASTER

"Princeton University," — President Woodrow Wilson

"The Tennessee Association," — Laps G. Walker, '76

"Princeton Around the Great Lakes," — H. S. Johnson, '76

"The Western Association," — James Mathers, '90

"The Trustees," — Jos. B. Shea, '85

"Yale," — Col. Luke W. Finlay, Yale '56

"The Southern Youth," — Prof. W. R. Webb, Sr.

"Princeton Men in Professional Life," — Judge O. B. Brown, '76

"Princeton in the East," — Dr. J. Madison Taylor, '76

"The Young Alumni," — Percy R. Pyne, II, '03.

PRINCETON ALUMNI ASSOCIATION BANQUET AGENDA. The invitation included both the speakers' names and the menu for the event. Sawney spoke about "The Southern Youth." Woodrow Wilson, then president of Princeton, was included in the list of toasts.

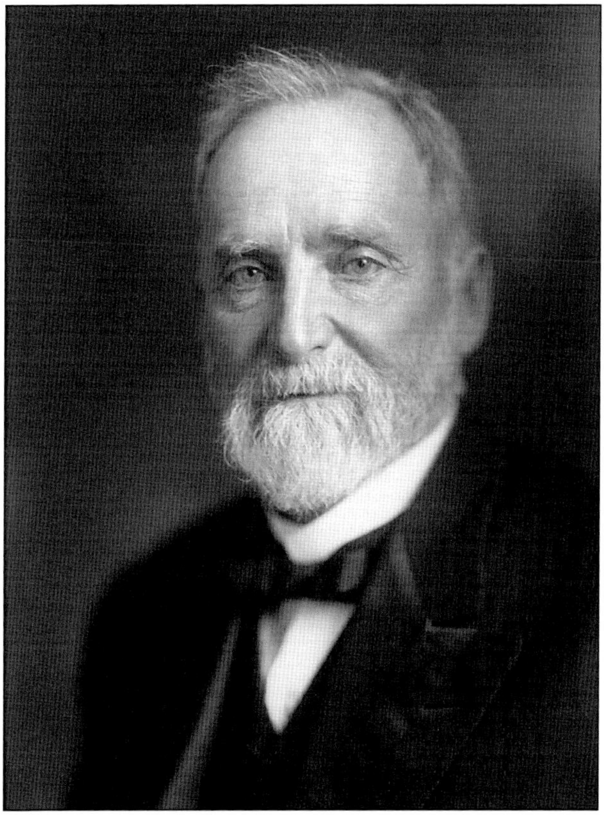

US Senator. Sawney Webb was elected on January 24, 1913, to fulfill the unexpired term of Sen. Robert L. Taylor. His term would last until March 3. He claimed this victory by receiving 73 votes, while his next-closest opponent, Judge M.T. Bryan, received 53 votes.

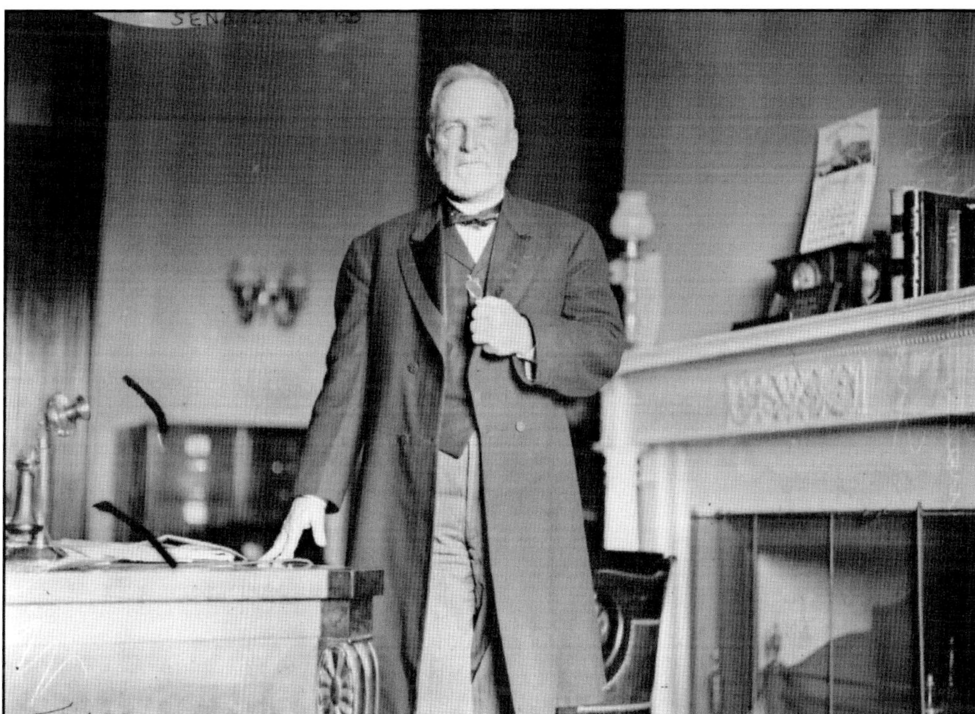

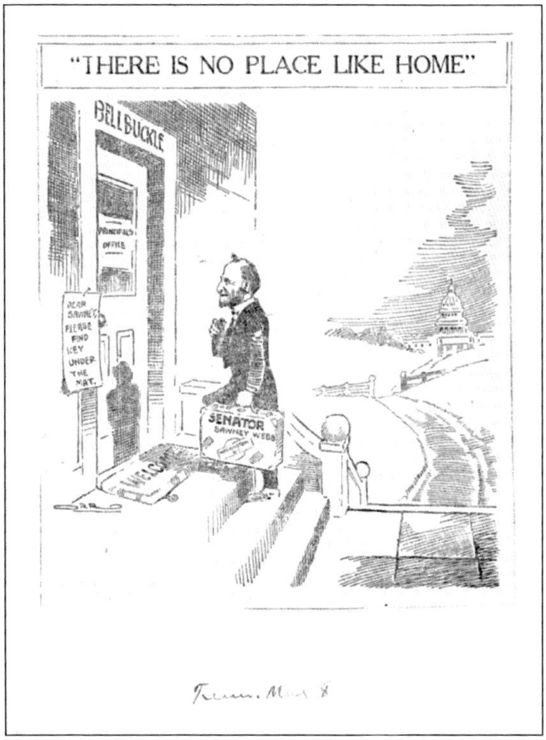

SENATE CARTOON. At least two of Sawney's former students were responsible for Sawney's declaration of election to the US Senate. They were 1878 Webb graduate Newton White and 1894 graduate Frank F. McCombs. Sawney was nominated by his boys; he did not choose to run for the Senate.

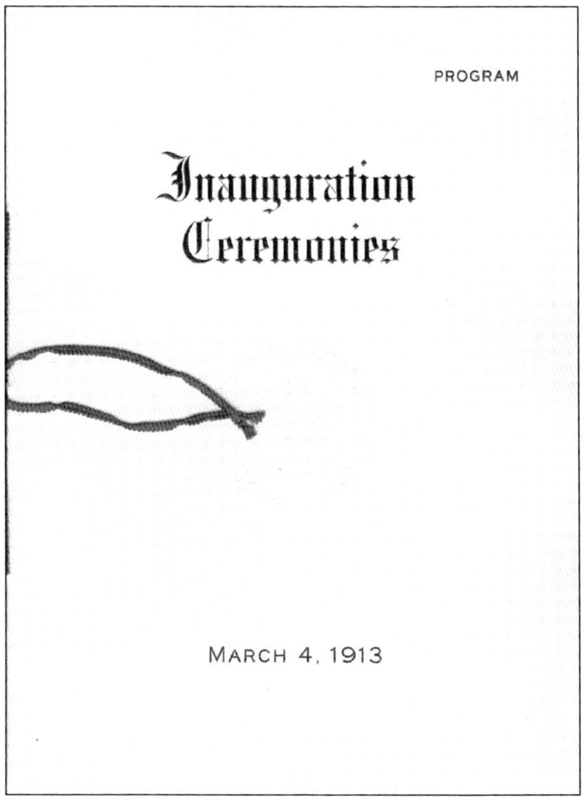

INAUGURATION. This program details the activities of the inauguration ceremony for Woodrow Wilson on March 4, 1913. Many items like this program can be found in Sawney's senatorial scrapbook, including news clippings, invitations, and other programs.

Young Alla. Alla Webb was the first daughter born to Sawney Webb Sr. and Martha Emma Clary Webb. She attended Webb School in Bell Buckle. Following that, she studied at Wesleyan College in Massachusetts. She then graduated from the University of Chicago in Illinois.

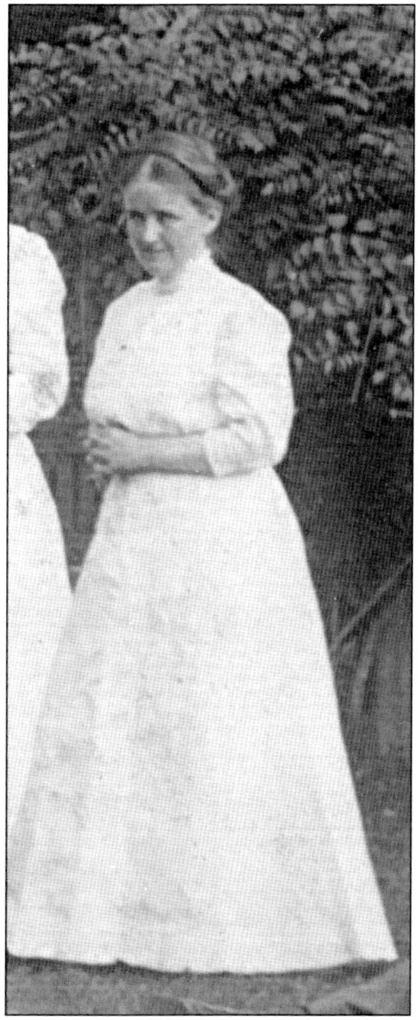

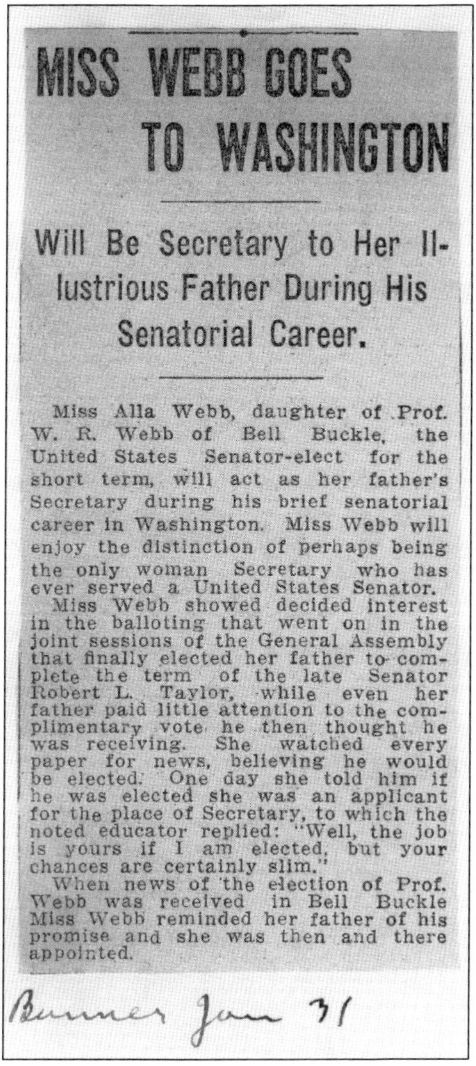

MISS WEBB GOES TO WASHINGTON

Will Be Secretary to Her Illustrious Father During His Senatorial Career.

Miss Alla Webb, daughter of Prof. W. R. Webb of Bell Buckle, the United States Senator-elect for the short term, will act as her father's Secretary during his brief senatorial career in Washington. Miss Webb will enjoy the distinction of perhaps being the only woman Secretary who has ever served a United States Senator.

Miss Webb showed decided interest in the balloting that went on in the joint sessions of the General Assembly that finally elected her father to complete the term of the late Senator Robert L. Taylor, while even her father paid little attention to the complimentary vote he then thought he was receiving. She watched every paper for news, believing he would be elected. One day she told him if he was elected she was an applicant for the place of Secretary, to which the noted educator replied: "Well, the job is yours if I am elected, but your chances are certainly slim."

When news of the election of Prof. Webb was received in Bell Buckle Miss Webb reminded her father of his promise and she was then and there appointed.

Banner Jan 31

Miss Webb Goes to Washington. Alla Webb held at least two teaching positions in her career, one as a teacher at Randolph-Macon Woman's College and another at Agnes Scott Academy. She also held the title of librarian at Flagler Memorial Library in Miami, Florida. She worked as an assistant to the librarian at Scripps College in Claremont, California. One of the most significant jobs that Alla held was secretary to her father when he went to Washington as a US senator. Having had experience as a librarian, Alla also cataloged by the Dewey decimal system all of the Webb library books when they were moved from the Senior Room to the newly built John Webb Library in 1928.

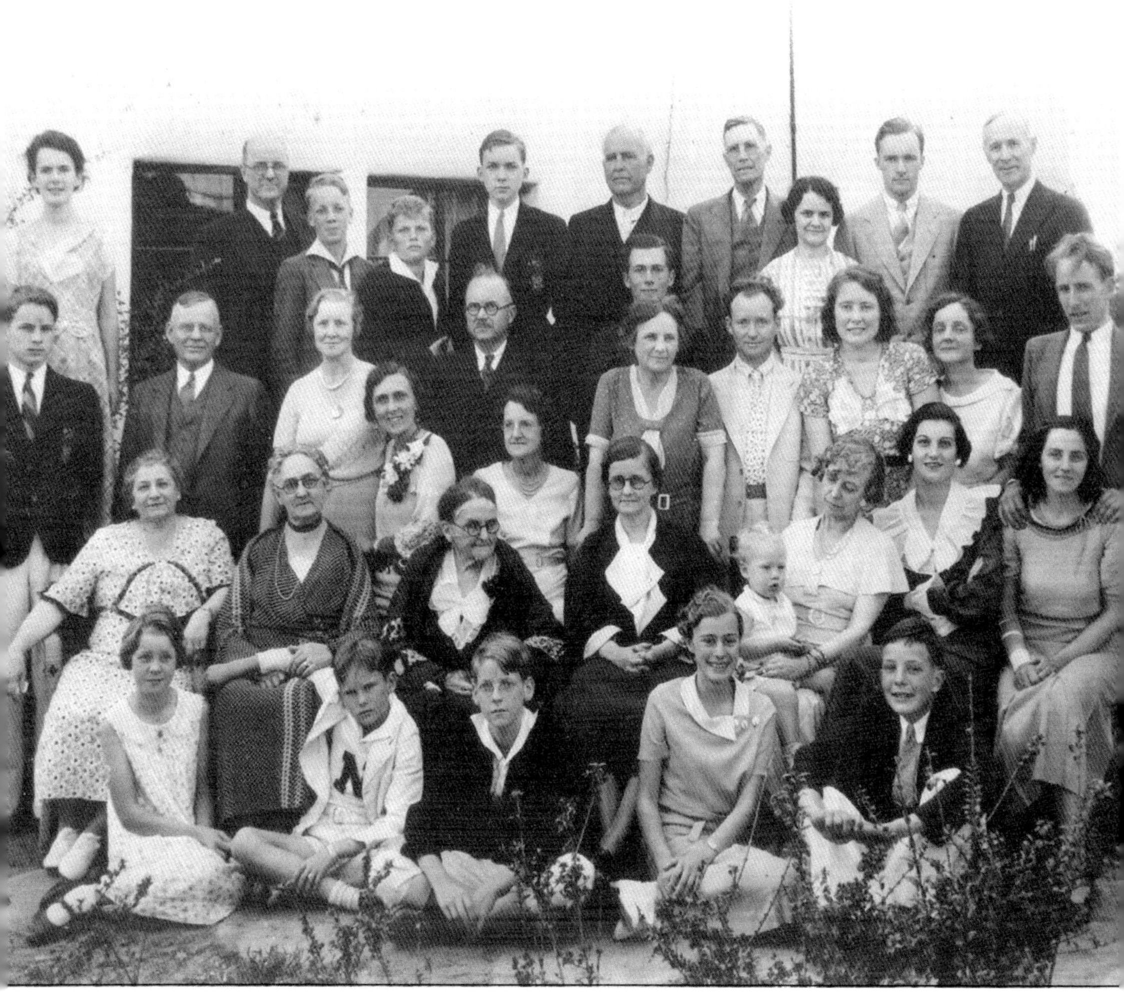

Webb Family Portrait. In 1934, Son Will was asked to be the commencement speaker at The Webb School in Claremont, California, the school that was founded by his brother, R. Thompson Webb. Several of the family members were already residing in California. At this occasion, many members of the family came together for a Webb family reunion. This is a picture of that gathering. From left to right are (first row) Margaret Webb, Jack Webb, George Webb, Emily Price, and Joe Sibley; (second row) Louise Webb, Loulie Howell, Emma Clary Webb, Alla Webb, Leno Webb, Philip Steed (baby), Lois Sibley, and Florence Webb; (third row) Tom Webb, Son Will Webb, Julia Webb, Vivian Webb, Thompson Webb, Susan Webb Price, Peyton Sibley, Adeline Webb Sibley, Victor Steed, Emma Webb Steed, Emma Webb McLean, and Sawney Ben Webb; (fourth row) Susanne McLean, Daniel Clary Webb, Bob Webb, Bill Webb, Howell Webb, John Stanford Webb, Richard Webb, Minnie Wilson Webb, Ed Price Jr., and Ed Price Sr.

Family Shakespeare Connection. William Shakespeare's grandmother Mary Webb was Sawney and John's ninth great-grandmother, born in 1512 in Stratford, England. Shakespeare's mother was Mary Arden, the brothers' eighth great-grand-aunt, born in 1537 in Warwickshire. Shakespeare was Sawney and John's first cousin nine times removed. This pedigree chart was created by George Webb.

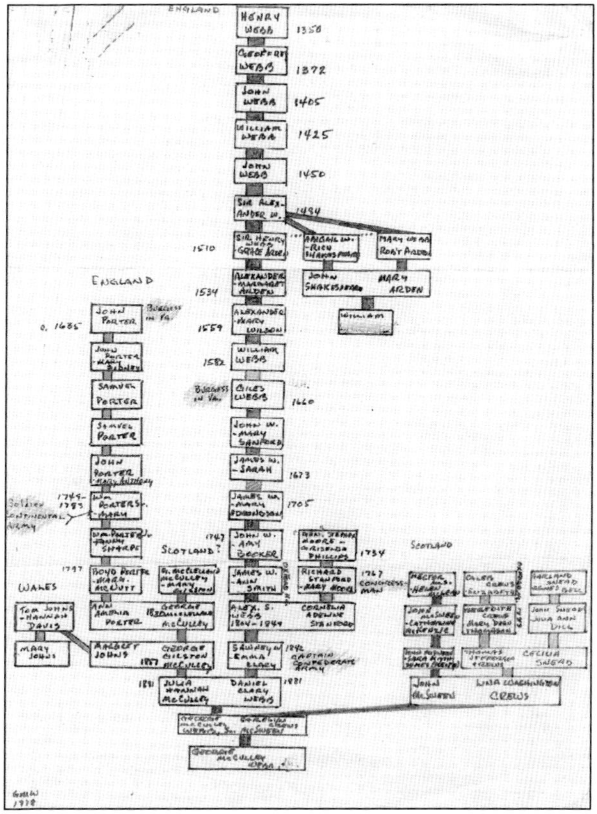

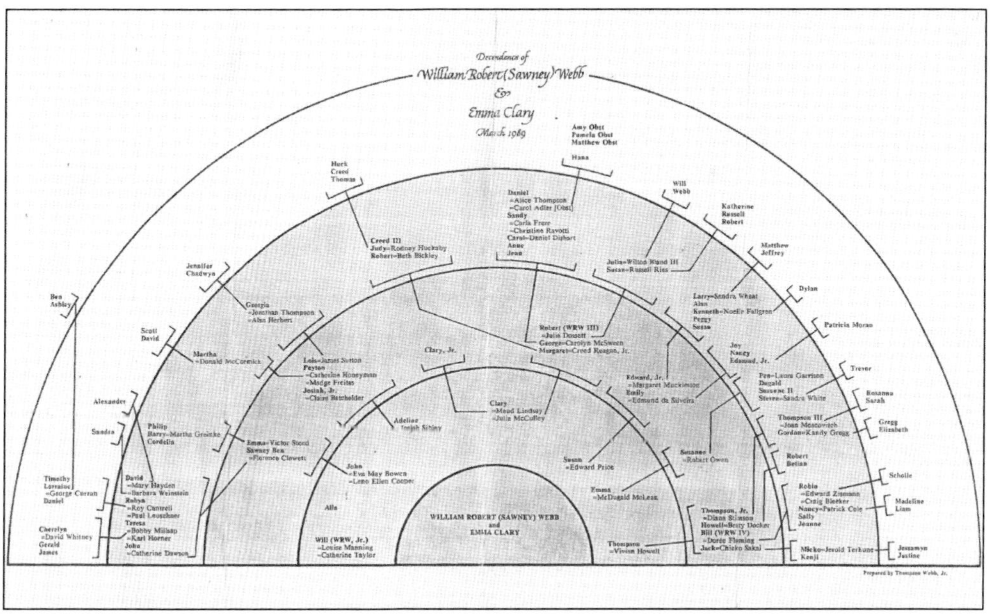

Family Tree. Sawney's son Thompson Webb with his wife, Vivian Webb, founded The Webb Schools in Claremont, California. Son Will did not have a biological child, so he mentored his nephew Bob Webb, his namesake. Sawney's grandson William R. "Bob" Webb III and his wife, Julie, founded The Webb School in Knoxville, Tennessee.

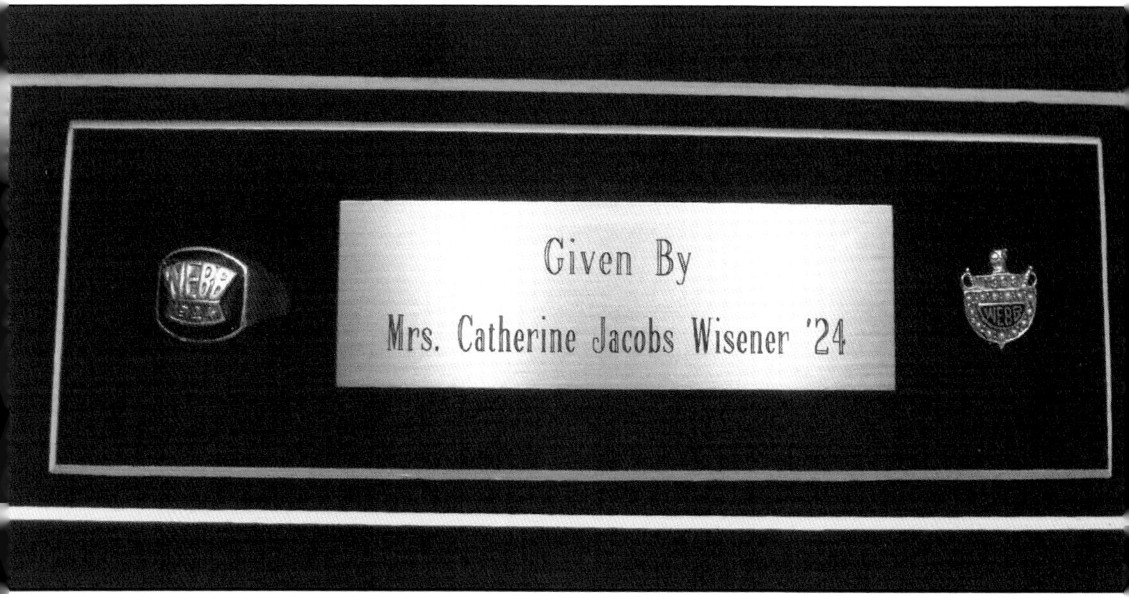

CLASS OF 1924 RING. Pictured is a ring and class pin given to the school archives by 1924 graduate Catherine Jacobs Wisener. The pin is ornate, and neither it nor the ring feature the school seal. Wisener was a textile artist whose yo-yo quilts were featured in the Charleston Museum in Charleston, South Carolina. Yo-yo quilts were popular during the Great Depression presumably because the pieces could be made with very small scraps of fabric. Wisener was one of three women in the class of 1924. The other two were Alison Webster and Dorothy Webb. Webb, Sawney's grandniece, was a Webb librarian and can be found in the 1953 yearbook as a sponsor of the Art Guild. She was also the dean of women at Birmingham Southern College.

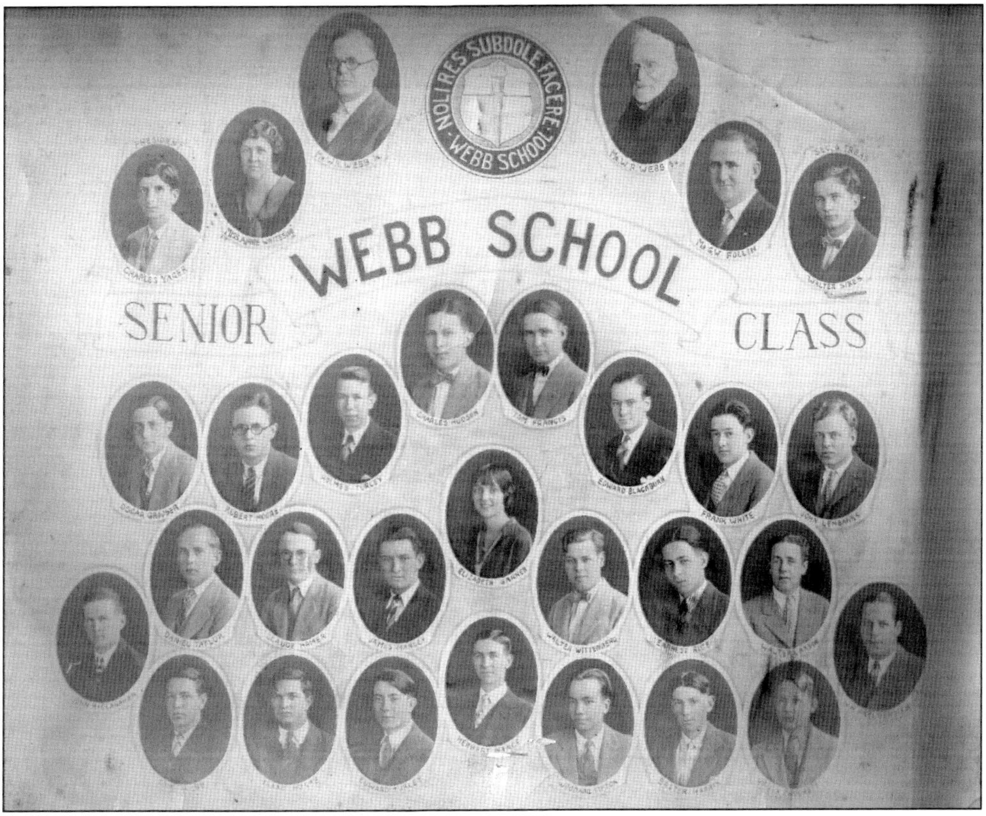

WEBB SCHOOL MOTTO AND SEAL ON THE 1926 CLASS COMPOSITE. One of the first documented uses of the seal is in the 1926 class composite. Ironically, this was the last school year Sawney was alive. "Noli Res Subdole Facere" is Latin for "Do Nothing on the Sly." This is something Sawney always emphasized to his students. It later became the school motto.

CLASS OF 1937 PIN. This pin belonged to 1937 graduate June Carroll. Her initials, JAC, are inscribed on the back. This simple, direct statement forms the basic foundation of Webb School's honor code. The sentence was a frequent admonition of the school's founder Sawney Webb and was translated into Latin as the school's motto.

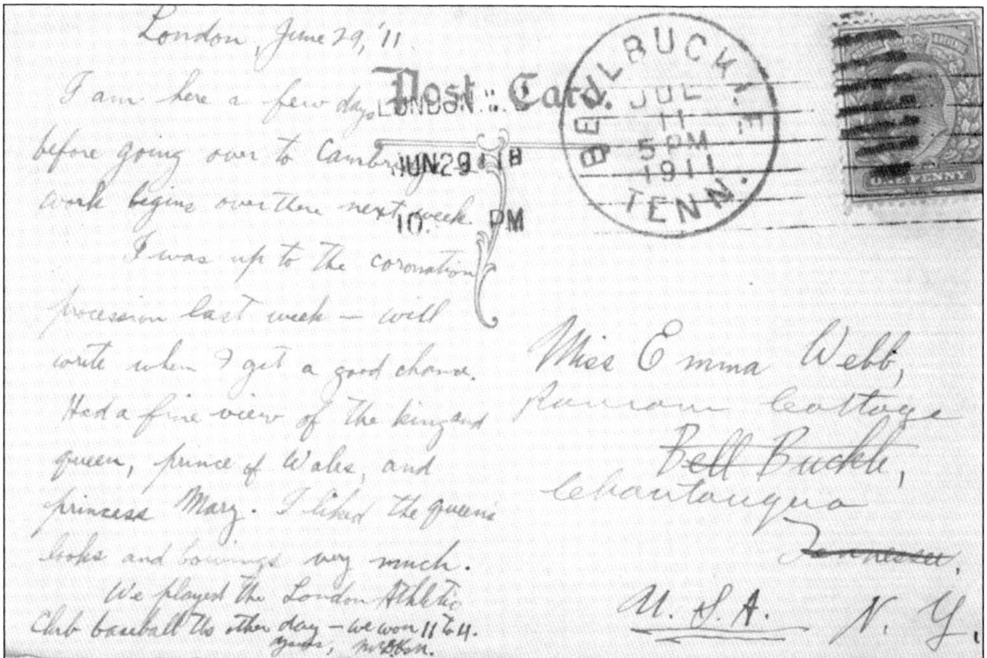

London, June 29, '11.

I am here a few days before going over to Cambridge. Work begins over there next week.

I was up to the coronation procession last week — will write when I get a good chance. Had a fine view of the king and queen, prince of Wales, and princess Mary. I liked the queen's looks and bowings very much.

We played the London Athletic Club baseball the other day — we won 11 to 4.

Yours,

Post Card

LONDON JUN 29 11 10 PM

BELLBUCKLE JUL 11 5 PM 1911 TENN.

ONE PENNY

Miss Emma Webb,
Ransom Cottage
~~Bell Buckle~~,
Chautauqua
~~Tennessee~~,
U.S.A. N.Y.

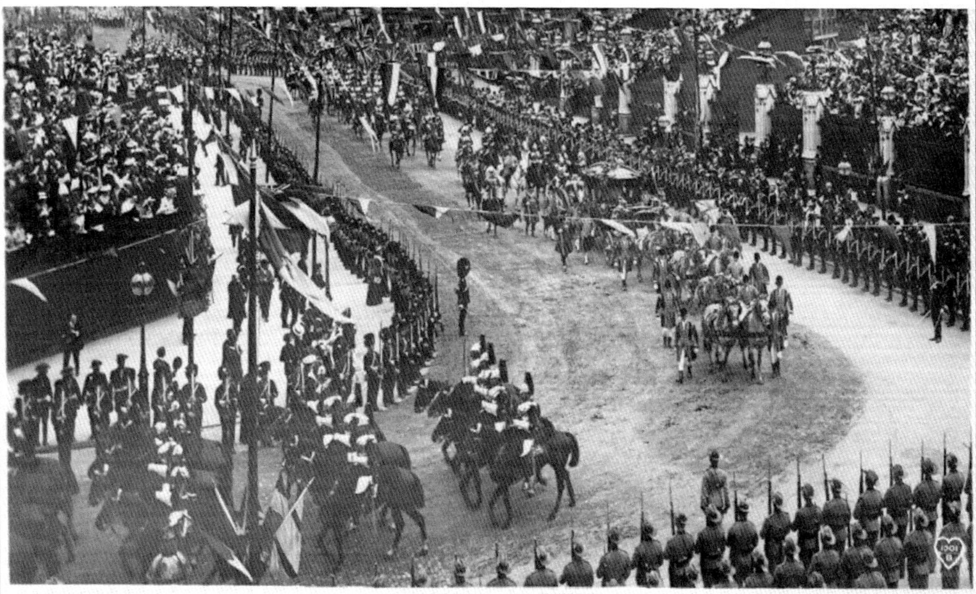

CORONATION PROCESSION.
ROYAL CARRIAGE.

POSTCARD FROM OXFORD. This is a postcard McDugald McLean (class of 1904) sent to Emma Webb (1902), Sawney's daughter, whom he later married. The postcard was written while McLean was studying as one of The Webb School's Rhodes scholars in England in 1911.

Two

WILLIAM R. "SON WILL" WEBB JR.

1926–1953

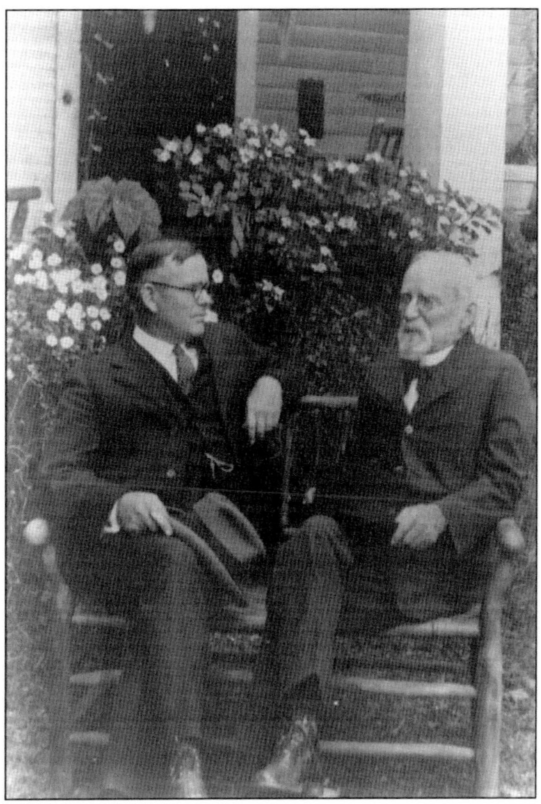

SON WILL WITH SAWNEY. William R. "Son Will" Webb Jr. was the oldest child of Sawney and Emma Webb. Son Will followed in his father's footsteps to become the head of The Webb School in Bell Buckle.

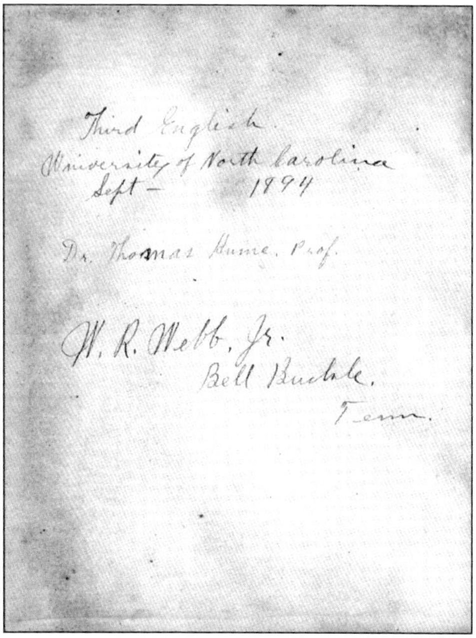

Third English
University of North Carolina
Sept – 1894

Dr. Thomas Hume, Prof.

W. R. Webb, Jr.
Bell Buckle.
Tenn.

The Education of Son Will. Following high school, Son Will attended the University of North Carolina at Chapel Hill, graduating magna cum laude in 1896. He was an instructor at UNC for one year before he returned to The Webb School in Bell Buckle and began working with his father and uncle John. Pictured is Son Will's English journal from 1894 when he was attending UNC.

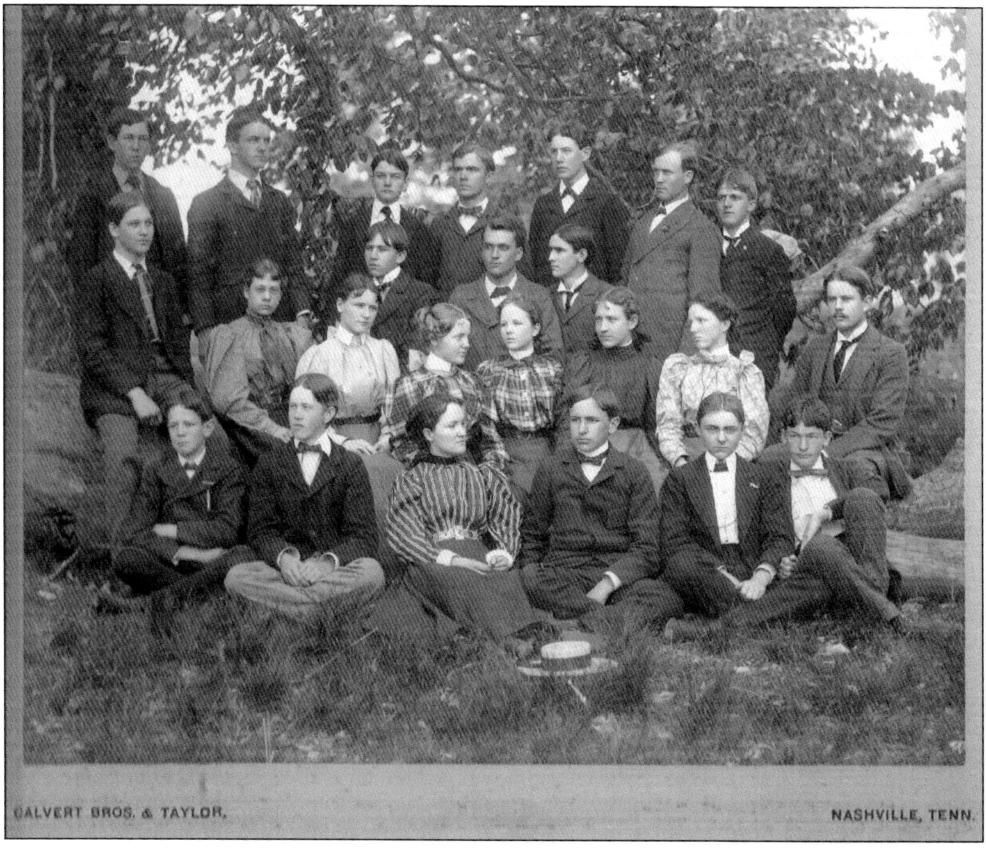

Son Will with Class. Son Will is pictured in the second row on the far right, sitting on the log. He was the teacher of this junior class of 1897–1898.

THE WEDDING. As the bride was the daughter of a renowned university professor in North Carolina, the guest list was a who's who of the education world at the time. Calling cards were left at their wedding representing those in attendance. Guests included the likes of Edwin Anderson Alderman, who served as the president of three universities.

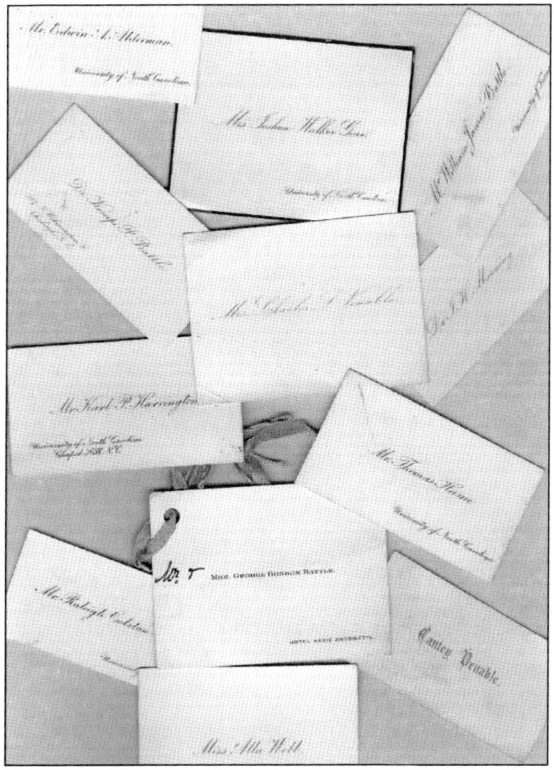

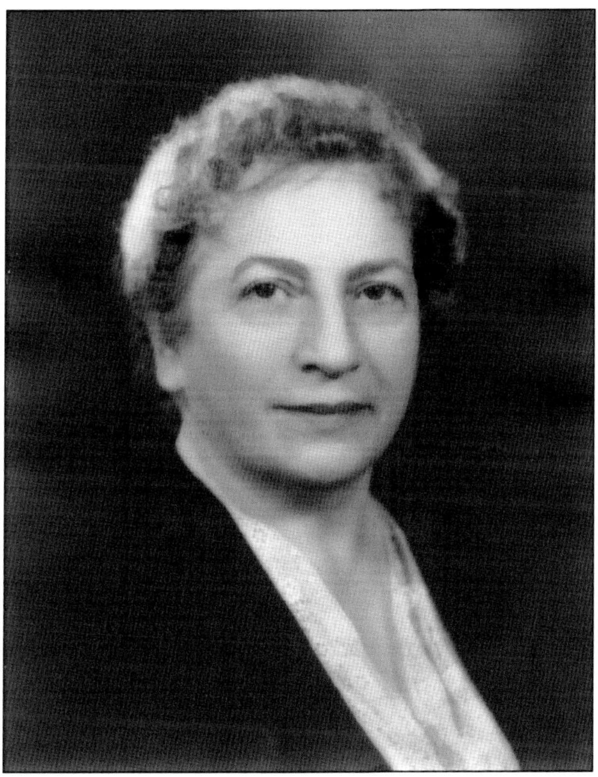

LOUISE MANNING WEBB. Son Will and Louise Hall Manning were married on October 19, 1898. Son Will absolutely adored Louise, as is seen through his letters to her.

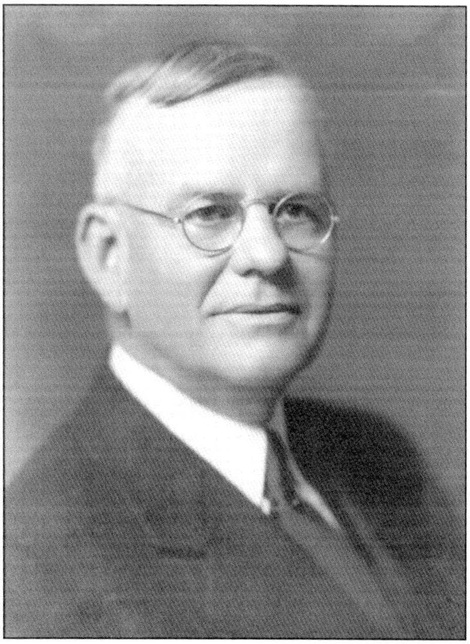

Son Will, Principal. Son Will was the principal of record from 1926 to 1953; however, he began assisting his father and uncle as early as 1908. His service as principal was nearly as long-serving as that of his father.

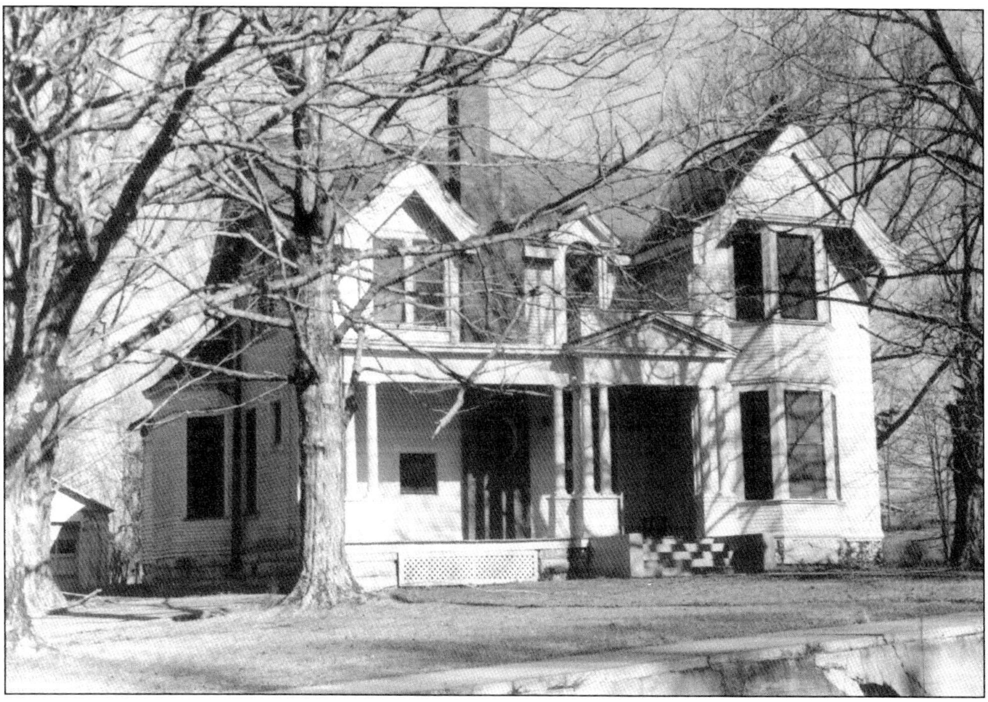

Will Webb House. Seen here is the home of William R. "Son Will" Webb Jr. and Louise Manning Webb, also known as the Will Webb House. Students would visit their home on Sunday nights. Susanne Webb McLean, Sawney's granddaughter and Son Will's niece, lived with Son Will and Louise while she was a student at Webb, so it was also used to board students. The home was remodeled in the mid-1960s as a new student recreation center. It was operated primarily by the students with minimal assistance from the faculty. It stood on campus until November 1970, when it burned down.

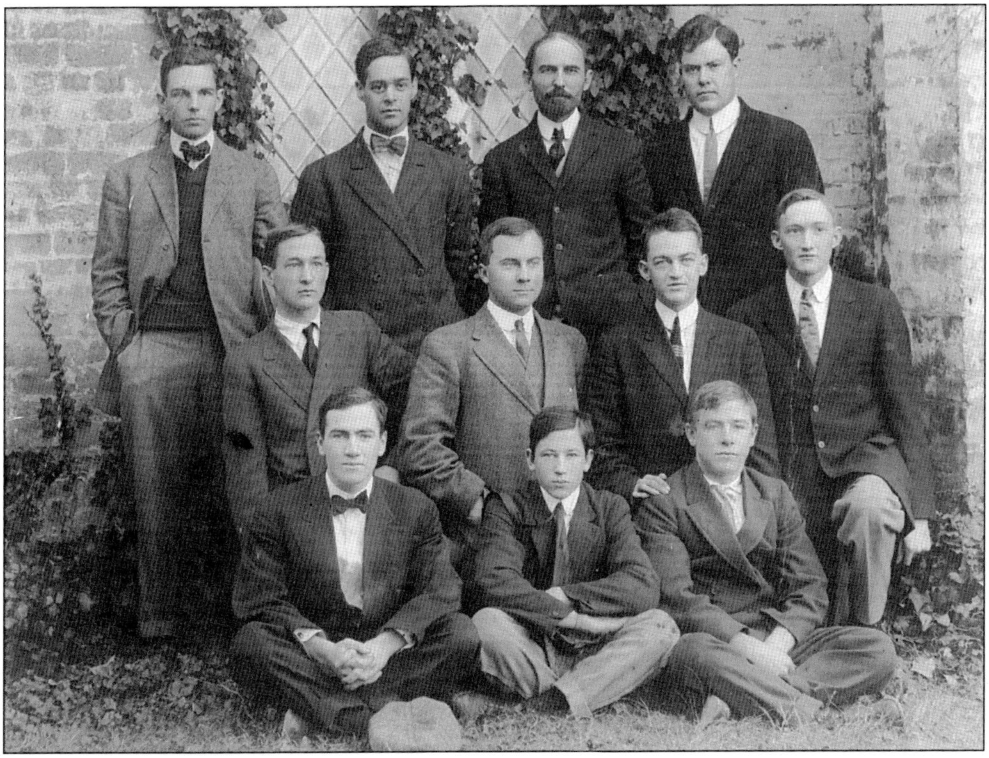

The Webb School Club at UNC, 1911. This photograph includes former Webb School students who were at UNC at that time. Thompson is in the second row, second from left. In the third row, second from right, is 1888 Webb graduate Edwin Mims, a professor at UNC at the time.

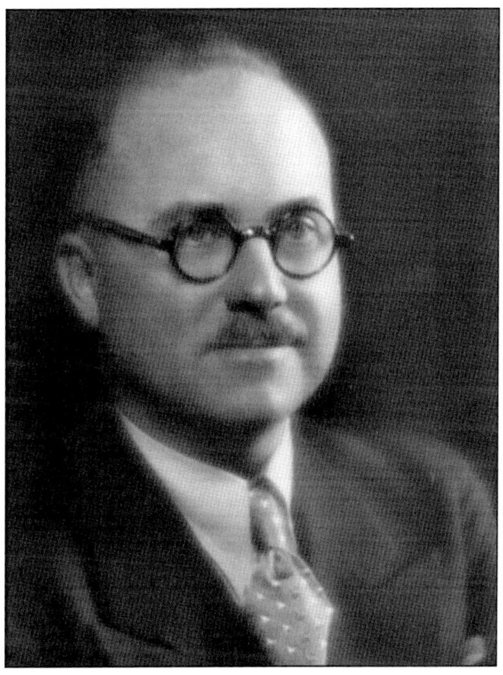

Thompson Webb. Richard Thompson Webb Sr. was the last child born to Sawney and Emma Clary Webb. He was a 1907 graduate of The Webb School in Bell Buckle and continued his education at UNC, graduating in 1911. He did some work in the Webb Summer Camps in Walling, Tennessee. He also did some farming with his brother John in California. In 1915, Thompson married Vivian Howell, and they had five children together. In 1922, Thompson decided to start his own school in Claremont, California, and named it The Webb School. (Webb Schools of Claremont.)

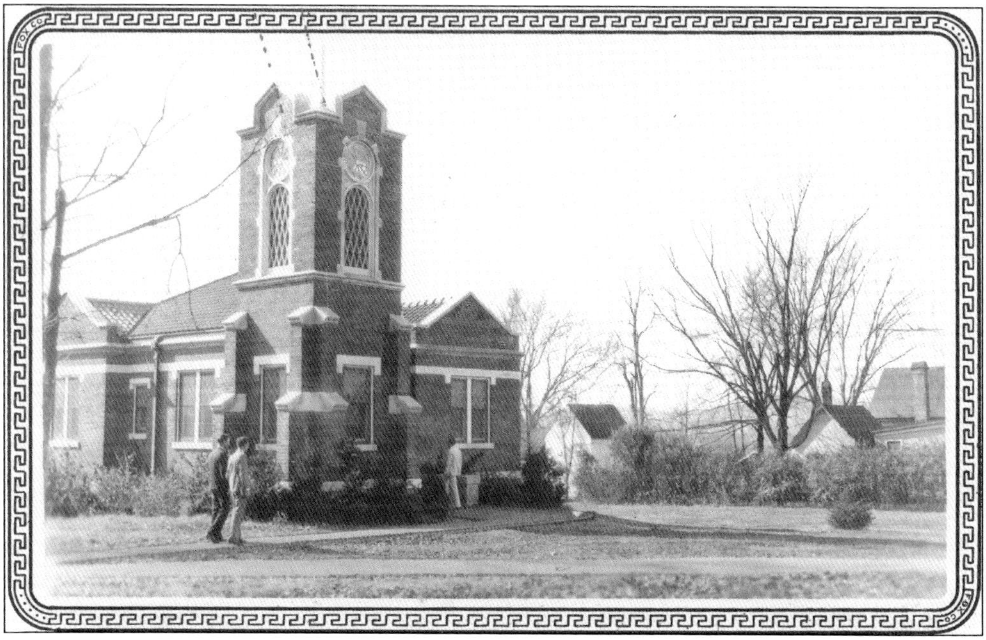

THE SON WILL BUILDING. The Son Will Building was erected in 1926, and was the first property constructed in the 1920s building campaign; it housed Webb's administrative offices. Many years later, a new administrative building was constructed during another campaign. Today, this building houses Webb's admissions office.

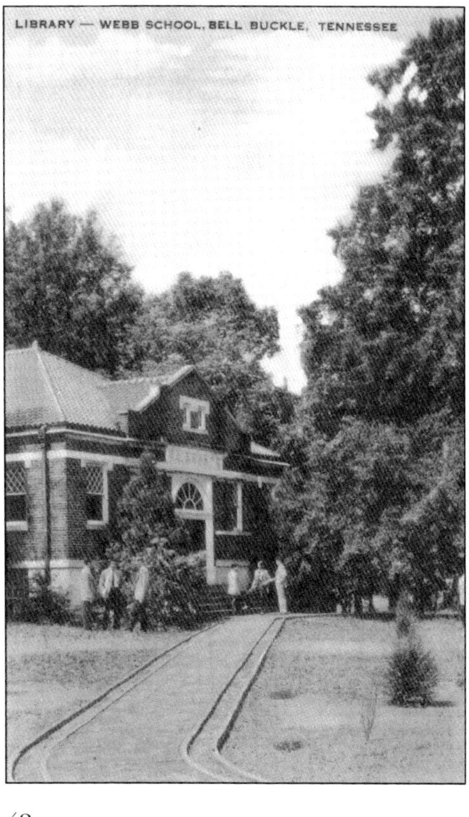

THE JOHN WEBB LIBRARY. Named after one of the founders, the John Webb Library was built in 1927. The graduating class of 1903 was responsible for the library being built, and J. Russell Simpson (class of 1903) was the principal donor. It was completed and dedicated in 1928. In the early 1930s, the first chemistry bench and equipment that started Webb's first modern science program was housed in the basement of the library. This science lab was used until the early 1950s, when it was moved to the Big Room. The library basement was then converted into a studio. In the early 1970s, the library basement was converted into a lounge for students.

TIGERS AND BULLDOGS THANKSGIVING DAY FOOTBALL GAME, 1935. In the early days at Webb, there were only intramural sports. Each year, Webb had a Thanksgiving Day football game. Pictured is the program from that game on November 28, 1935, when the Tigers took on the Bulldogs.

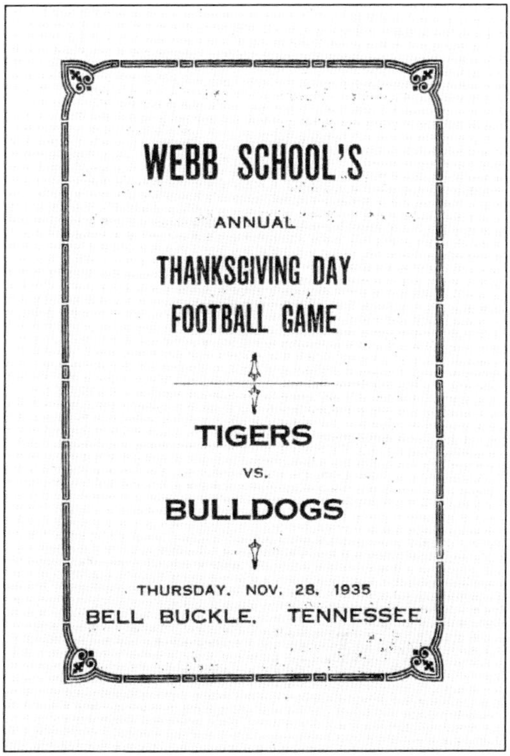

TIGERS. Sawney established a system of intramural sports a year after a fighting incident that occurred while Webb and Vanderbilt were playing baseball. Students were divided into teams; two of the more commonly known teams were the Tigers and the Bulldogs. Pictured here is the 1922 Tigers football team.

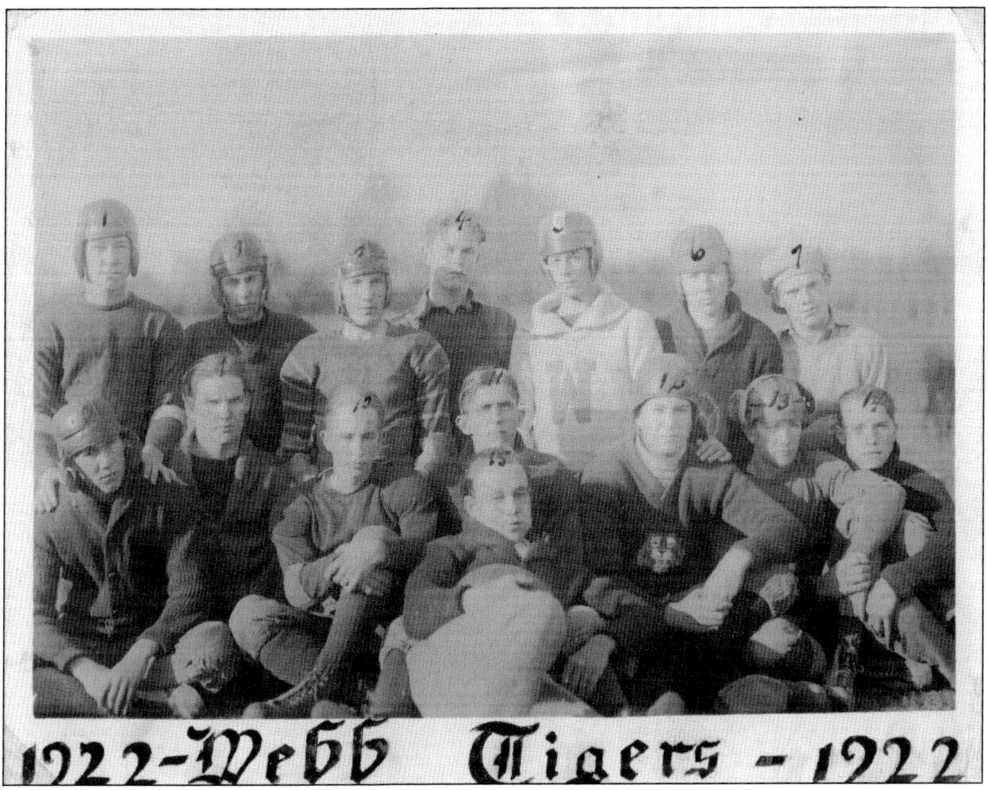

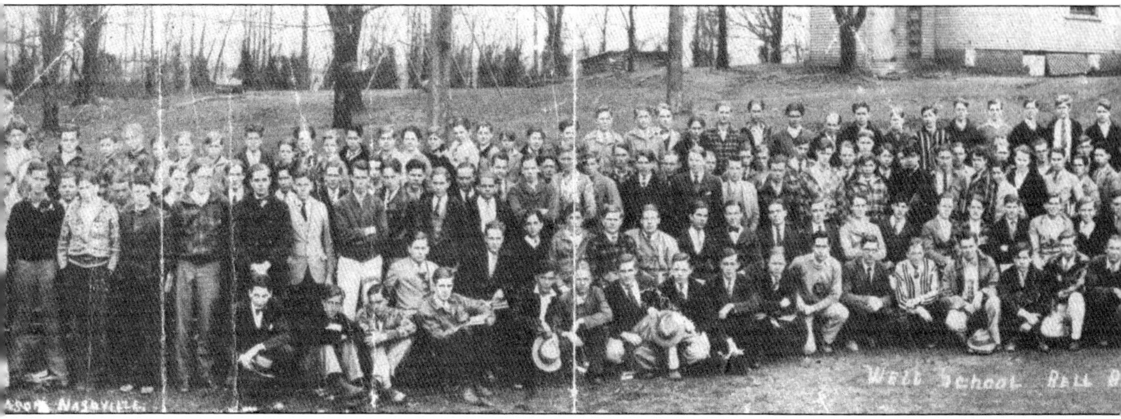

All-School Photograph, c. 1927. The all-school photograph is a longtime tradition at The Webb School and is taken in a panoramic style; they have continued to be taken up until the last few years. The original camera was in use until 2015. After that year, the school employed modern panoramic digital cameras. The only sad part about the change is that a student could run behind the group and appear in the photograph twice with the antique method. This photograph was taken in 1927 and included a prominent Webb graduate, Jac

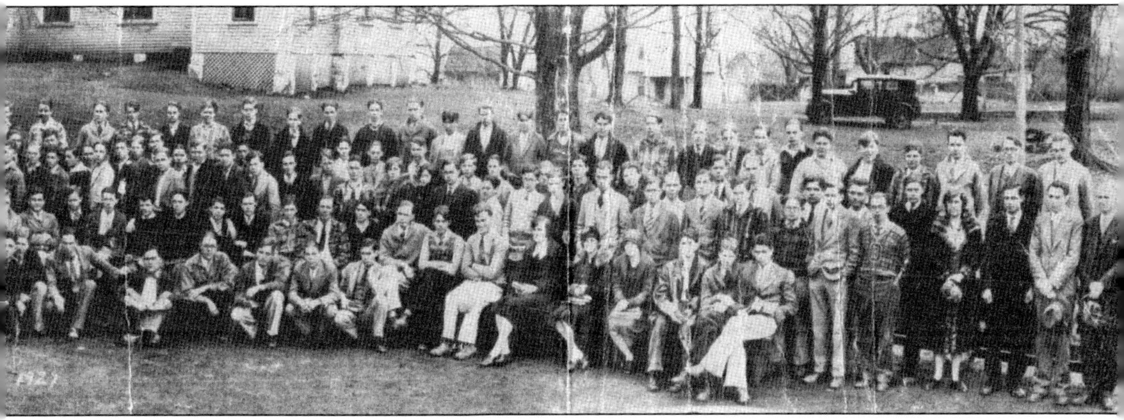

Chambliss. Chambliss was a Webb trustee, a gunnery officer in the Navy in World War II in the South Pacific, a trial lawyer, a poet, and a fellow of the Royal Society of Arts of London. The class of 1927, with 41 members, rivaled the size of modern-day senior classes at Webb. The class of 2019 has 45 members. These all-school photographs capture not only the senior class but the whole school, including faculty and staff. With the new format, the picture is now available in color.

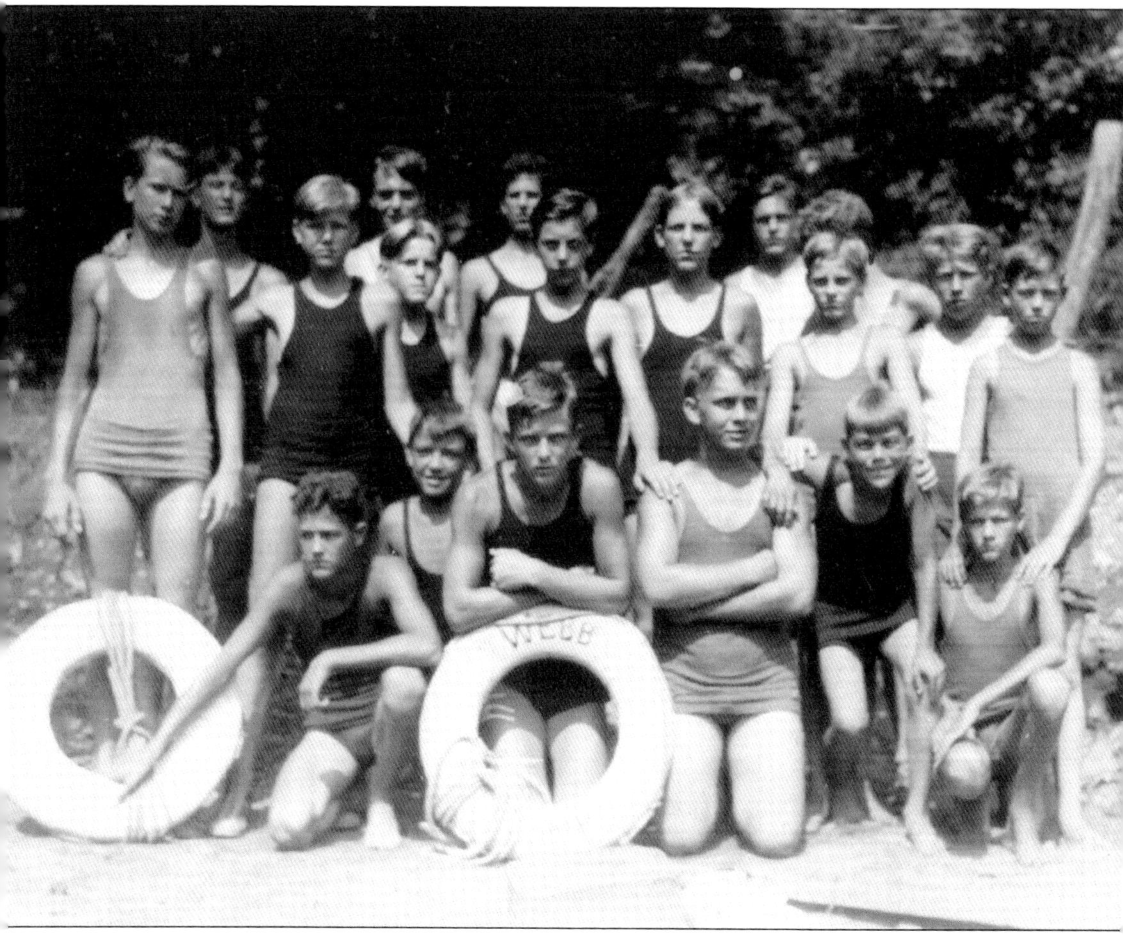

Webb Camp. Webb Summer School or Webb Camp began in 1898 and continued through 1939. It was located in the Cumberland Mountains near Walling, Tennessee. Ed T. Price was a director, and there were others who worked at the camp as well. From 1925 to 1939, G.W. Follin directed the camp. Webb Summer School resumed in 1975, except that it took place on the school's campus. This time, it was directed by faculty member Glenn Holliman.

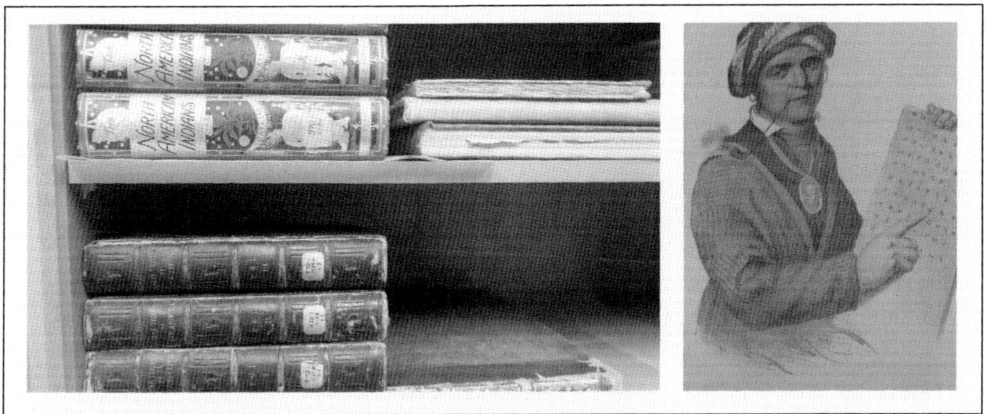

Son Will's Rare Book Collection. The Webb School Library and Archives is home to the collection and papers of the founder's firstborn Son Will. The library and archives provide education and access to the many pursuits of William R. Webb Jr., including but not limited to World War I support and propaganda, Native American research, Tennessee highways, and Webb summer camps. Pictured are rare books from the extensive Native American collection.

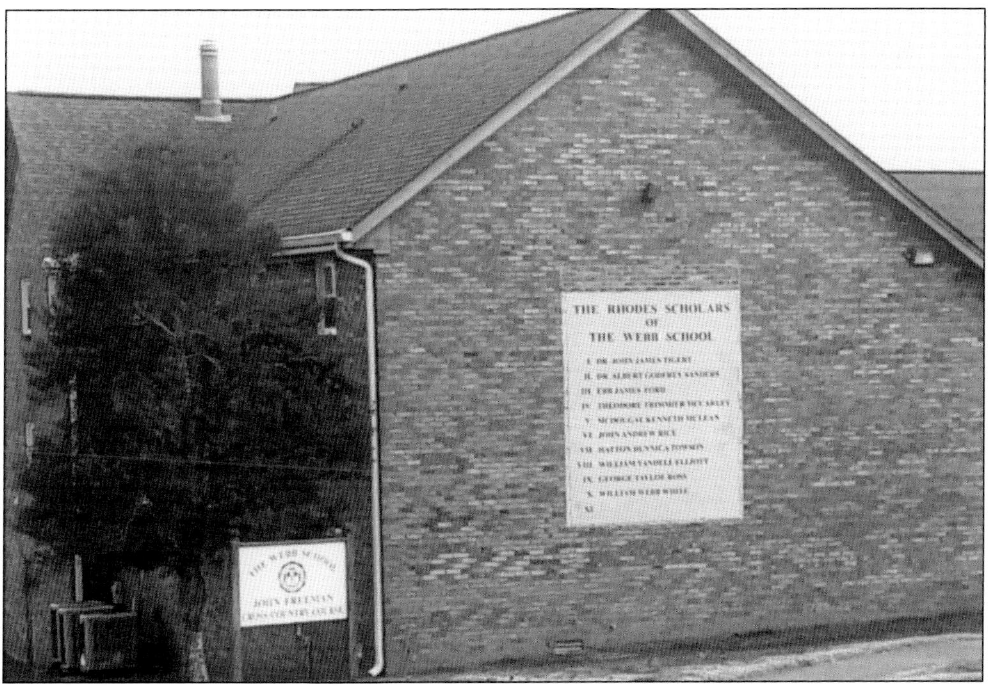

Rhodes Scholars. Engraved in stone on the side of Davis Dormitory are the names of all the Rhodes scholars from The Webb School. By 1917, Webb had more Rhodes scholars than any other secondary school at that time. In fact, the first Rhodes scholar from Tennessee was a Webb graduate.

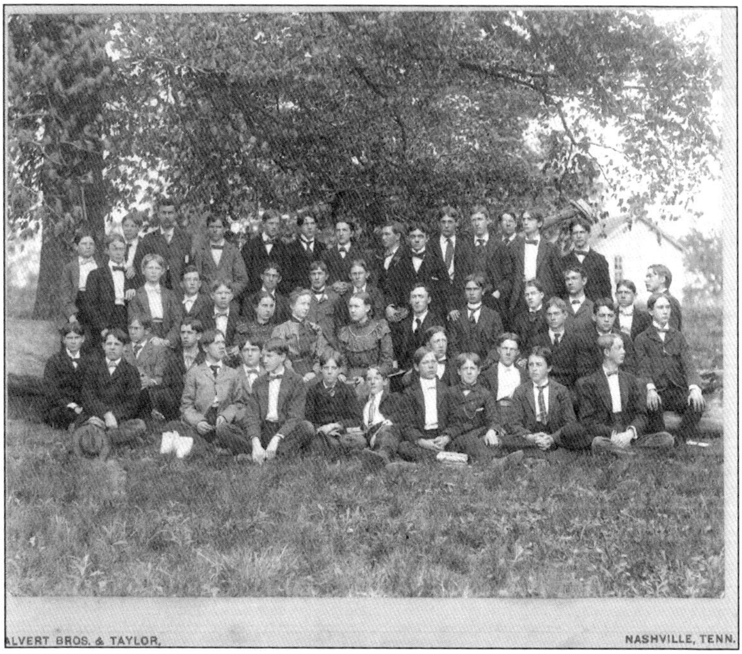

JOHN JAMES TIGERT. Dr. John James Tigert was a 1900 Webb graduate. He was also Webb's first Rhodes scholar. Pictured is Webb's Caesar class of 1897–1898 with teacher R.G. Peoples. Dr. John James Tigert stands in the back row, fourth from the left.

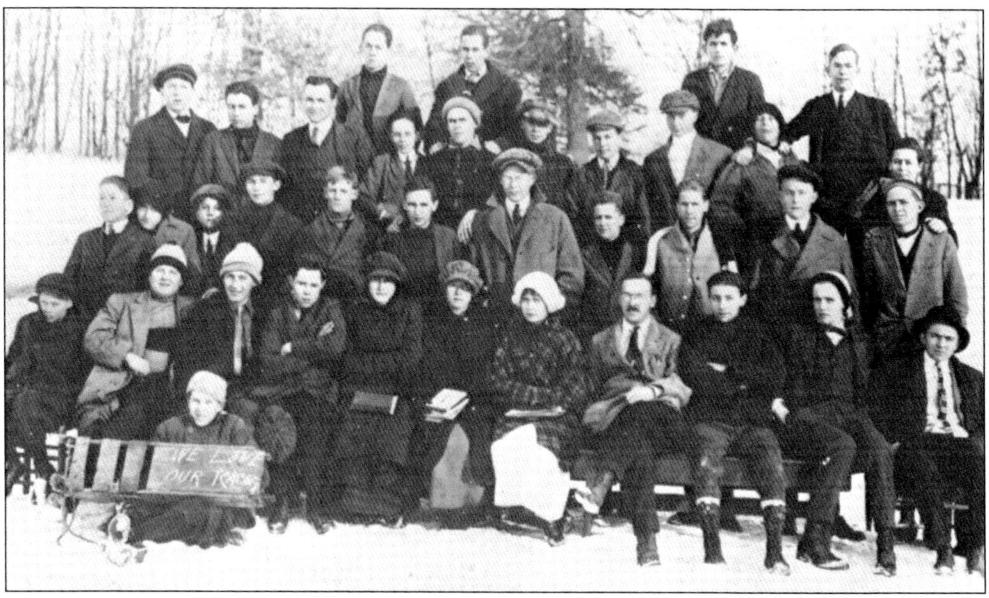

JOHN ANDREW RICE. One of the Rhodes scholars from Webb went on to found Black Mountain College near Asheville, North Carolina. The Caesar class of 1914–1915 is pictured here with John Andrew Rice, their teacher and 1908 Webb graduate. John Andrew Rice favored John Webb over Sawney. Though Black Mountain College was successful for a short time with the scholar at the helm, it could have benefitted from an administrative partner. Schools need a dynamic like that of Sawney and John for long-term success.

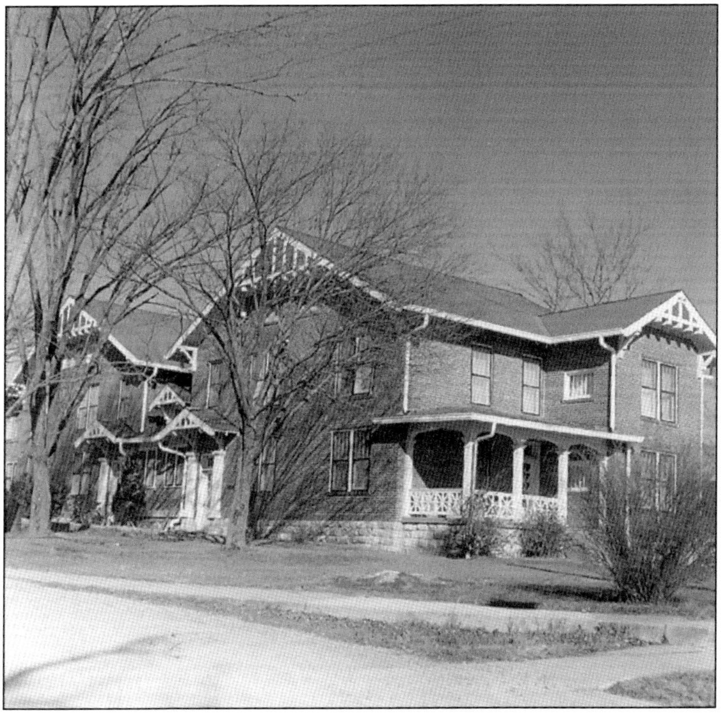

JACKSON HALL. Jackson Hall was the first dormitory built on The Webb School campus, in 1920. The late A.E. Jackson Jr. of Hartsell, Alabama, a 1900 Webb School graduate, was largely responsible for the construction of this building; therefore, it was named for him. A complete renovation took place on this building in the summer of 1956, partly to accommodate the rising enrollment.

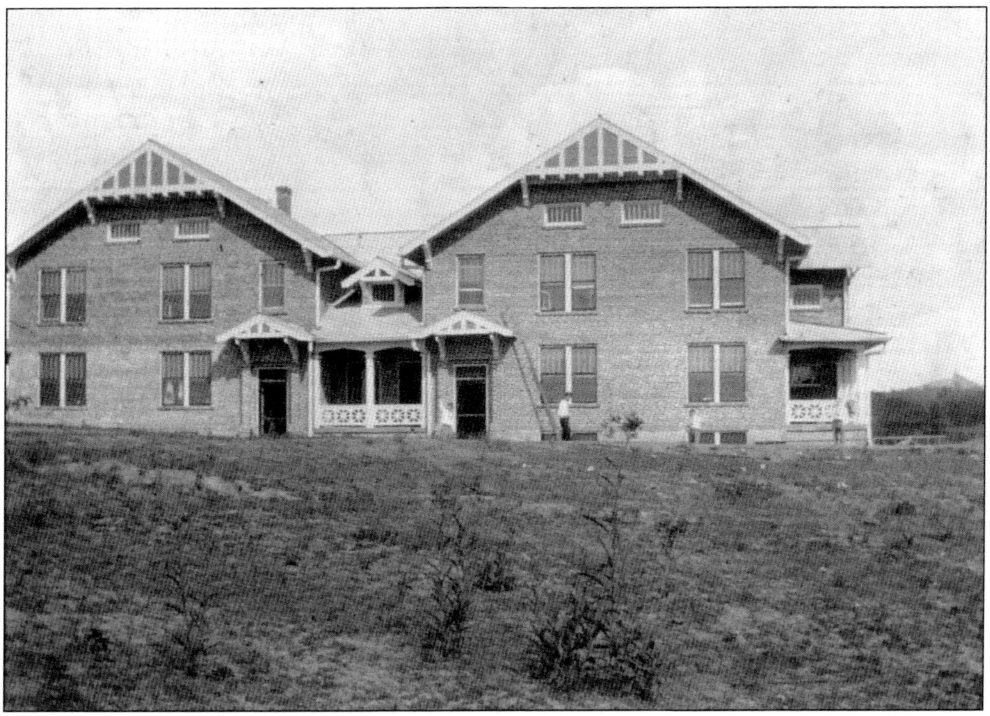

RAND HALL. Rand Hall, built in 1923, was named for Frank C. Rand, an 1894 Webb graduate. The basement of this dormitory was one of the two dining halls on campus at the time. It stood until 1969, when its roof was destroyed by a tornado.

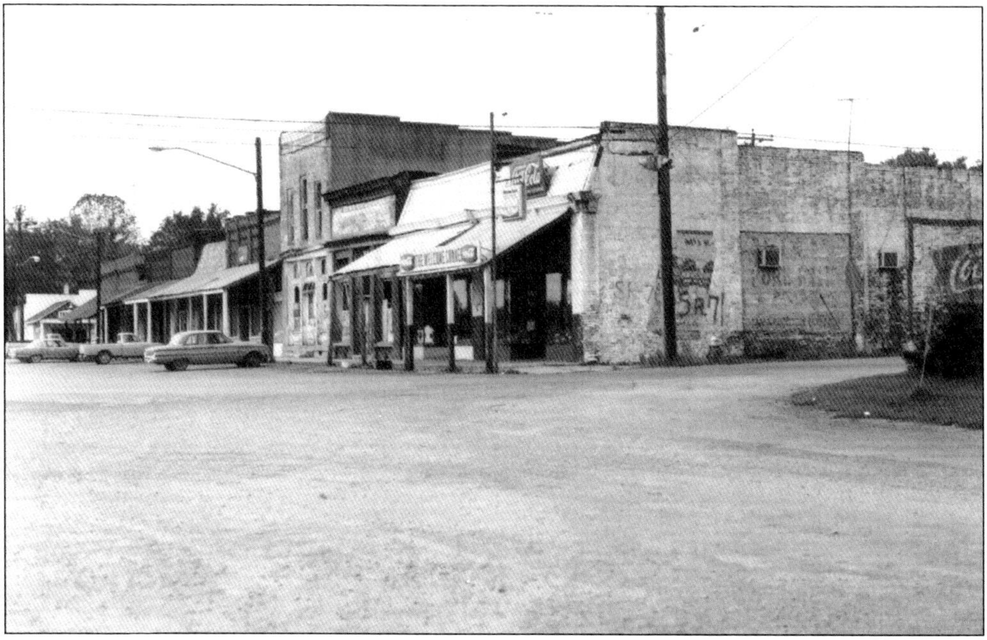

Downtown Bell Buckle. The downtown storefront area of Bell Buckle has always been one of the town's focal points. The quaintness of Bell Buckle is part of what makes it attractive to residents and visitors alike. It was founded in 1852 by A.D. Fugitt. In the late 1800s, there were feed stores, banks, drugstores, a post office, and more. Today, Bell Buckle still has a post office, antique shops, a coffee shop, an ice-cream shop, and the Bell Buckle Café, for which it is well known, in addition to The Webb School Arts & Crafts Fair, held every October. It also has a tea room and a small market with a diner.

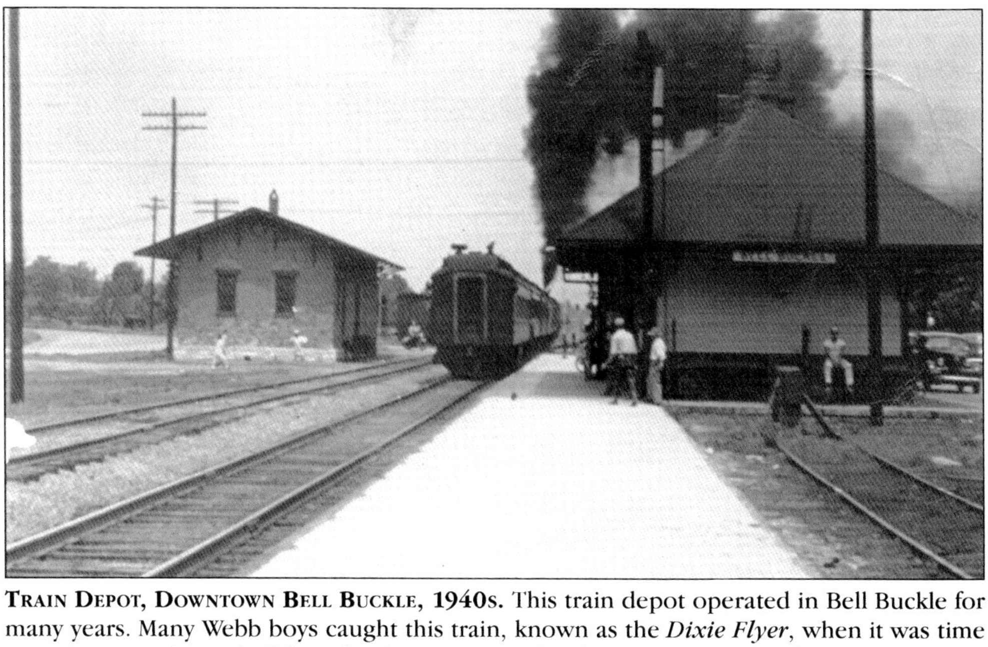

Train Depot, Downtown Bell Buckle, 1940s. This train depot operated in Bell Buckle for many years. Many Webb boys caught this train, known as the *Dixie Flyer*, when it was time to go home at the end of the school year. It was also the primary mode of transportation at that time.

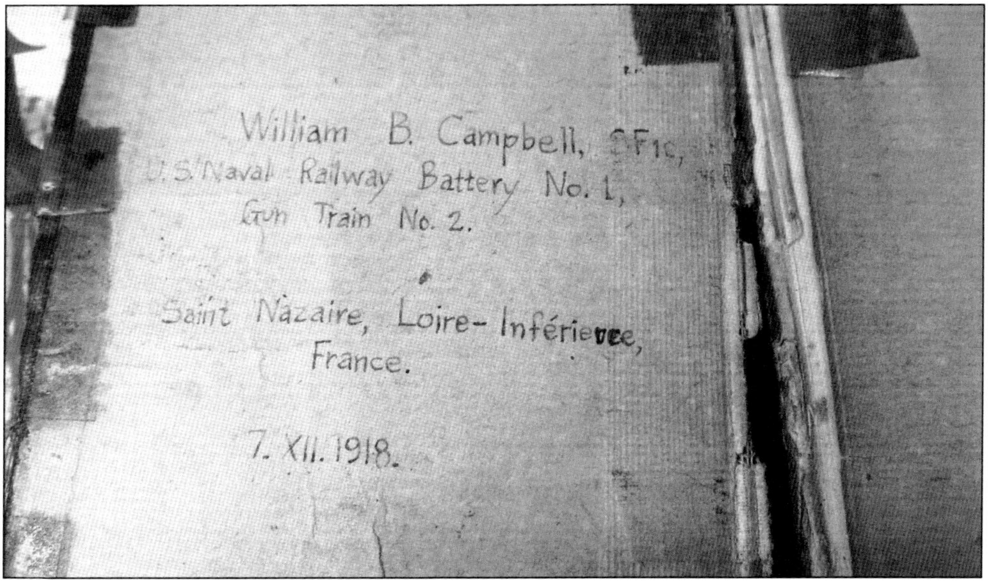

FRENCH-ENGLISH DICTIONARY. This French-English dictionary, donated to the archives by a local man, belonged to William B. Campbell. There were several handwritten definitions, including one for "hoodlum." Campbell, a 1911 Webb graduate, was listed in the 1917 *Alumni Bulletin* as a soldier from Webb.

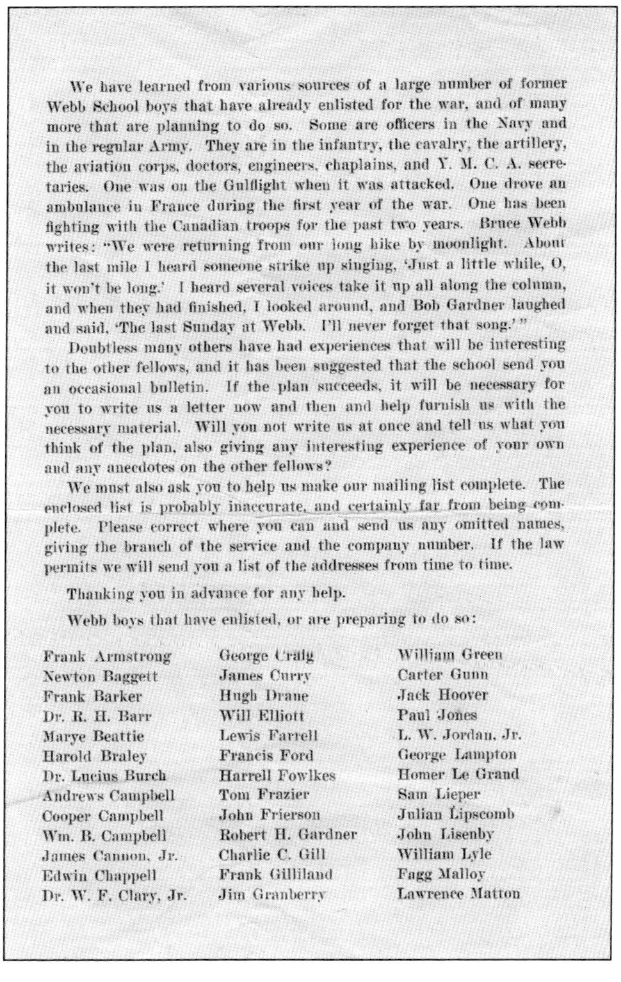

We have learned from various sources of a large number of former Webb School boys that have already enlisted for the war, and of many more that are planning to do so. Some are officers in the Navy and in the regular Army. They are in the infantry, the cavalry, the artillery, the aviation corps, doctors, engineers, chaplains, and Y. M. C. A. secretaries. One was on the Gulflight when it was attacked. One drove an ambulance in France during the first year of the war. One has been fighting with the Canadian troops for the past two years. Bruce Webb writes: "We were returning from our long hike by moonlight. About the last mile I heard someone strike up singing, 'Just a little while, O, it won't be long.' I heard several voices take it up all along the column, and when they had finished, I looked around, and Bob Gardner laughed and said, 'The last Sunday at Webb. I'll never forget that song.'"

Doubtless many others have had experiences that will be interesting to the other fellows, and it has been suggested that the school send you an occasional bulletin. If the plan succeeds, it will be necessary for you to write us a letter now and then and help furnish us with the necessary material. Will you not write us at once and tell us what you think of the plan, also giving any interesting experience of your own and any anecdotes on the other fellows?

We must also ask you to help us make our mailing list complete. The enclosed list is probably inaccurate, and certainly far from being complete. Please correct where you can and send us any omitted names, giving the branch of the service and the company number. If the law permits we will send you a list of the addresses from time to time.

Thanking you in advance for any help.

Webb boys that have enlisted, or are preparing to do so:

Frank Armstrong	George Craig	William Green
Newton Baggett	James Curry	Carter Gunn
Frank Barker	Hugh Drane	Jack Hoover
Dr. R. H. Barr	Will Elliott	Paul Jones
Marye Beattie	Lewis Farrell	L. W. Jordan, Jr.
Harold Braley	Francis Ford	George Lampton
Dr. Lucius Burch	Harrell Fowlkes	Homer Le Grand
Andrews Campbell	Tom Frazier	Sam Lieper
Cooper Campbell	John Frierson	Julian Lipscomb
Wm. B. Campbell	Robert H. Gardner	John Lisenby
James Cannon, Jr.	Charlie C. Gill	William Lyle
Edwin Chappell	Frank Gilliland	Fagg Malloy
Dr. W. F. Clary, Jr.	Jim Granberry	Lawrence Matton

***Alumni Bulletin*.** This 1917 *Alumni Bulletin* discusses the recent Webb graduates who had enlisted as part of the Great War efforts.

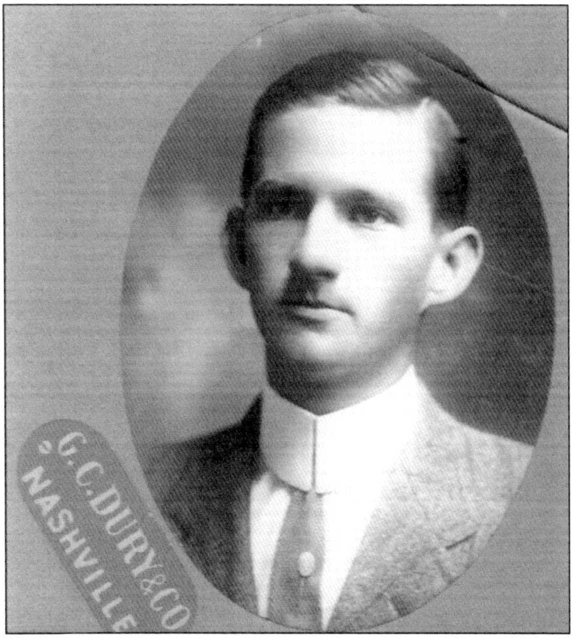

John Manning Battle. From the Son Will glass-slides collection, this is a portrait of John Manning Battle, who attended Webb and was an adopted son of Louise and Son Will. Sadly, he died overseas in World War I.

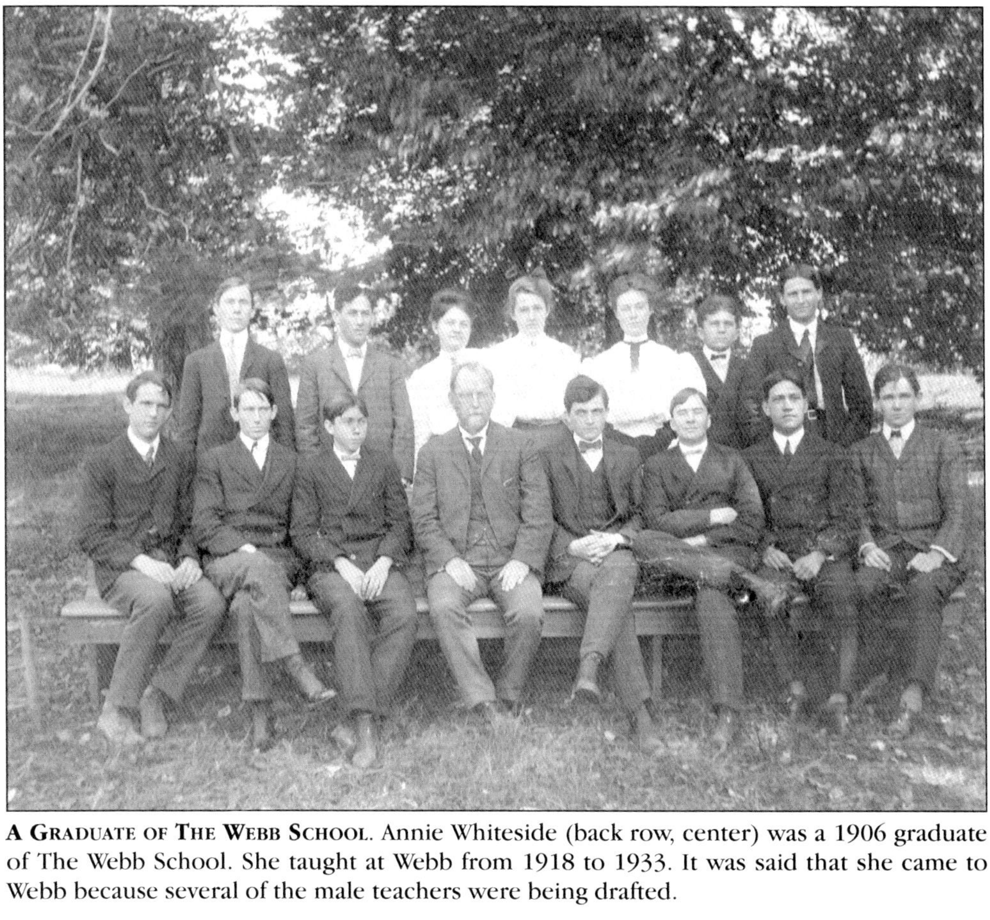

A Graduate of The Webb School. Annie Whiteside (back row, center) was a 1906 graduate of The Webb School. She taught at Webb from 1918 to 1933. It was said that she came to Webb because several of the male teachers were being drafted.

Annie Whiteside. Whiteside was Webb's first documented female teacher. This image came from the July 1975 *Alumni Bulletin*.

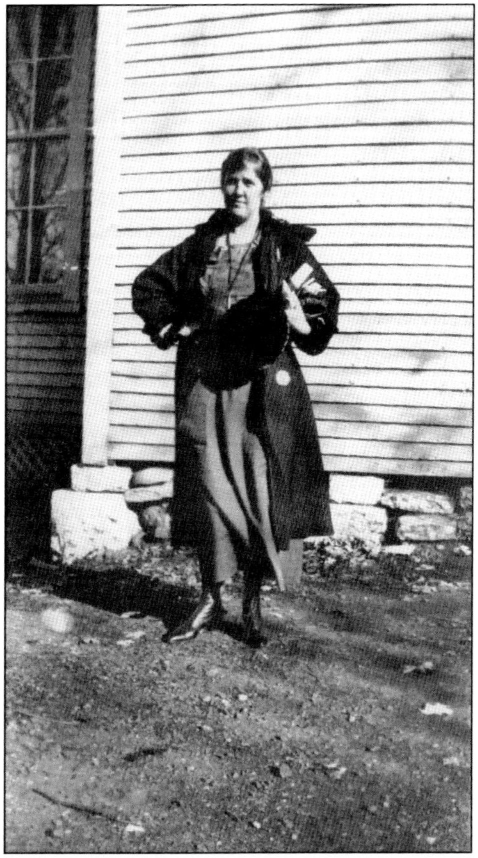

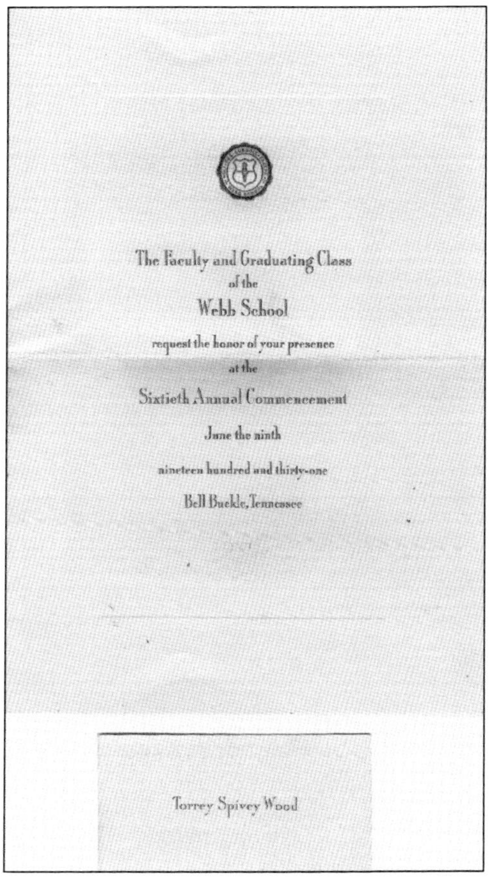

The Faculty and Graduating Class
of the
Webb School
request the honor of your presence
at the
Sixtieth Annual Commencement
June the ninth
nineteen hundred and thirty-one
Bell Buckle, Tennessee

Torrey Spivey Wood

Commencement Invitation, 1931. This is a graduation announcement for Torrey Spivey Wood from the 60th commencement of the school from the Torrey Wood scrapbook, a valuable addition to the school's archives.

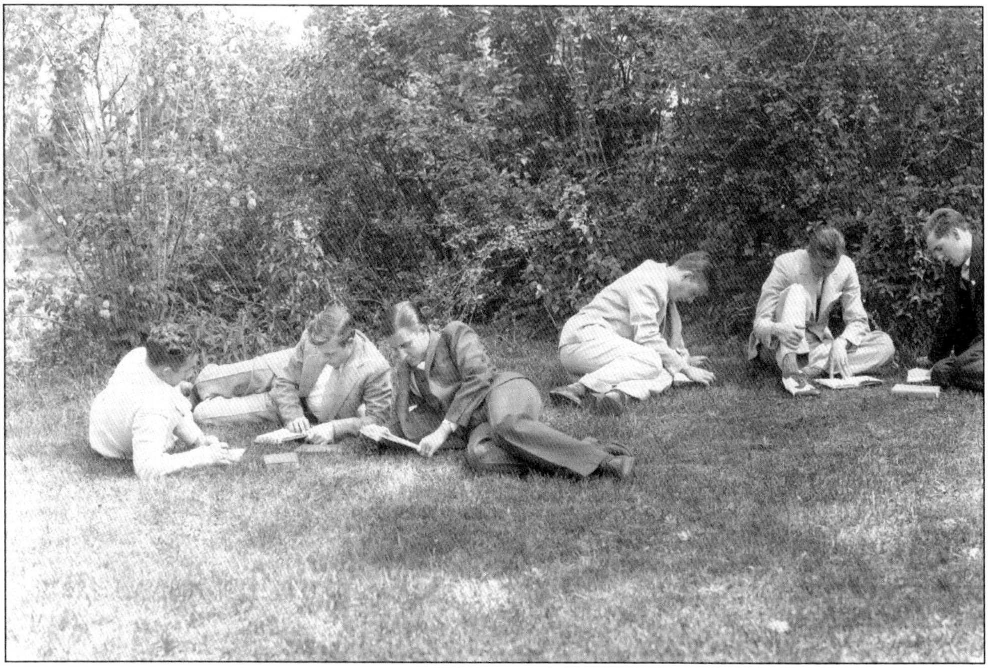

Outdoor Classroom, May 1932. Classes are still held today in one of the many outdoor classrooms. From left to right are boys Bob Beasley, Tom Malone, Bob Thompson, Pryor Plumlee, Thomas Happel Jr., and Lynwood Sanford.

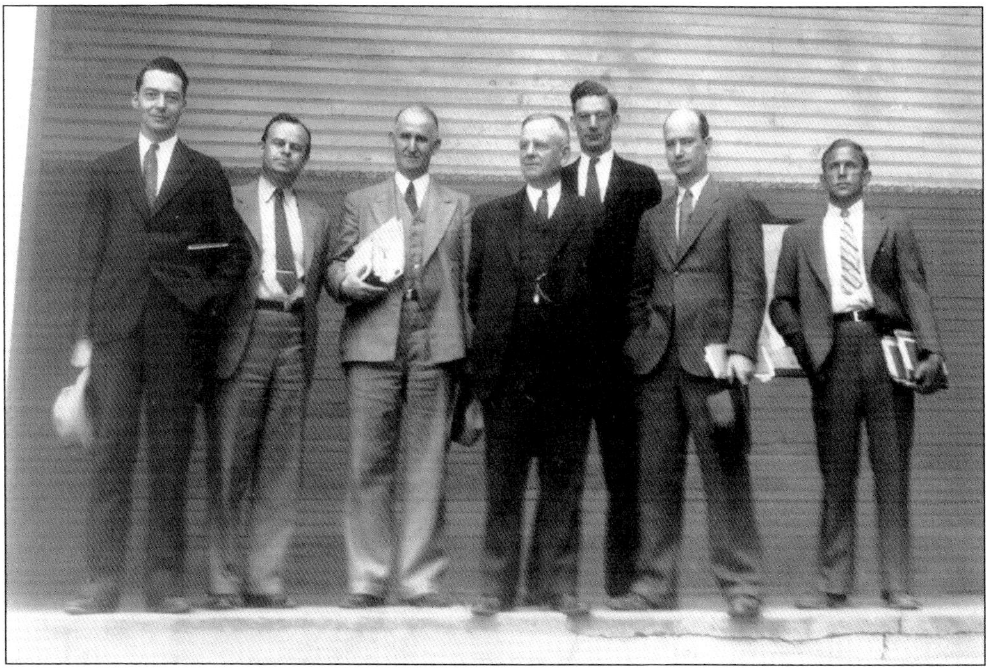

Faculty Group, c. 1934. From left to right are David McQuiddy (class of 1921), Hunter Buford, Gerald Webb Follin Sr. (1908), William Robert "Son Will" Webb Jr. (Sawney's son and headmaster), Paul Raker (behind William Webb Jr.), John Lewis Morgan, and Harry C. "Mike" Milligan.

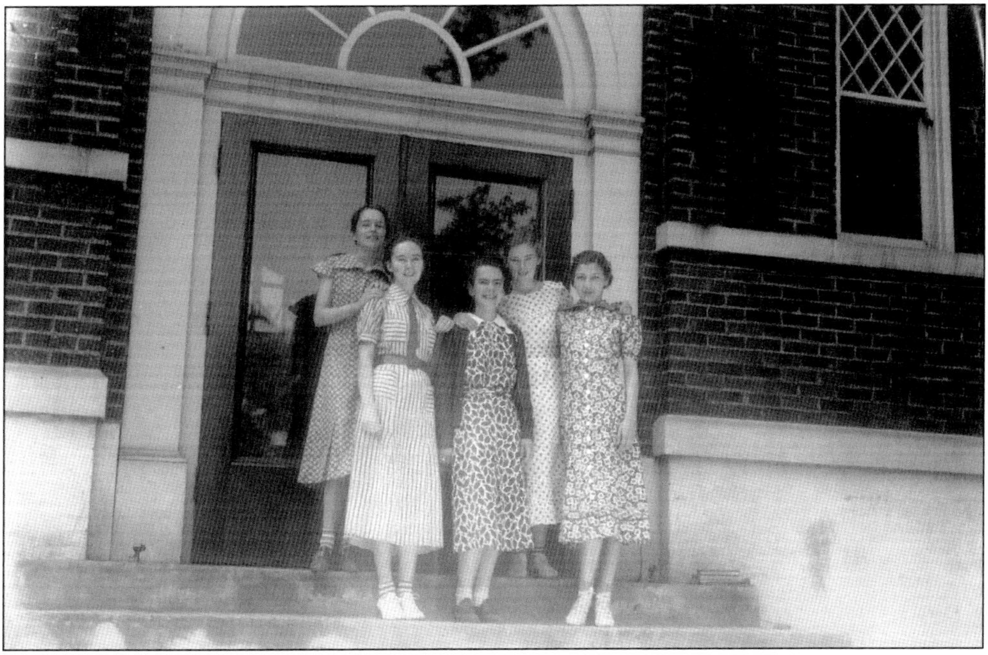

SPRING, 1937. This group picture was taken on the steps of the John Webb Library; from left to right are Emily Paty (class of 1939), June Carroll (1937), Susanne Webb McLean (1937), Evelyn Carroll (attended Webb), and Olive Jean Paty (1937). Susanne was the granddaughter of Sawney Webb.

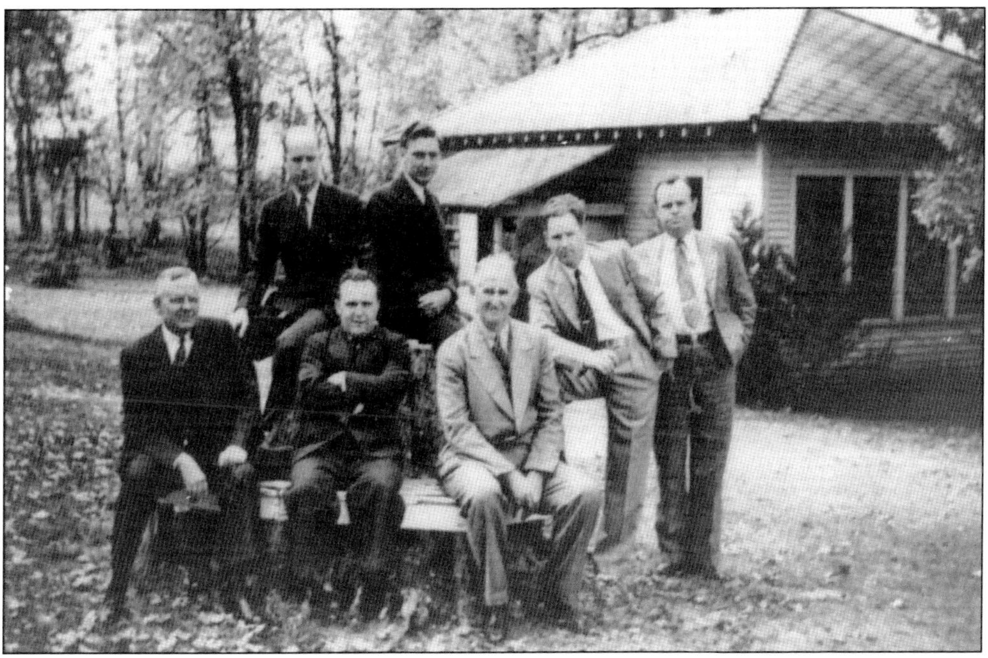

WEBB SCHOOL FACULTY, C. 1938. From left to right are (first row, seated) Son Will, Dr. Thomas Cutt, and Gerald Webb Follin Sr. (class of 1908); (second row, standing) John L. Morgan, Paul Raker, Philip Milhous, and Hunter Buford.

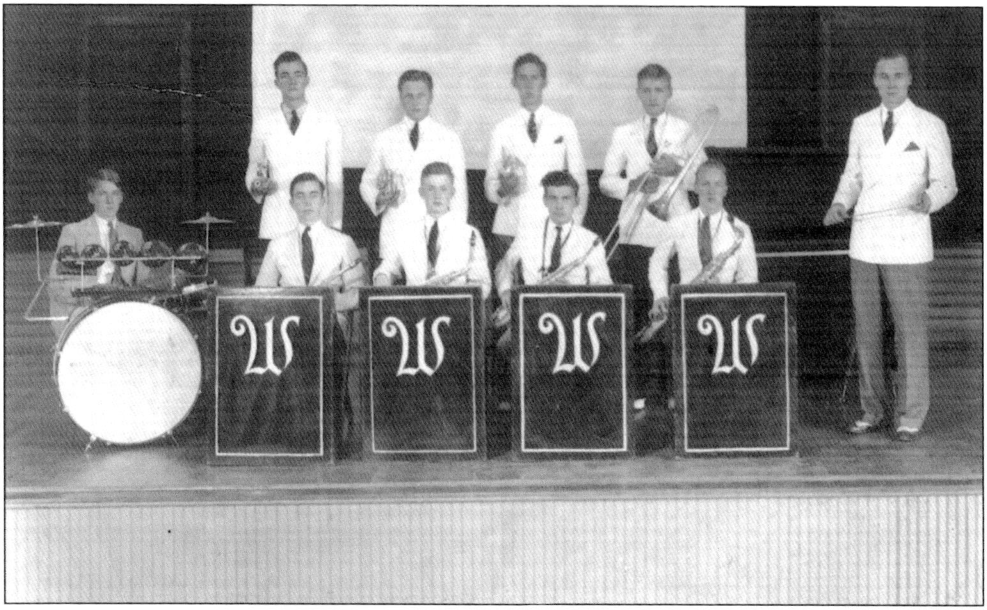

WEBB SCHOOL BAND, LATE 1930S. One of the activities available to Webb students in the 1930s was the band. Pictured are Charles Markum Berry (class of 1938), Stanley Horton (Bunt) Robertson Jr. (1938), Walter L. Gilbert (attended Webb), Joseph G. Brownlee Sr. (attended Webb), J. Hunter Peak (1937), Bourne Bean (1938), Julius Harrell (1938), George M. Webb (1938), W. Robert Webb III (1937), and William F. Murrah Jr. (1937).

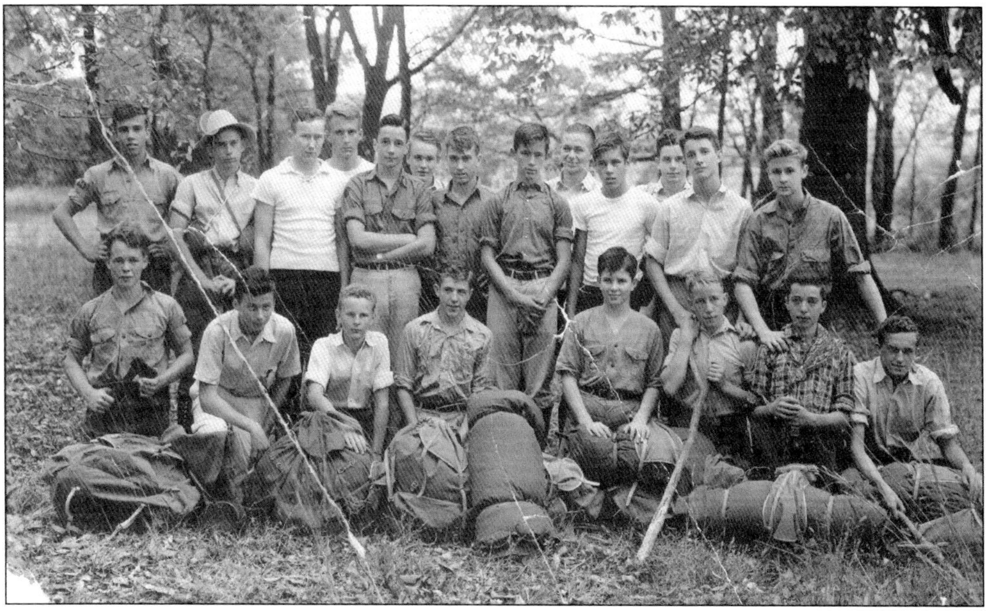

WILDERNESS CLUB, 1938–1939. Another one of the activities available to Webb boys was the Wilderness Club, pictured here after returning from a hike. From left to right are (first row) Cecil Sims, John Bennett, Phillip McKinne, Bob Campbell, Charlie McKenzie, Homer Ellis, Wilson Sims, and Don McIntyre; (second row) Hunter McDonald, Tommy Howard, Wallace Mabrey, Benton Sellars, Stanton Tubbs, Bob Fitch, Lester Baggett, Frank Upchurch, Clayton Pierce, Tommy Kesterson, Billy Hutton, Buck Baylor, and Rumsey Lewis.

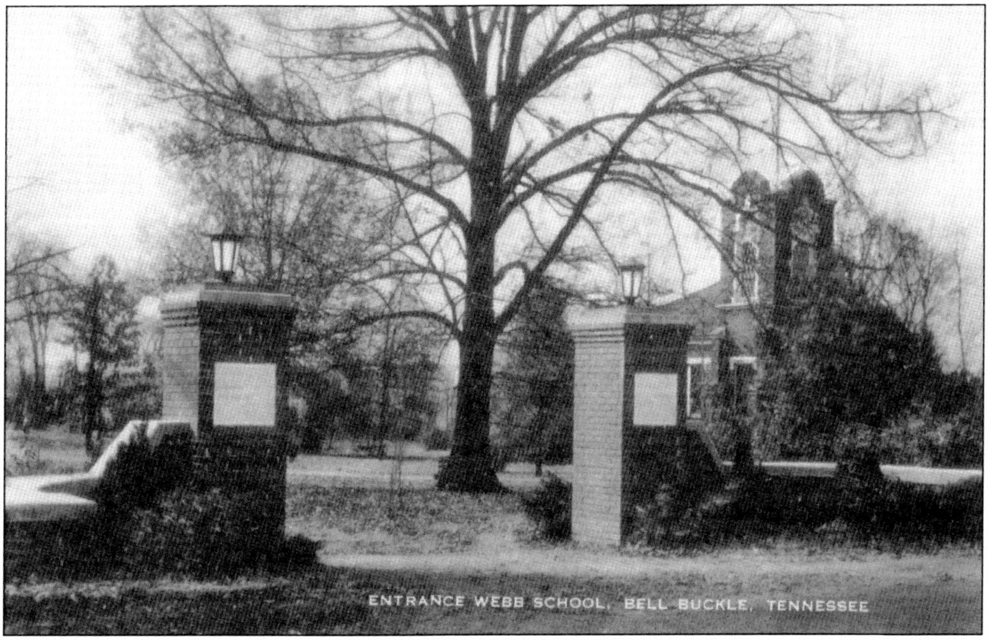

POTEAT GATES. The Poteat gates on Webb's campus were built in the fall of 1942. In addition to the gates, there was also a long brick wall added. The funds for these gates were donated by Thomas Arnold Turner Jr. (class of 1940), Charles W. Upchurch Jr. (1940), and McNeil Upchurch (1943). The gates were presented in memory of their grandfather Edwin McNeil Poteat, who was a well-known educator, clergyman, and Christian gentleman.

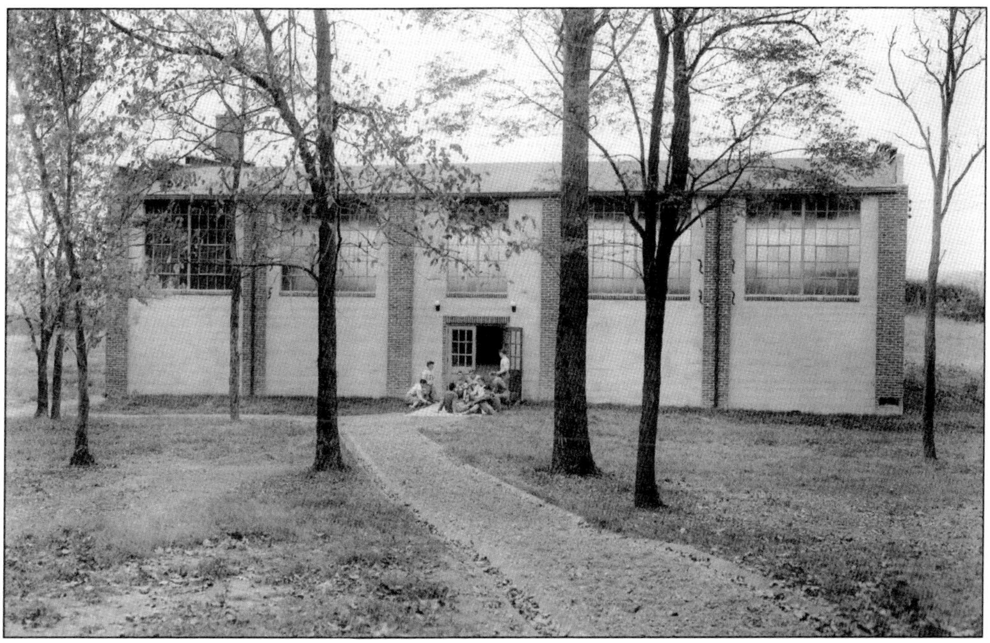

CECIL SIMS GYMNASIUM. Built in 1938, the Cecil Sims Gymnasium was named in memory of Cecil Sims Jr., who died during World War II. The gym was used for various student activities from the beginning. It was where Webb held its first grand ball in 1963 and a tag-team wrestling event in December 1965.

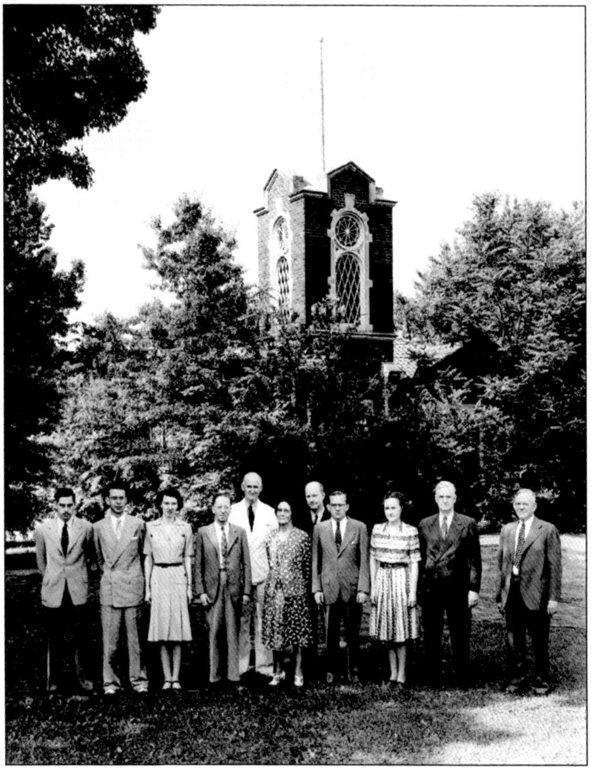

Webb Faculty and Staff, 1940s. This picture was taken in the early to mid-1940s in front of the Son Will Building. From left to right are coach Harry Airy, Milton Hodnette (class of 1938), unidentified, Dr. Otto Rosenberg, G. Webb Follin Sr. (1908), Emma Rosenberg, Dr. John Lewis Morgan, Cartledge Williams (1932), unidentified, Wilson Puryear, and Son Will.

Bob Webb III. William Robert "Bob" Webb III (right) was a 1937 graduate of The Webb School. He was not just any graduate though—he was Sawney's grandson. He returned to teach at Webb in 1942. After teaching for only a month, he went into the Army. At the end of the war, he returned to Webb to teach. While there, Bob lived in the Sawney House. As a teacher and faculty advisor, he was given the nickname "Bobo" by students. Bob married Mary Julia "Julie" Dossett in July 1949. He remained at Webb until 1954. During the 1954–1955 school year, he taught at The Webb School in Claremont, California, founded by his uncle Thompson Webb. In September 1955, Bob, with the support of Julie, opened his own school in a church building. That school is what is known today as The Webb School in Knoxville. To the left is his uncle, and in the framed portrait is founder Sawney.

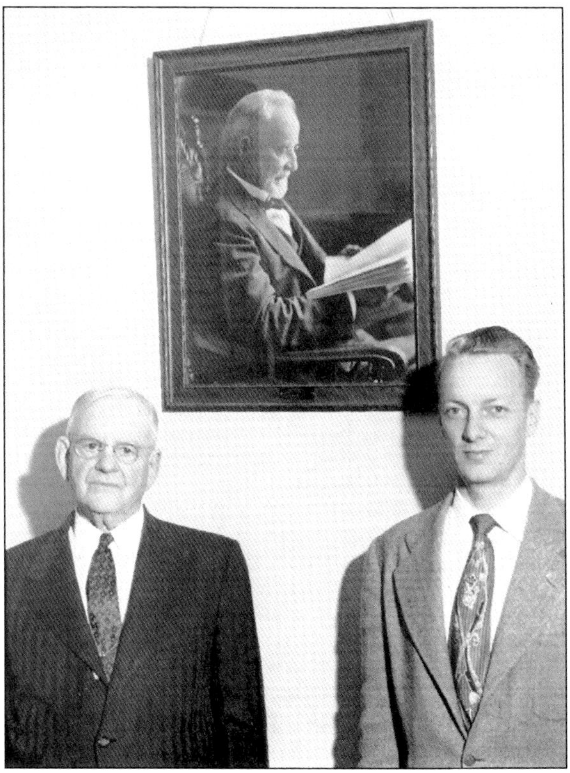

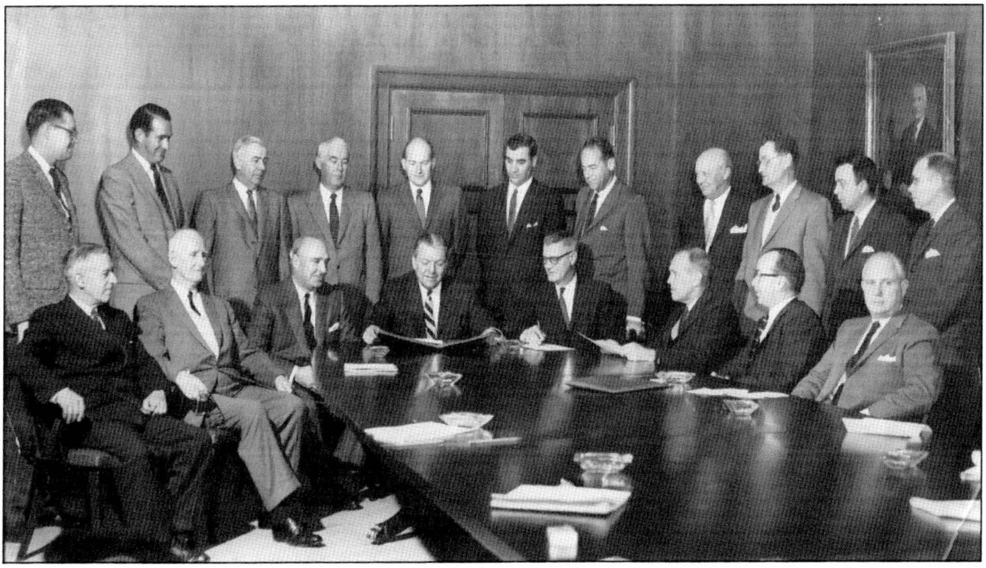

BOARD OF TRUSTEES, 1957. In 1922, a board of self-perpetuating trustees was elected and incorporated under the laws of Tennessee. The charter description reads, "this corporation is the owner of the real estate and property of the school. This board of trustees will have no voice in the operation of the school during the life of the then existing principals, but at their death or resignation, the board will have full charge of the operation of the school, including the selection of the principal." Frank Rand became chairman of the board of trustees in 1930. He organized the board and built a dormitory that bears his name.

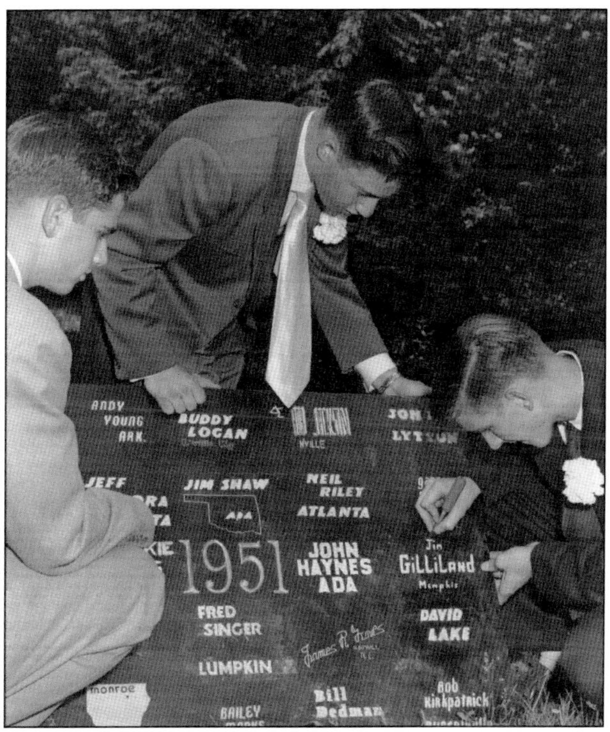

SENIOR BOARD, 1951. Each year, seniors carve something personal into a large wooden board. This tradition began in 1940 and was established based on rules that began with Sawney, who prohibited the students from damaging the plants and trees, carving or drawing on furniture and buildings, and general vandalism. Boys still had the desire to whittle on things, and the idea for a senior board came about. The wood was placed on a table in the Senior Room, and each graduating senior was permitted to carve their name. The year of that senior class was carved in the middle. At the end of the year, the carving was hung in the Big Room. Today's senior boards are not only carved, but also painted.

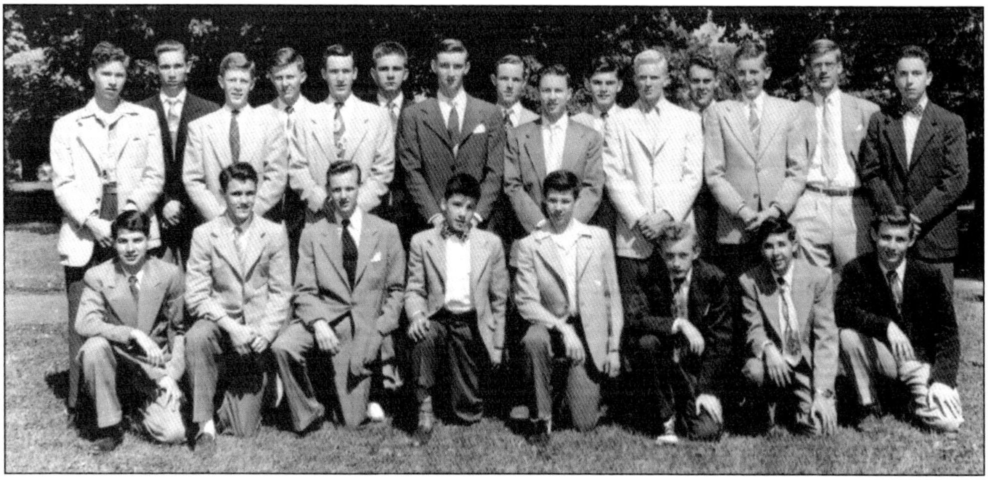

THE PLATONIC DEBATING SOCIETY, 1950–1951. Debating societies date all the way back to the Culleoka days of Webb School. At one time, there were three debating societies, with the Platonic and Hamilton being the upper school, and the Jeffersonians being the lower school.

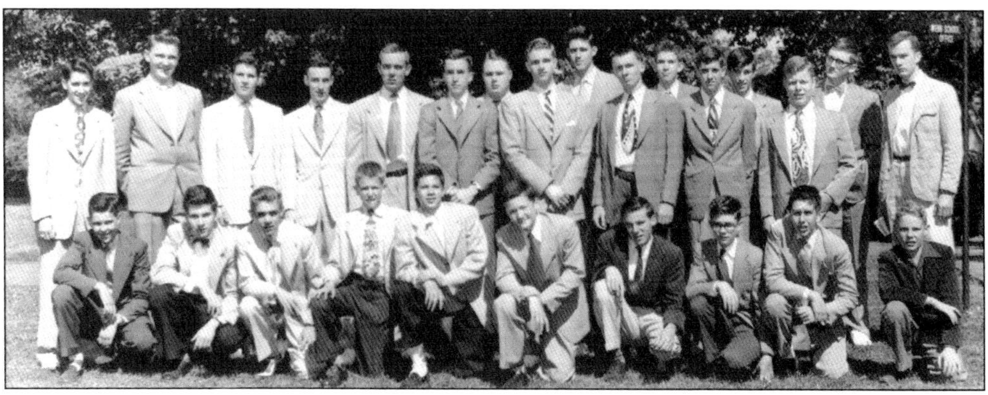

THE HAMILTON DEBATING SOCIETY, 1950–1951. Under the administration of Henry Whiteside (class of 1929), the lower school debating society was abolished. The debates were always a part of commencement week.

CAMPUS INFIRMARY EXTERIOR. Construction on this building began around December 1948 and it opened in September 1949. It was located east of Jackson Hall. The building was erected and named in memory of McNeal Bond McDonnell, a 1945 Webb graduate. President of the Memphis Furniture Manufacturing Company Dwight Morrow and his sister offered to give the furnishings for the infirmary.

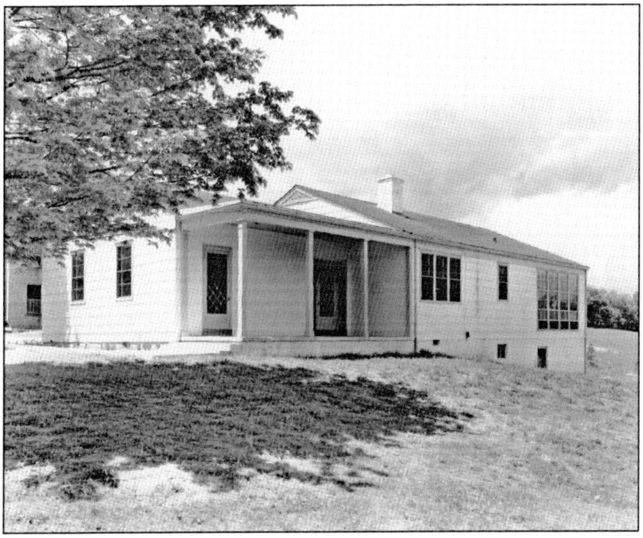

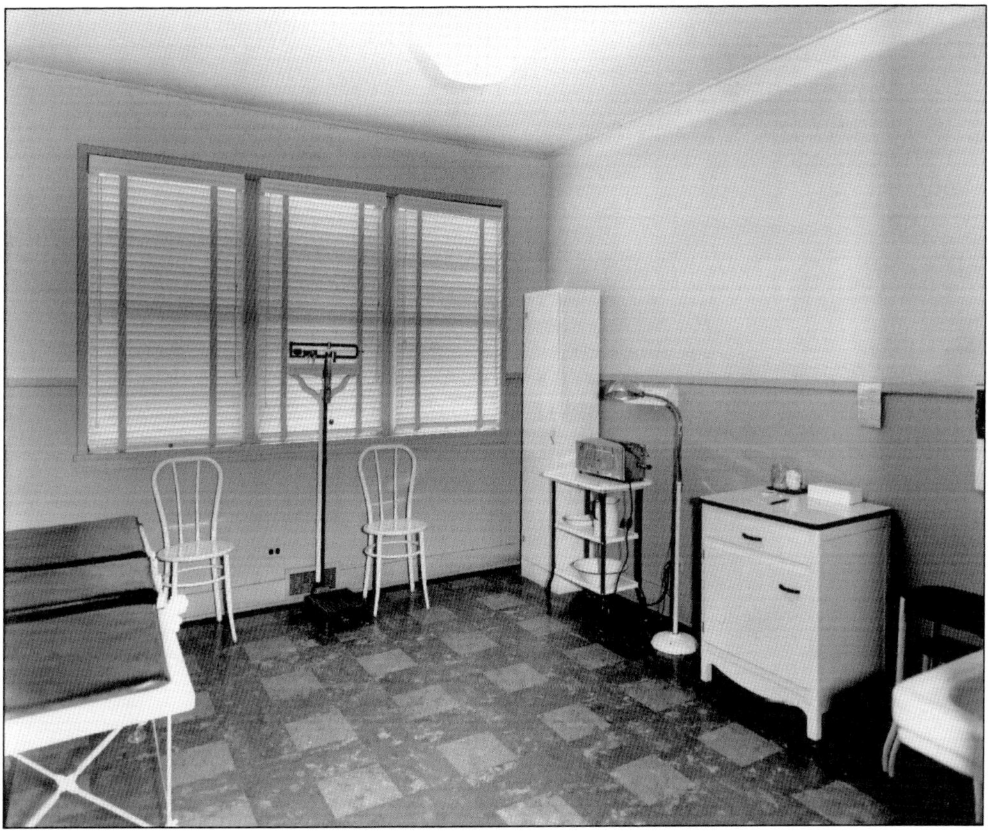

CAMPUS INFIRMARY INTERIOR. Many donations for the infirmary were also given by Henry Jamison, Bryant Woosley (class of 1922), Thomas Cartwright, and Bert Brush (architect) to furnish the infirmary as well. A senior class at Webb donated the Venetian blinds, and Son Will Webb donated two framed pictures. It was later moved to its current location to make room for a new dormitory. One of the Webb nurses who took care of sick students was Mary Catherine Taylor (1930), who would later become the second wife of Son Will.

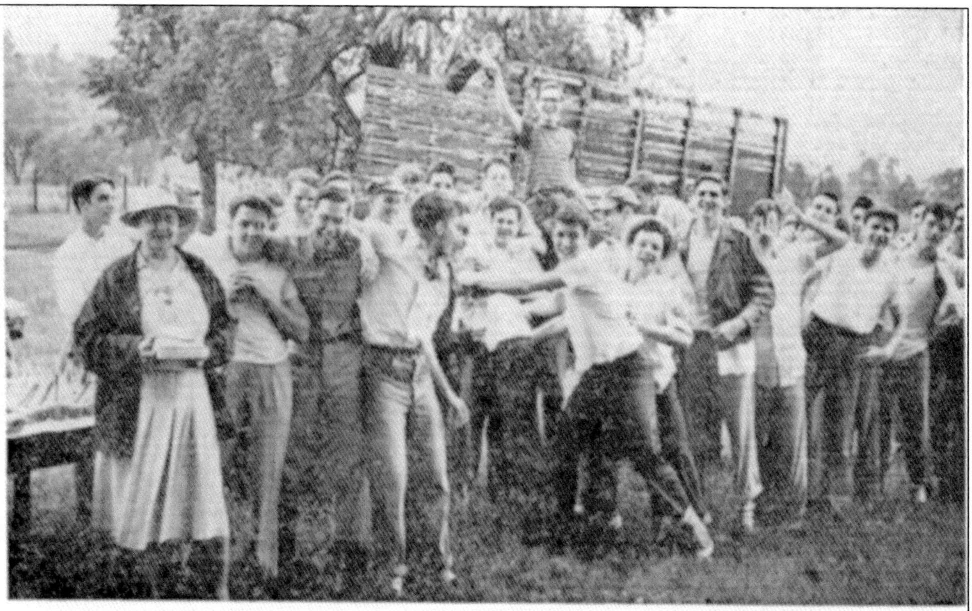

"EVERYONE LINES UP"

Only lady is Miss Esther, co-author of party. Boy with head turned away is Allison who was shy. Below: Enjoying the good food are (left to right) Bell, Liner, Duncan, Tucker and Looney.

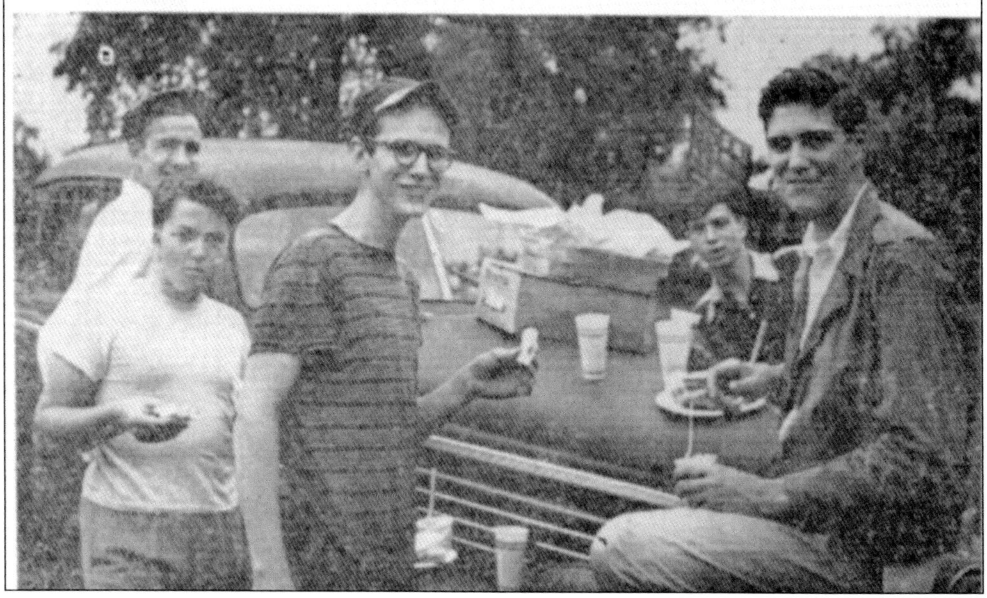

Miss Jeanne's Picnic. Jeanne Haynes held an annual picnic for many years for the juniors and seniors of Webb School. This tradition began on April 12, 1942. There was a lot of food and fun. The event that made Miss Jeanne's parties so famous was the water fight. The seniors battled the juniors in a small creek that ran through the farm. These pictures were taken from the 1949 senior edition of the *Oracle*.

Three

Building the Residential Campus 1953–1973

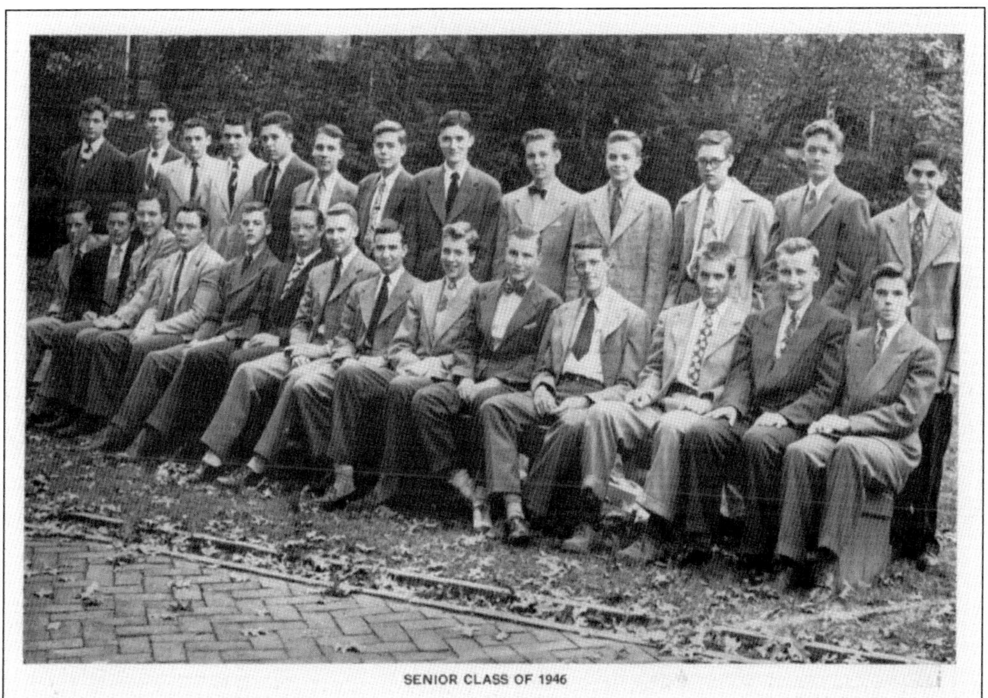

All-Male Senior Class, 1946. From 1946 until 1969, Webb went from a coeducational institution to all-male. During the years of 1953–1973, the trustees concentrated their efforts on building dormitories and other supporting buildings for the residential campus.

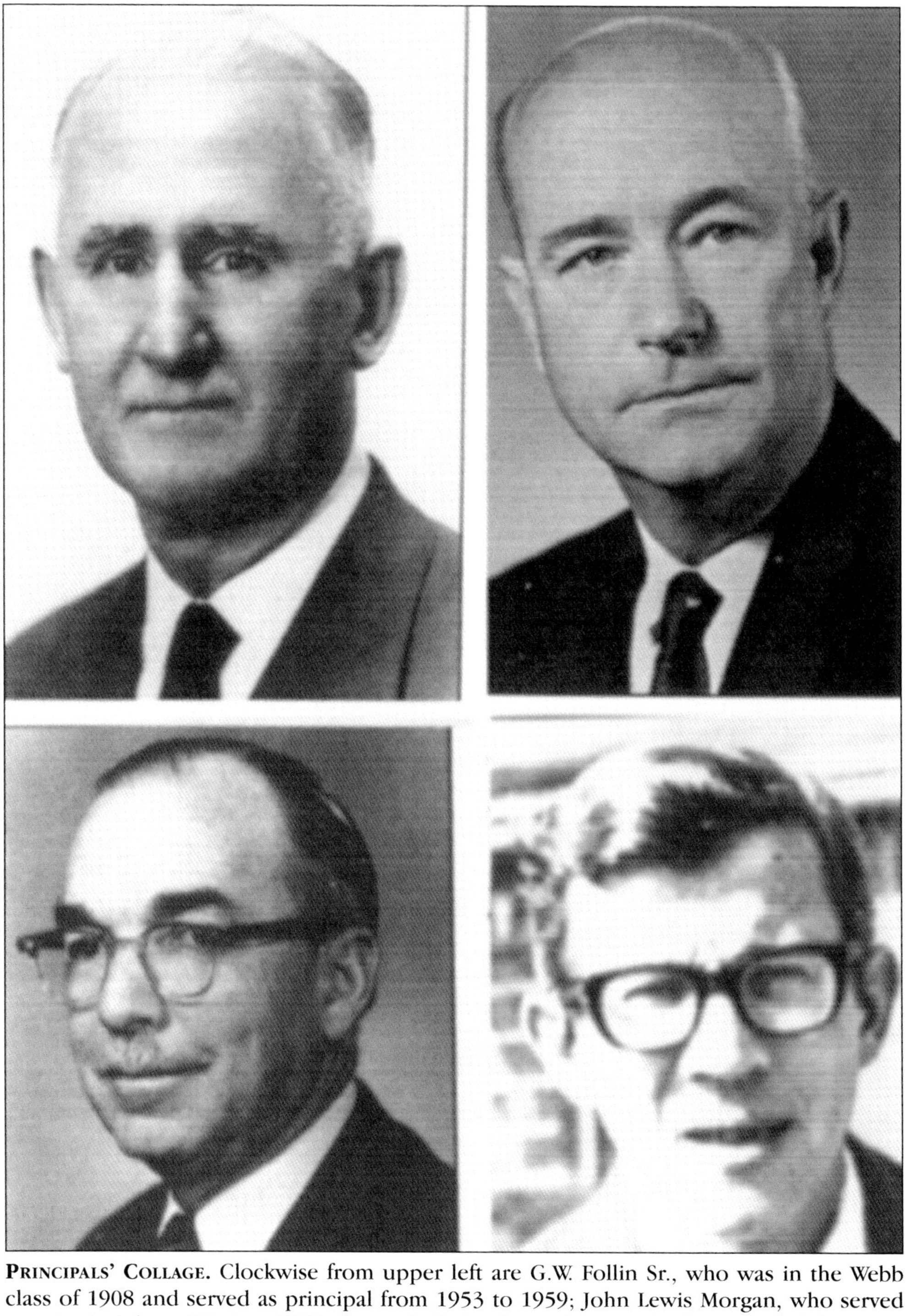

Principals' Collage. Clockwise from upper left are G.W. Follin Sr., who was in the Webb class of 1908 and served as principal from 1953 to 1959; John Lewis Morgan, who served as principal from 1959 to 1963; Kenneth F. Stuckey, who rang in the centennial year as principal from 1970 to 1973; and Henry O. Whiteside, who was in the Webb class of 1929 and served as principal from 1963 to 1970.

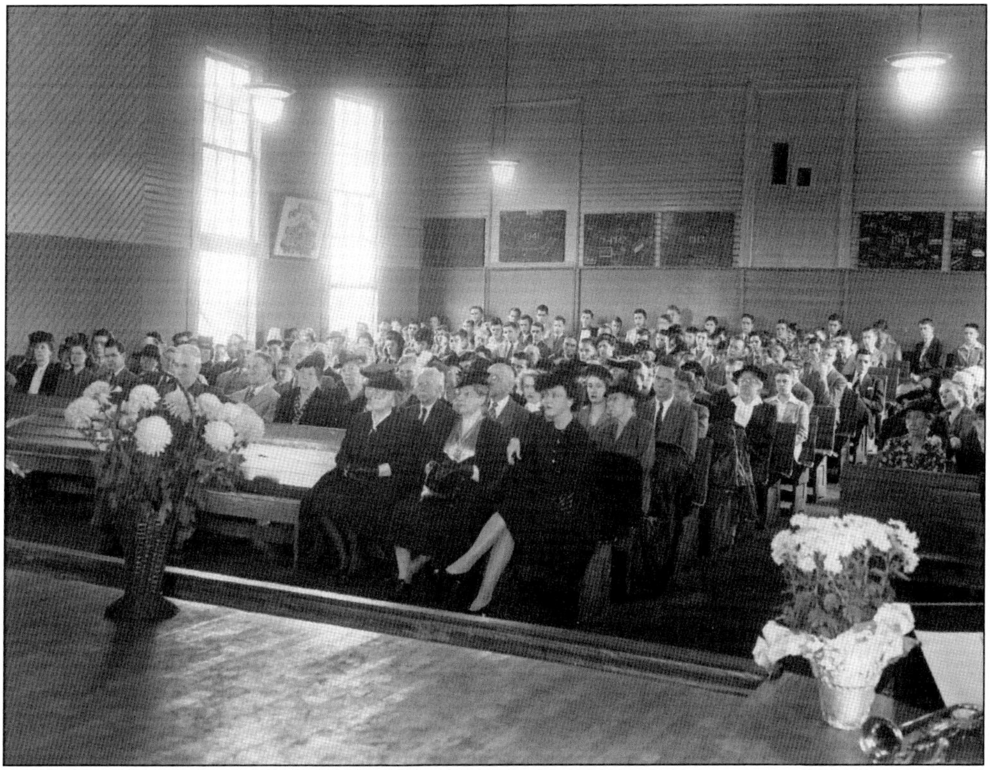

Big Room Auditorium. This photograph captures an event during the Follin administration. The auditorium was a part of the Big Room, not in a separate structure. Note the senior boards hanging on the back and side walls.

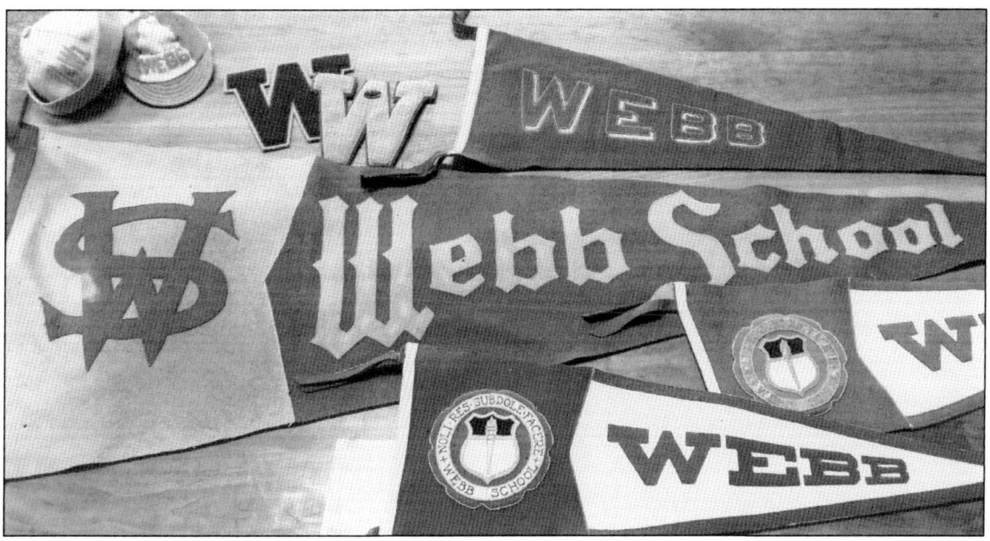

Pennants and Letters. The school colors throughout the 1940s, 1950s, and 1960s were purple and gold. This later changed to navy blue and gold. The pennants, letters, and hats pictured are all bright purple and gold.

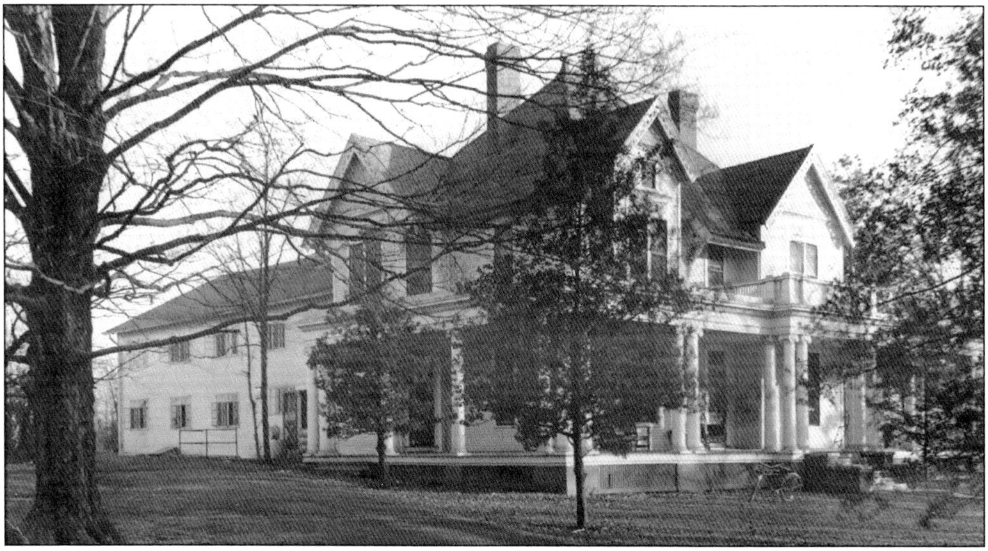

Sawney Webb Hall. Sawney Webb Hall was the original house that Sawney had built for his family when he moved the school to Bell Buckle in 1886. This picture shows how it had been remodeled to be used as a dormitory in 1940. There were rooms added on the back of the house to accommodate about 13 students. When it opened, the dorm parents were Philip G. and Anne Milhous.

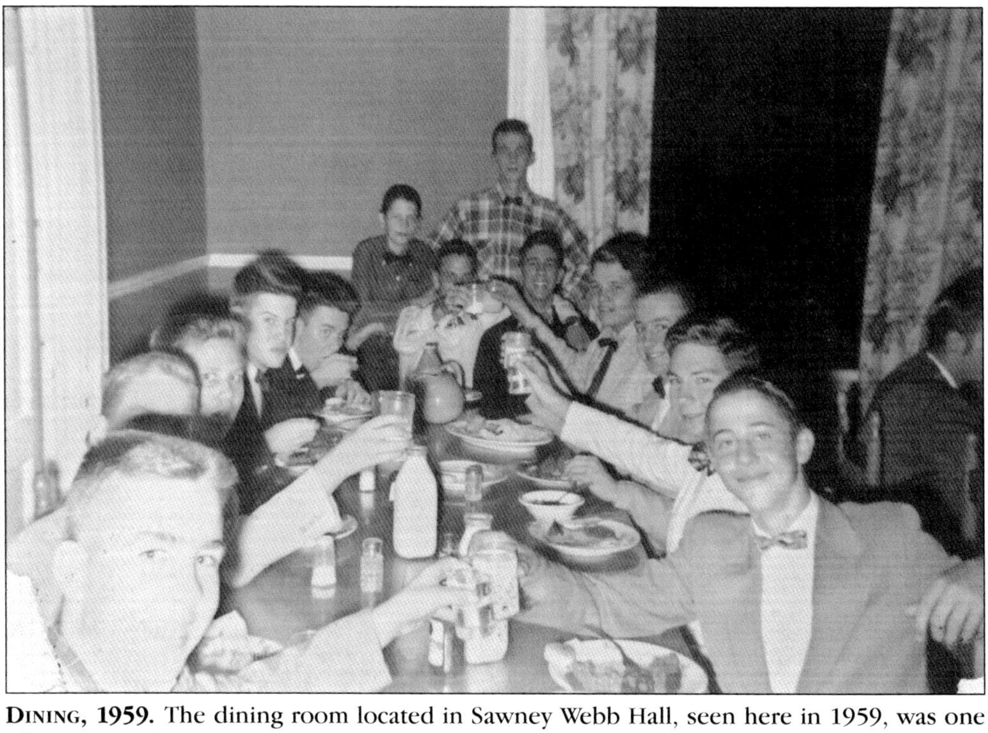

Dining, 1959. The dining room located in Sawney Webb Hall, seen here in 1959, was one of two located on campus.

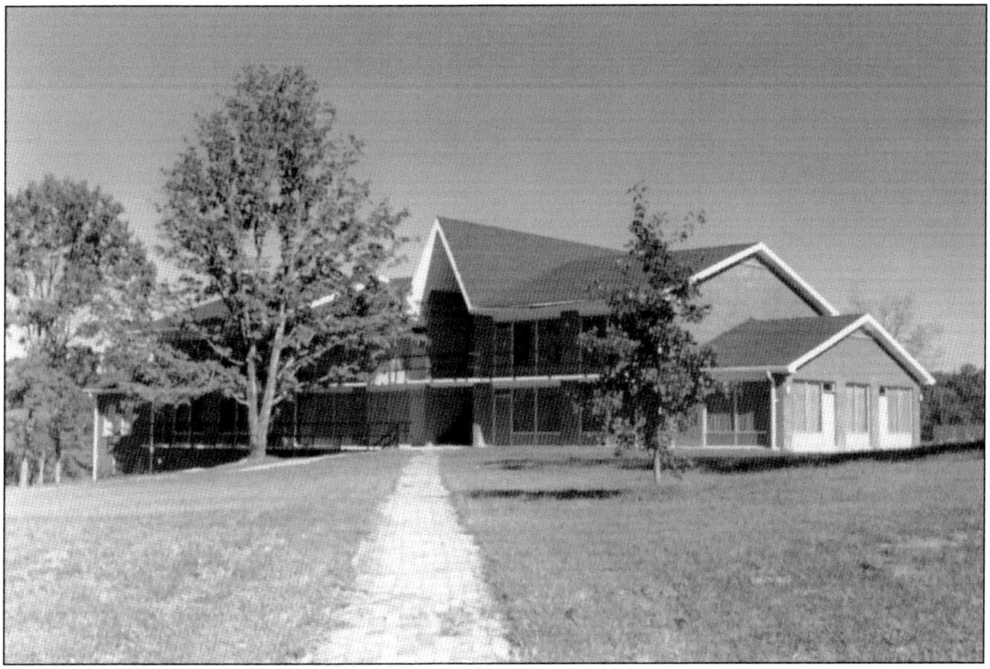

JAC CHAMBLISS DORMITORY. Jac Chambliss Dormitory was constructed in 1970. It was named after Jac Chambliss, a 1927 graduate and one of Webb's longtime dedicated alumni and trustees.

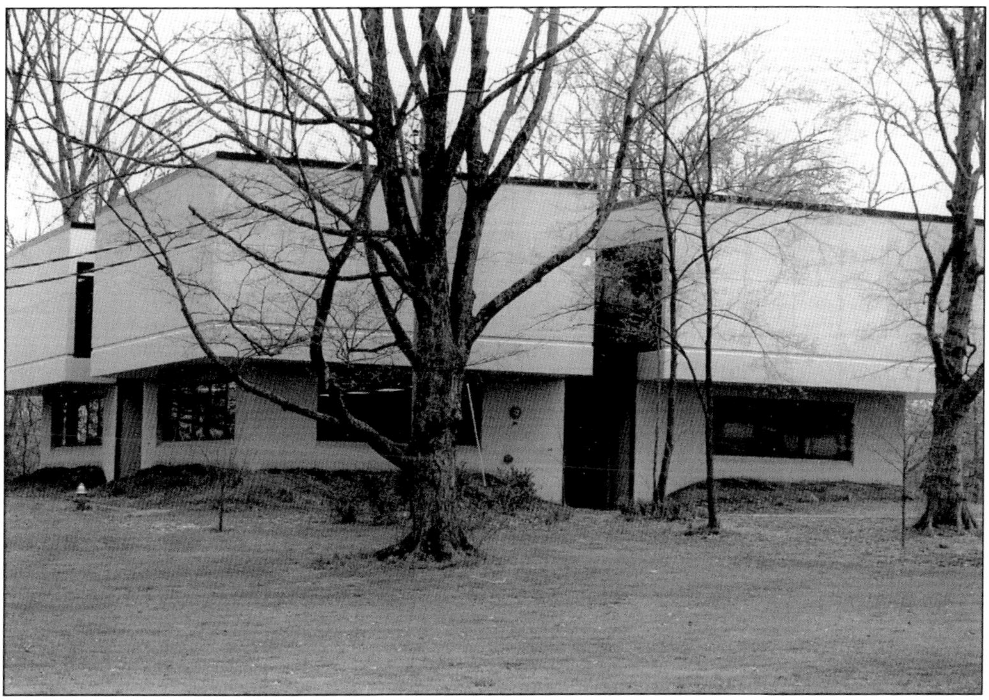

DAVIS-WOOSLEY COMPUTER SCIENCE BUILDING. This building was completed during the summer of 1987. A large monetary gift from the family of a student who graduated from Webb in 1893 helped make this building become a reality.

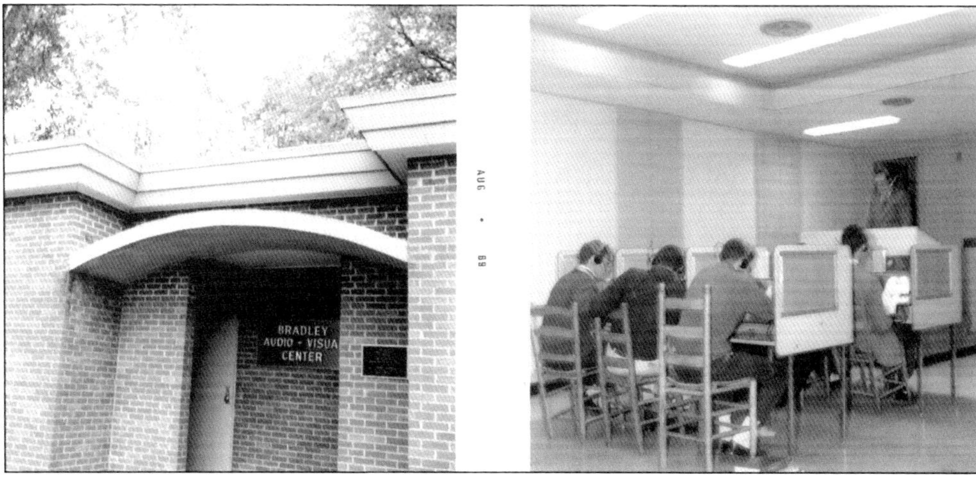

Bradley Audio-Visual Center. Originally built in 1962 as a state-of-the-art audiovisual lab, the Bradley Building is now the location of the sixth-grade classroom.

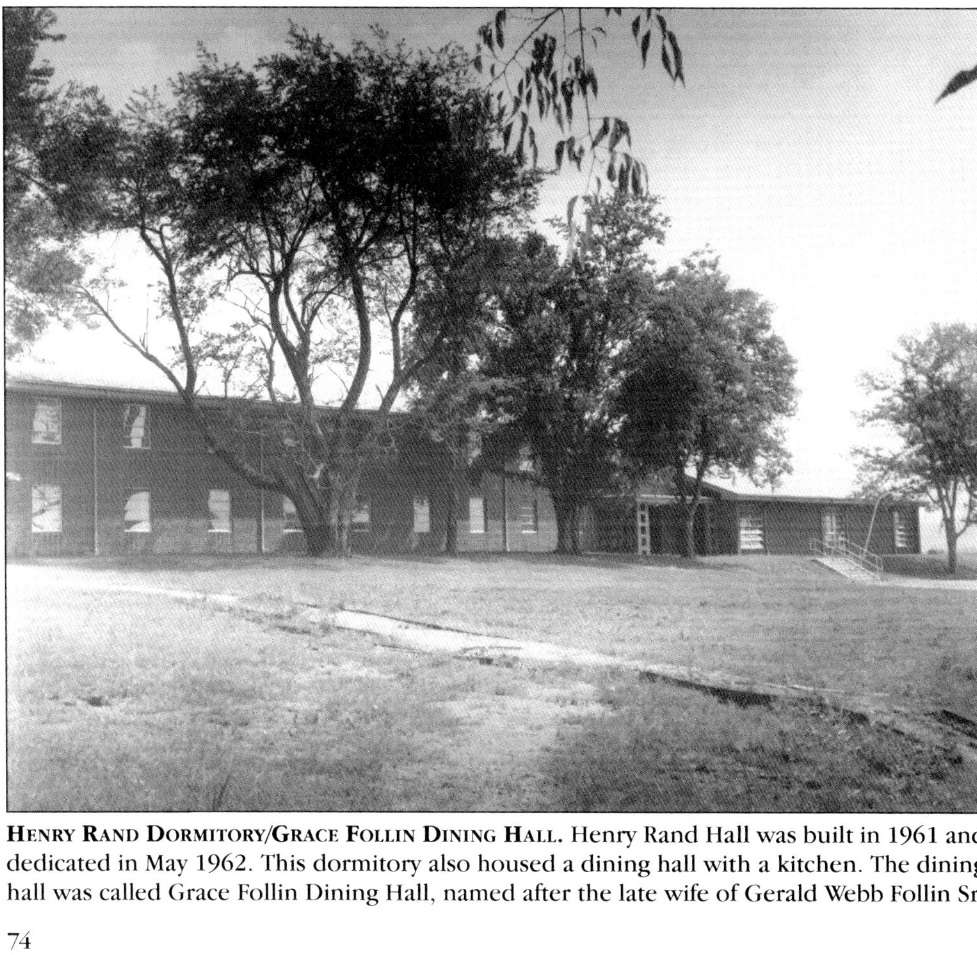

Henry Rand Dormitory/Grace Follin Dining Hall. Henry Rand Hall was built in 1961 and dedicated in May 1962. This dormitory also housed a dining hall with a kitchen. The dining hall was called Grace Follin Dining Hall, named after the late wife of Gerald Webb Follin Sr.

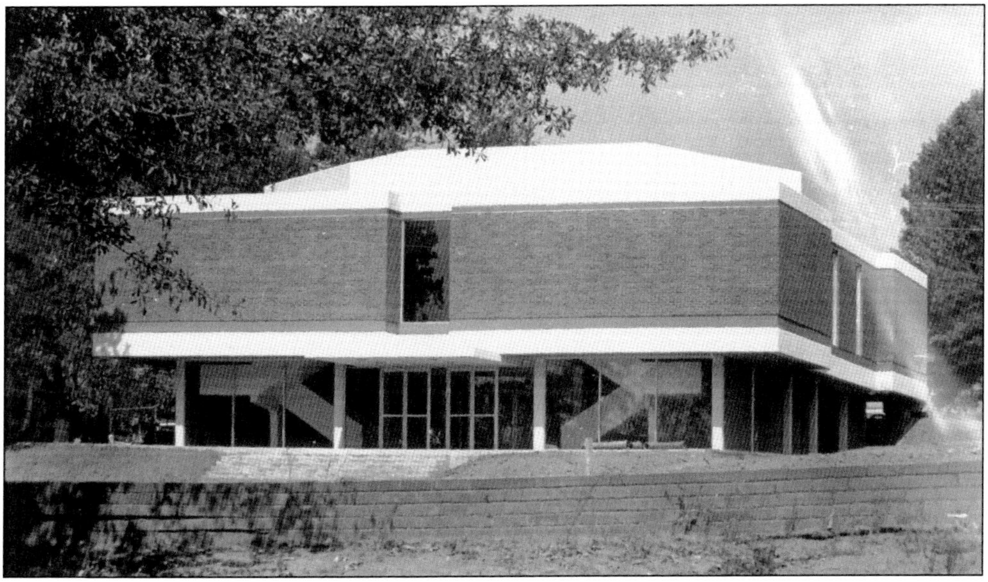

FOLLIN ADMINISTRATION BUILDING AND CHAPEL, OCTOBER 1964. Construction on this building began in 1964 on the site of the home of the late G. Webb Follin Sr. on campus. It was in full operation by 1966 and was named for the late G. Webb Follin Sr., a 1908 Webb graduate and former teacher and principal of the school.

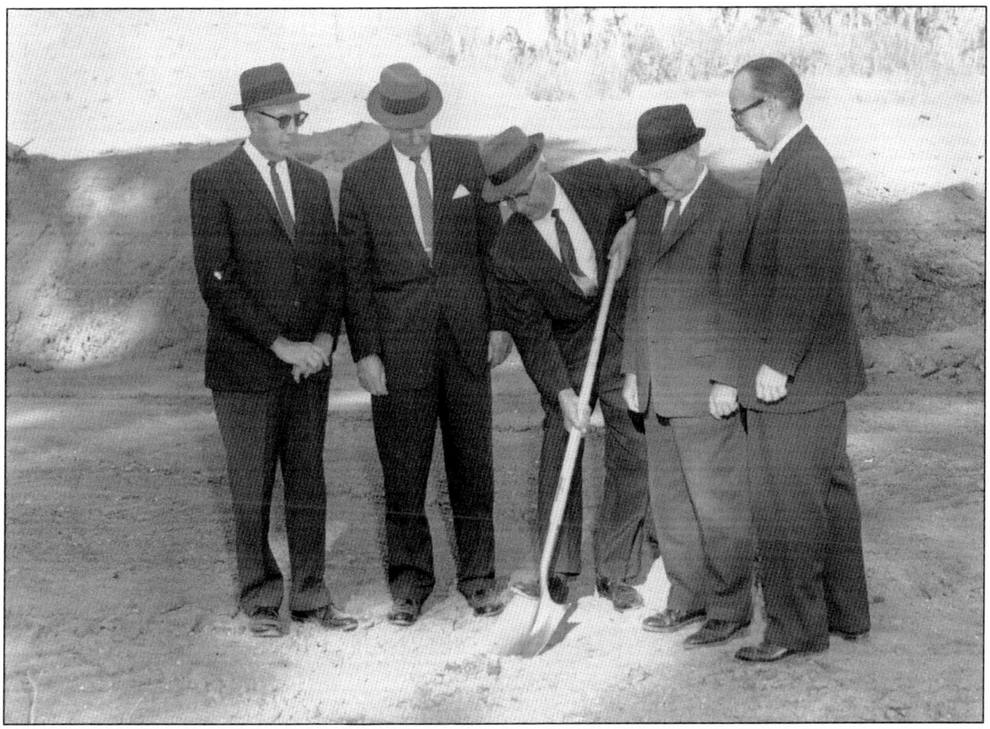

GROUND BREAKING OF FOLLIN ADMINISTRATION BUILDING AND CHAPEL, OCTOBER 1964. Pictured from left to right are contractor Sam Melson, G. Webb Follin Jr. (class of 1938), building committee chairman W. Bryant Woosley Sr. (1922); Charles S. Ragland (1913); and principal Henry Whiteside (1929).

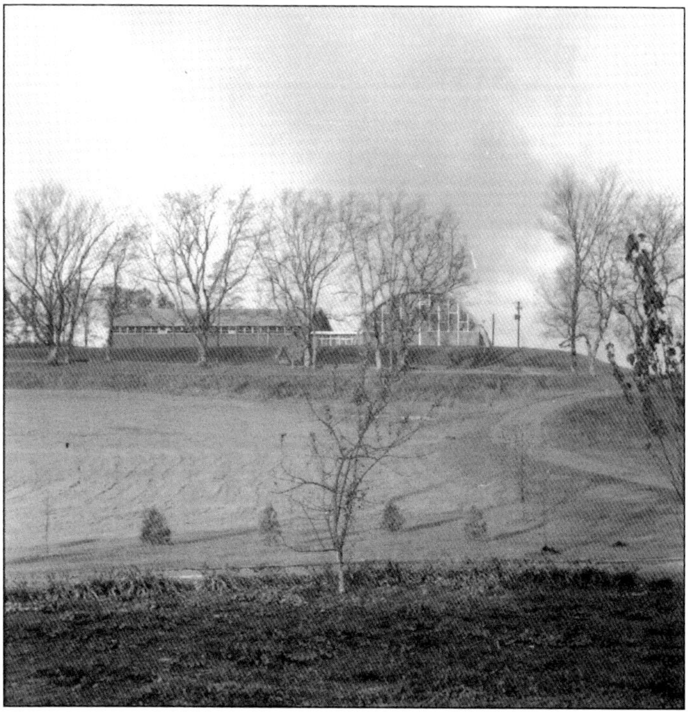

Haun-Ragland Gymnasium. In about 1961, the Haun-Ragland Gymnasium, which included an indoor swimming pool, was built. It was dedicated in May 1962.

Graduation, 1951. A group of Webb boys stands proud after receiving their Bibles at the 1951 commencement.

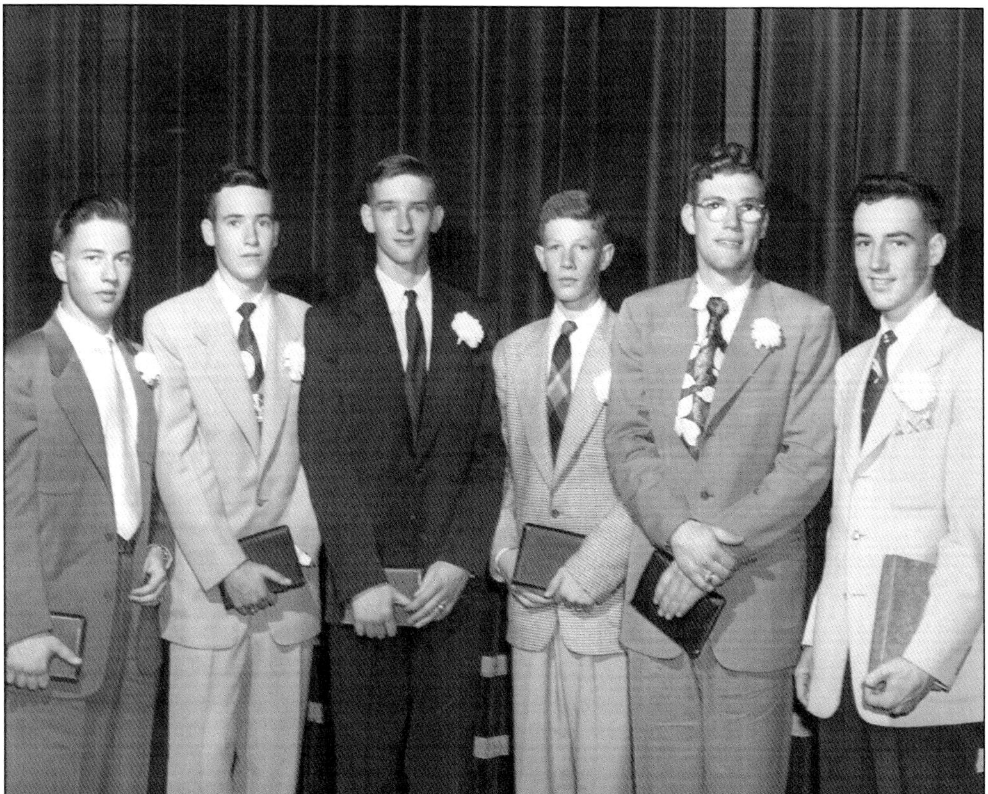

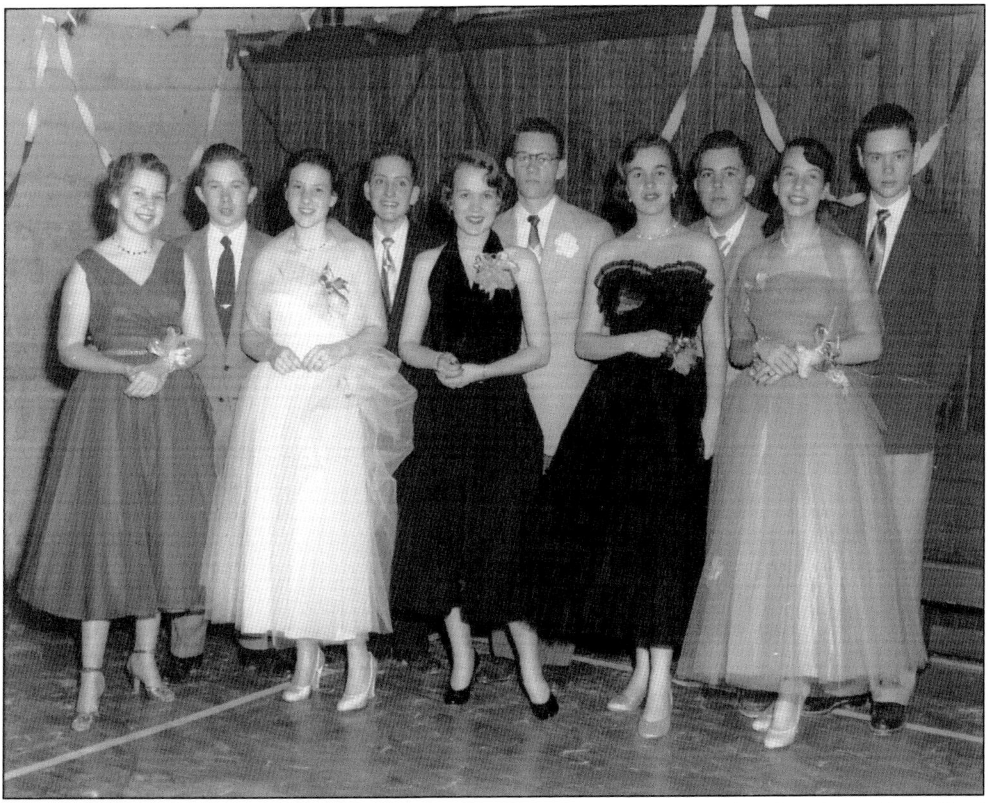

Dance. When interviewed about the 1950s dances, Julie Webb, wife of Bob Webb, talked about a dance held where approximately 80 girls from Shelbyville, Murfreesboro, and Nashville attended.

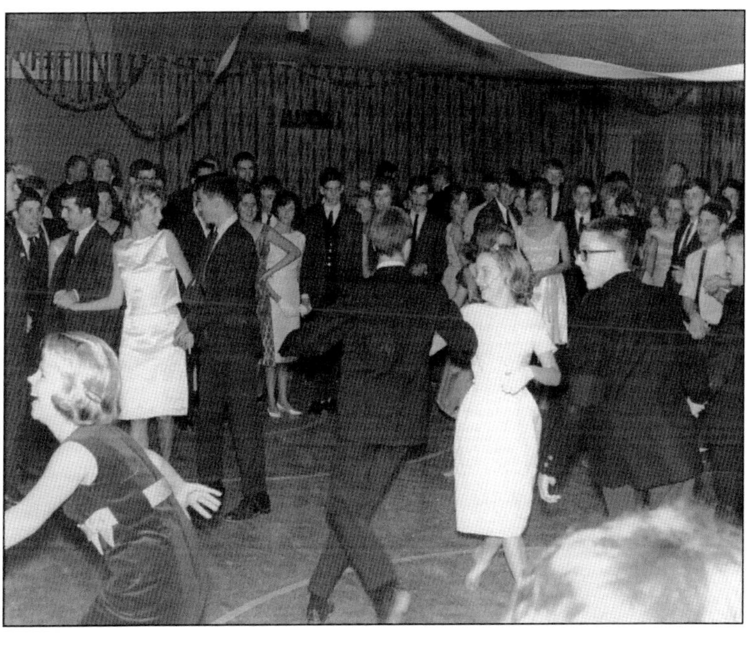

Webb Dance, 1965–1966. Dances were another activity that took place from time to time on the Webb campus.

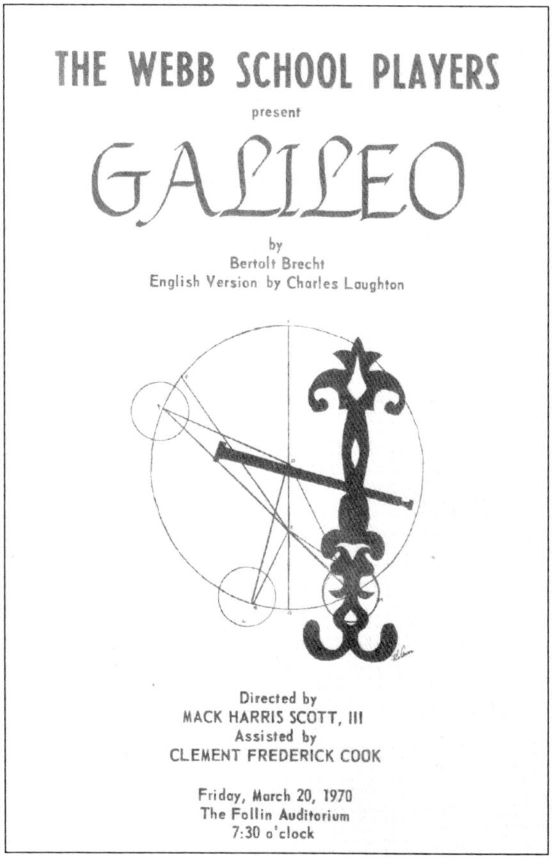
THE WEBB SCHOOL PLAYERS
present
GALILEO
by
Bertolt Brecht
English Version by Charles Laughton

Directed by
MACK HARRIS SCOTT, III
Assisted by
CLEMENT FREDERICK COOK

Friday, March 20, 1970
The Follin Auditorium
7:30 o'clock

Galileo. Set in the 1600s, the play *Galileo* by Bertolt Brecht was The Webb School Players performance for the spring centennial play in 1970.

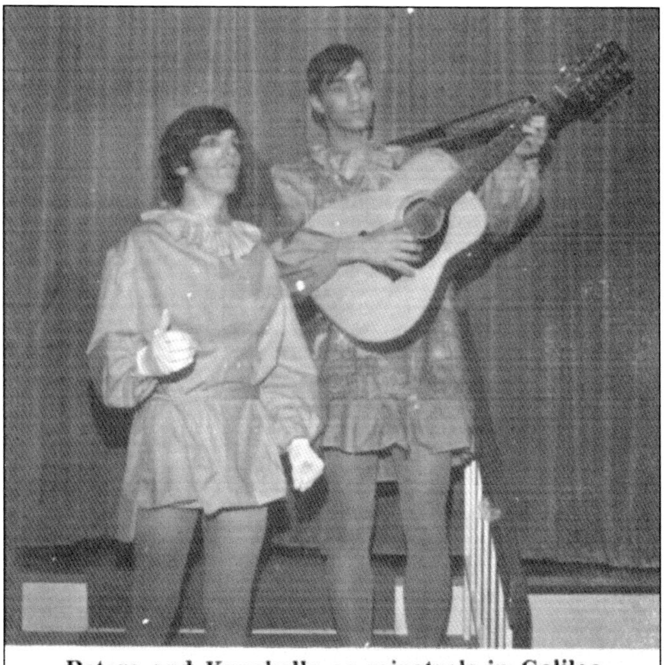
Peters and Knuckolls as minstrels in Galileo

A* Scene from *Galileo. Pictured here are two actors in the play that follows the career of Galileo Galilei. This version by Samuel French Inc. called for 27 male actors and 4 female actors. Many of the faculty, staff, and students participated in some way. The art classes, under the direction of Flo Ann Norvell, designed the sets.

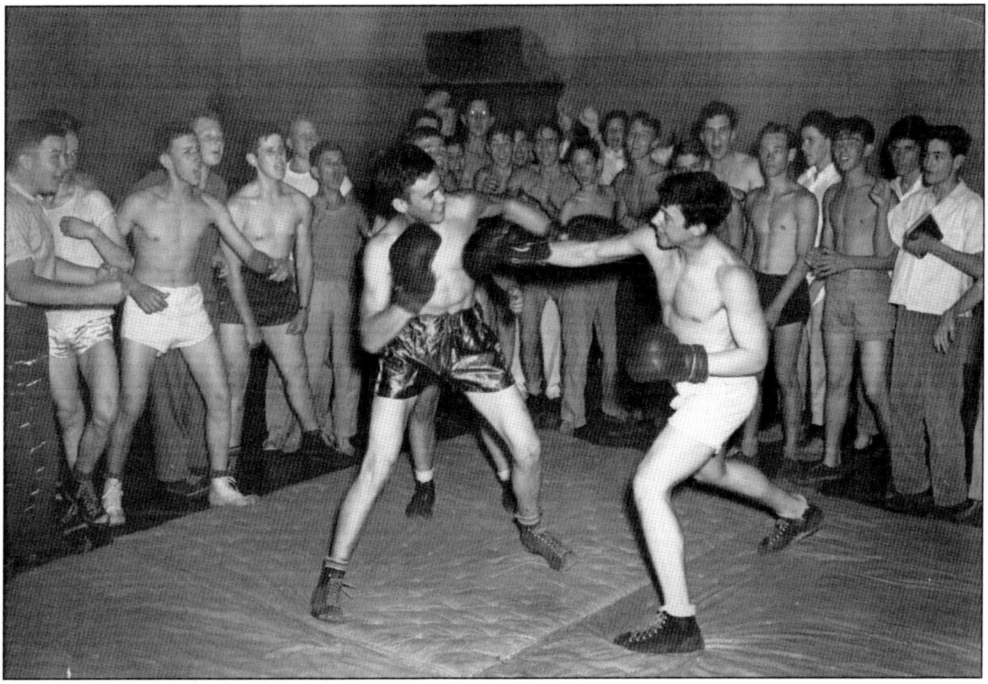

Boxing at Webb. Boxing first began as a sport at Webb in the 1939–1940 school year. Pictured here is one of the matches.

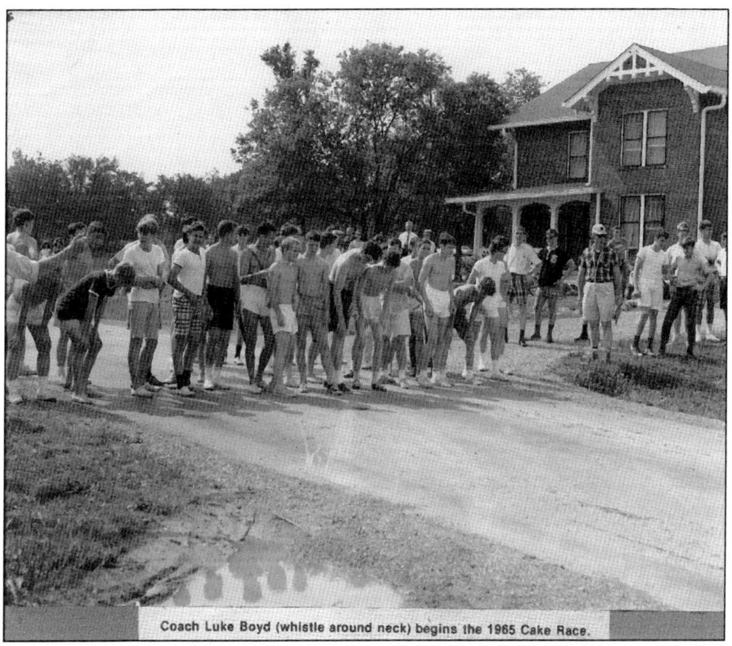

The Webb Cake Race, 1965. One of the yearly events at Webb during the 1960s and 1970s was the cake race.

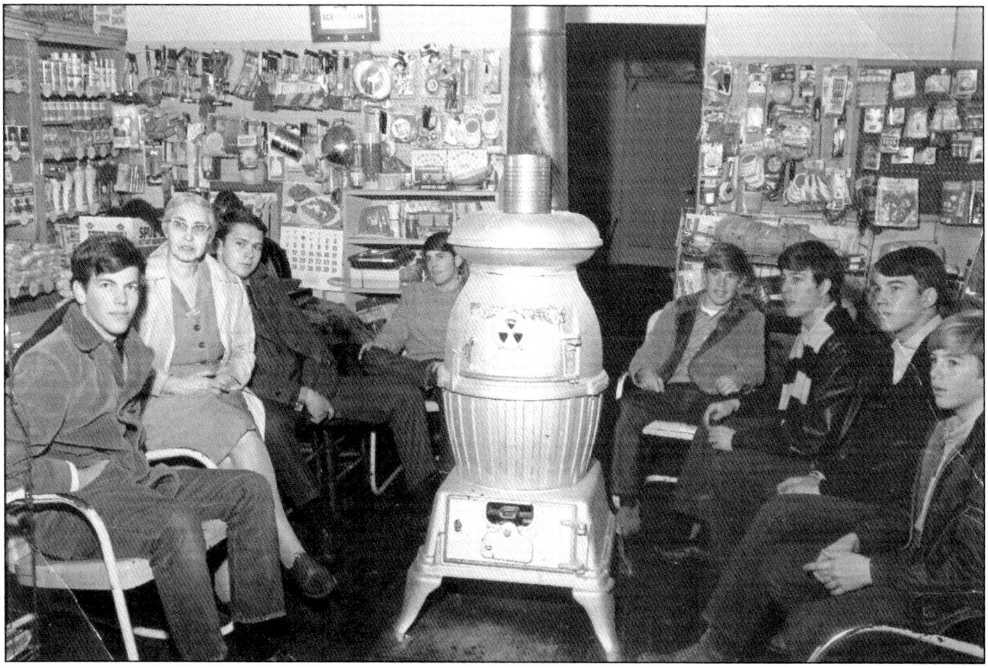

MISS JEANNE. Miss Jeanne's mementos include a bulletin board with pictures of children, snapshots of alums and their families enclosed in Christmas notes, and thank-you notes. If names are forgotten, which they rarely are, it has nothing to do with the heart. For it is with the school that a good part of Miss Jeanne's heart lies. She has many memories of Webb, but none compare to the night in 1974 when she received her Bible. Pictured here from left to right are Cham Johnston Jr., Miss Jeanne, Preston Murrey, Norfleet Rand Jr., Bill Abernathy, Wilson Sims Jr., John Murrey, and Webb Follin III.

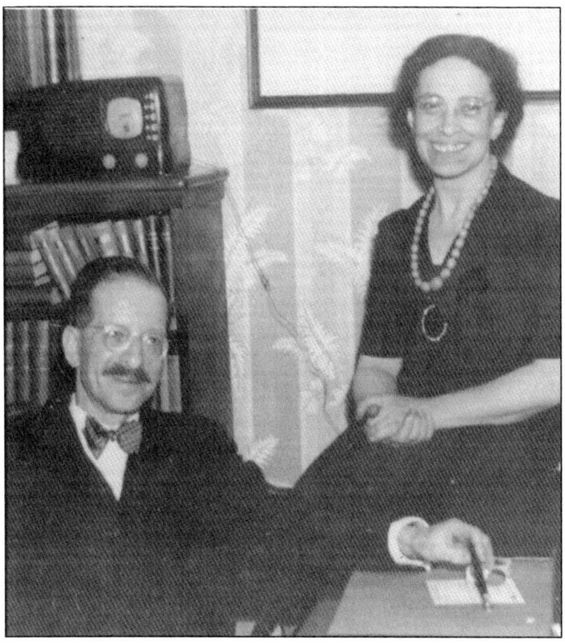

THE ROSENBERGS. In 1942, Will Webb Jr. traveled to Nashville to attend a series of lectures given by a group of "displaced" German scholars. He was so impressed that afterward, he invited them to come to Webb to speak before the student body. One man from the group, an Austrian rather than a German, immediately fell in love with the school and the town of Bell Buckle. Son Will discovered this and, as he had just lost a teacher, asked this Austrian scholar if he was interested in a job. He was, and he called his wife in New York to see if she was interested in moving south. She was indeed, and shortly after, they moved to Bell Buckle. This was how Dr. Otto Rosenberg and his wife, Emma, came to Webb.

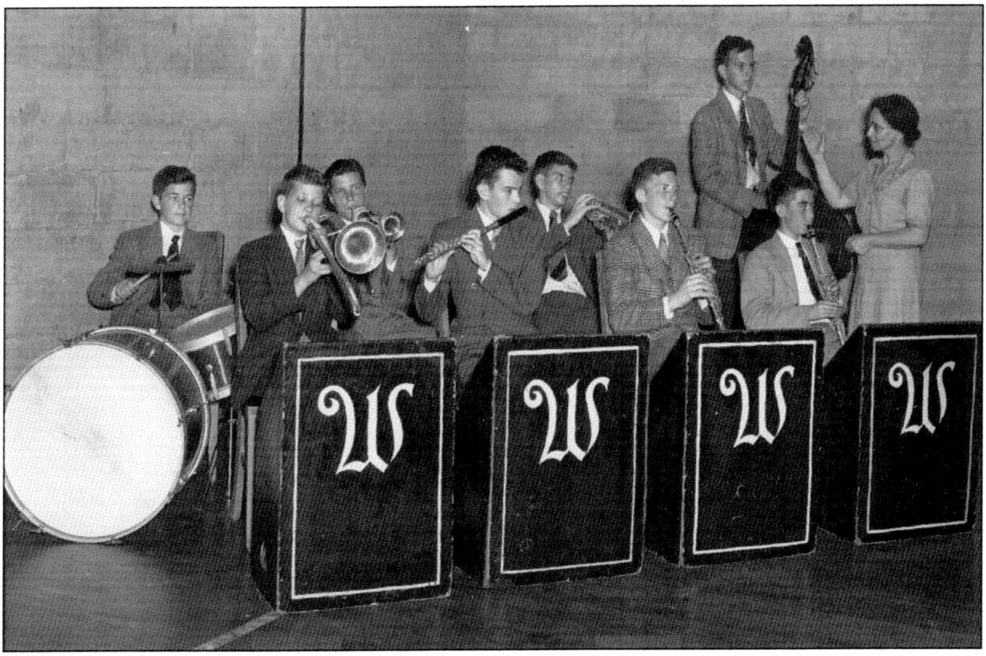

EMMA ROSENBERG AND THE WEBB SCHOOL ORCHESTRA, C. 1940S. The Webb School Orchestra was an activity made available to Webb students and directed by Emma Rosenberg.

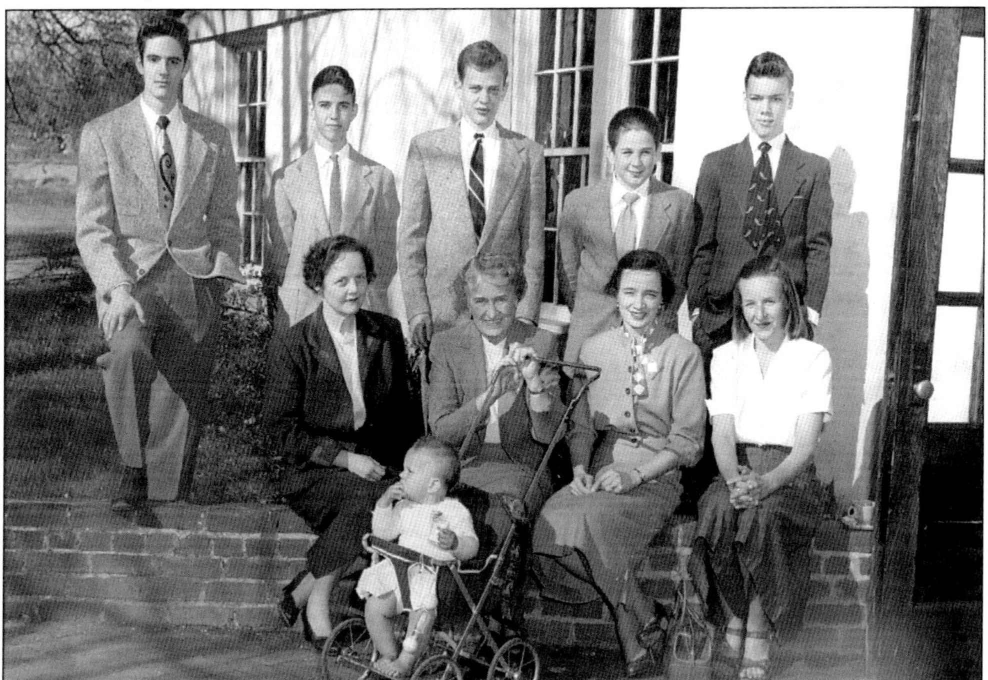

THE ART GUILD. One of the clubs in the 1952–1953 school year was the Art Guild. Pictured are the students and faculty sponsors. From left to right are (first row) faculty Dorothy Webb, Abbie (baby), Miriam Ames, Julie Webb, and Helen Iversen; (second row) students Bob Finley, Bill Counts, Barstow Brownson, Tim Martin, and Pat Nesbit.

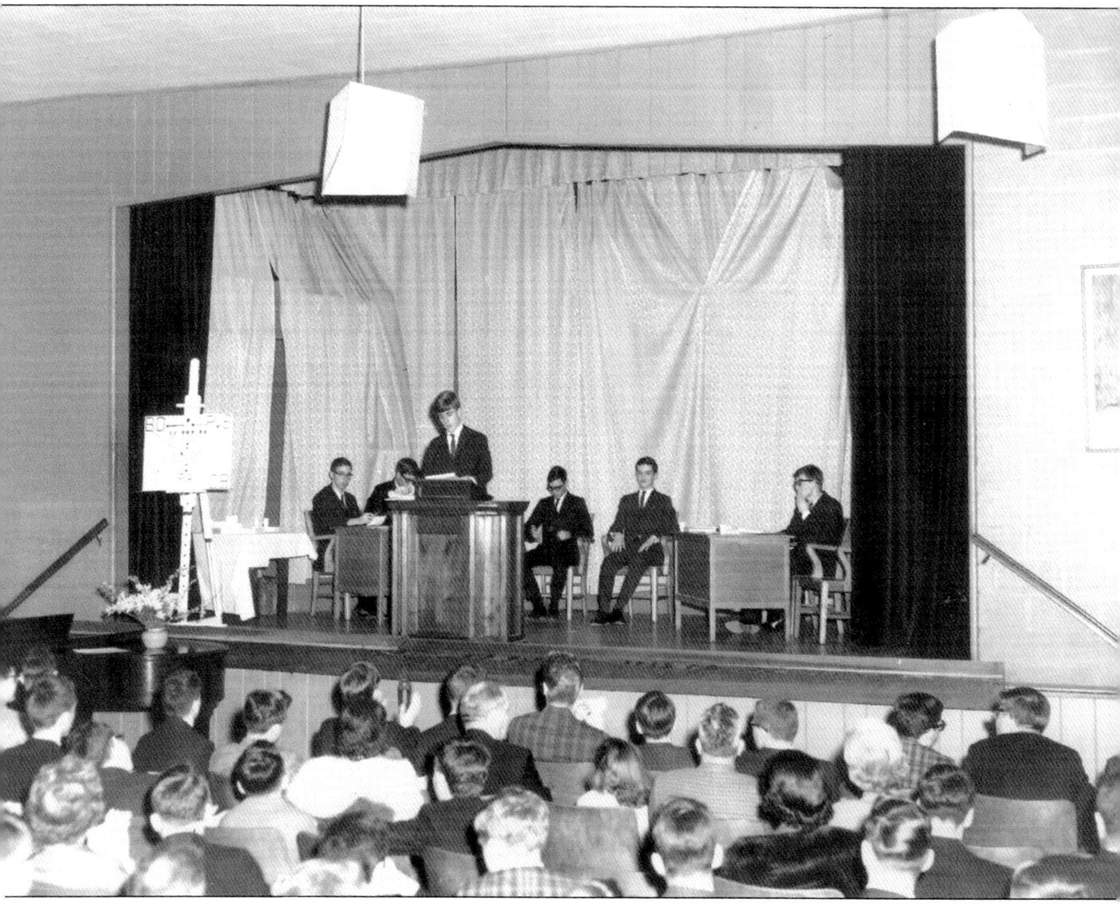

W.P. Cooper Auditorium Debate, c. 1960s. This auditorium was part of the new Big Room that was built in 1952. It was erected as a result of W.P. Cooper Jr., a 1913 Webb School graduate, and was named after his father, W.P. Cooper Sr., who graduated from Webb in 1890. This space included a stage and a projection booth. Many debates, chapel talks, and school assemblies took place in this building. Pictured is a mid-year debate in the auditorium.

THE JUNIOR ROOM. The Junior Room was one of the first three buildings erected on the grounds when The Webb School moved to Bell Buckle. The juniors were taught in this building. Throughout the school's history, it has been placed in multiple locations on campus. It was restored in the 1970s, transforming it into a school museum. In 1987, it was listed in the National Register of Historic Places.

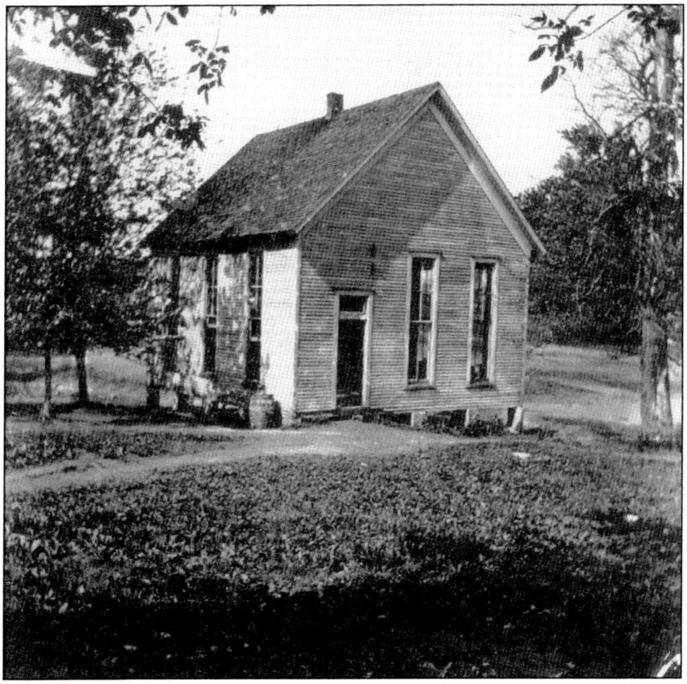

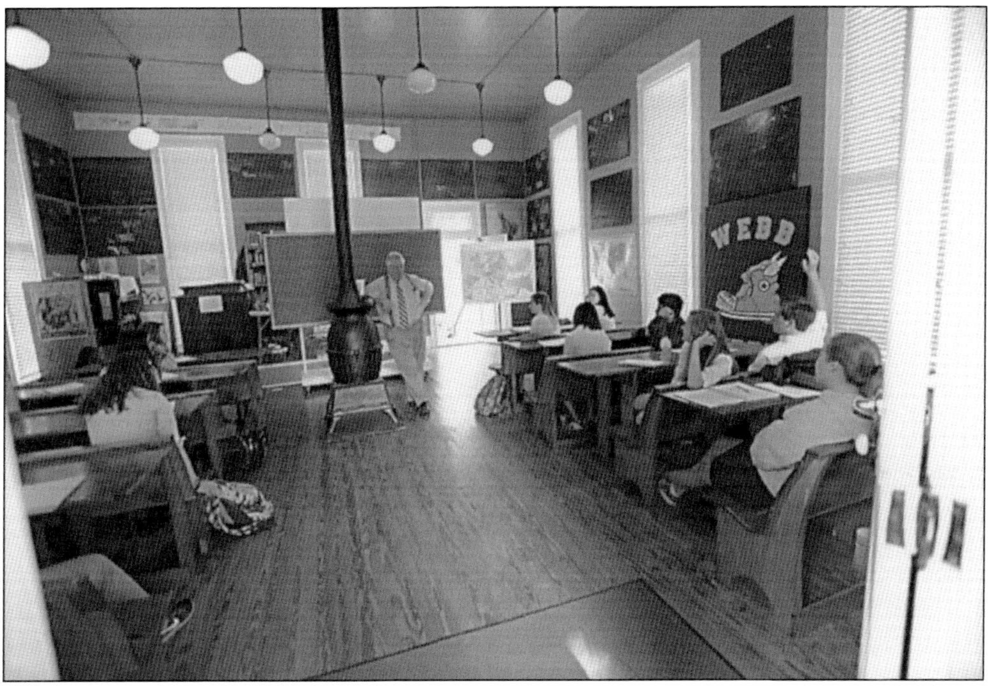

THE JUNIOR ROOM AS A CLASSROOM. The Junior Room today is a classroom. This room has always been a significant part of campus history. It began as a classroom in 1886; longtime teacher L.R. Smith is seen here using it once again for its original purpose.

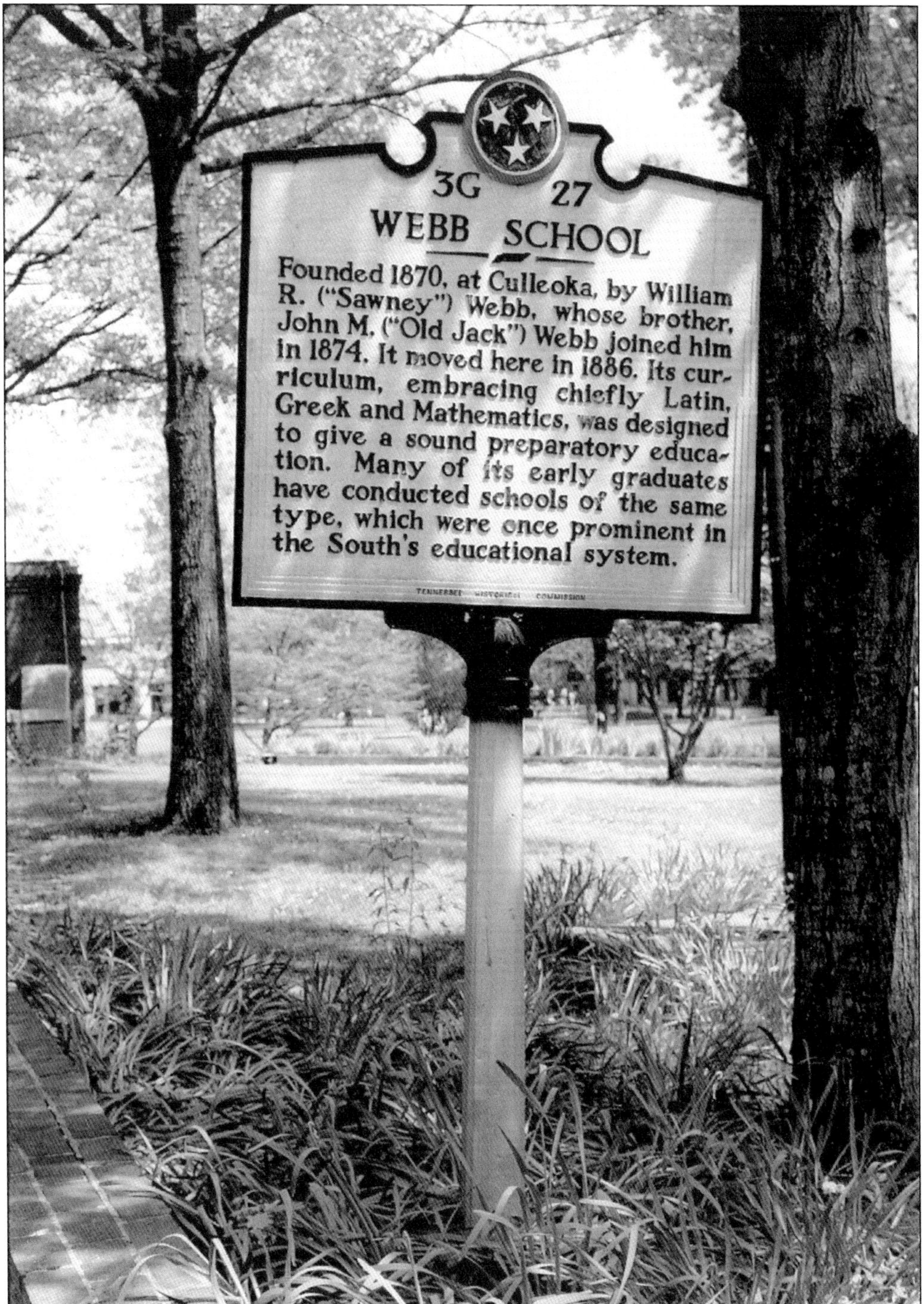

HISTORICAL MARKER. The Bell Buckle Historic District was listed in the National Register of Historic places in 1976. The school's historical marker was granted by the Tennessee Historical Commission.

Four

International Coeducational Day and Boarding School 1973–2020

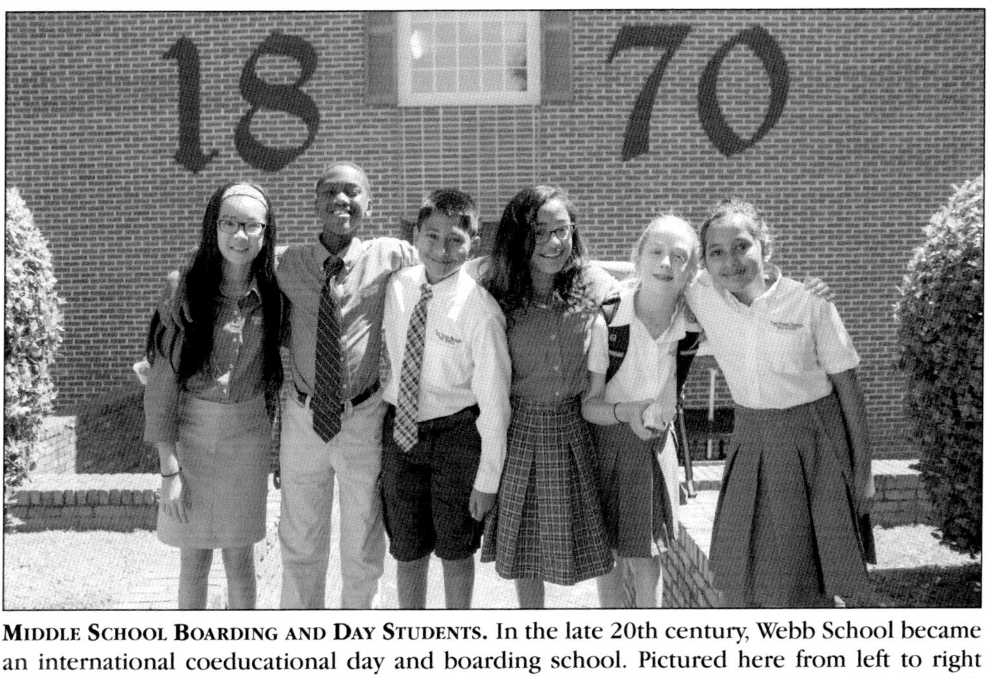

Middle School Boarding and Day Students. In the late 20th century, Webb School became an international coeducational day and boarding school. Pictured here from left to right are middle school students Mai Phan, class of 2024; Koen Edwards, 2023; Shiv Patel, 2024; Nataja Siva, 2023; Elle Rhea Goco, 2024; and Nysa Chaudary, 2023.

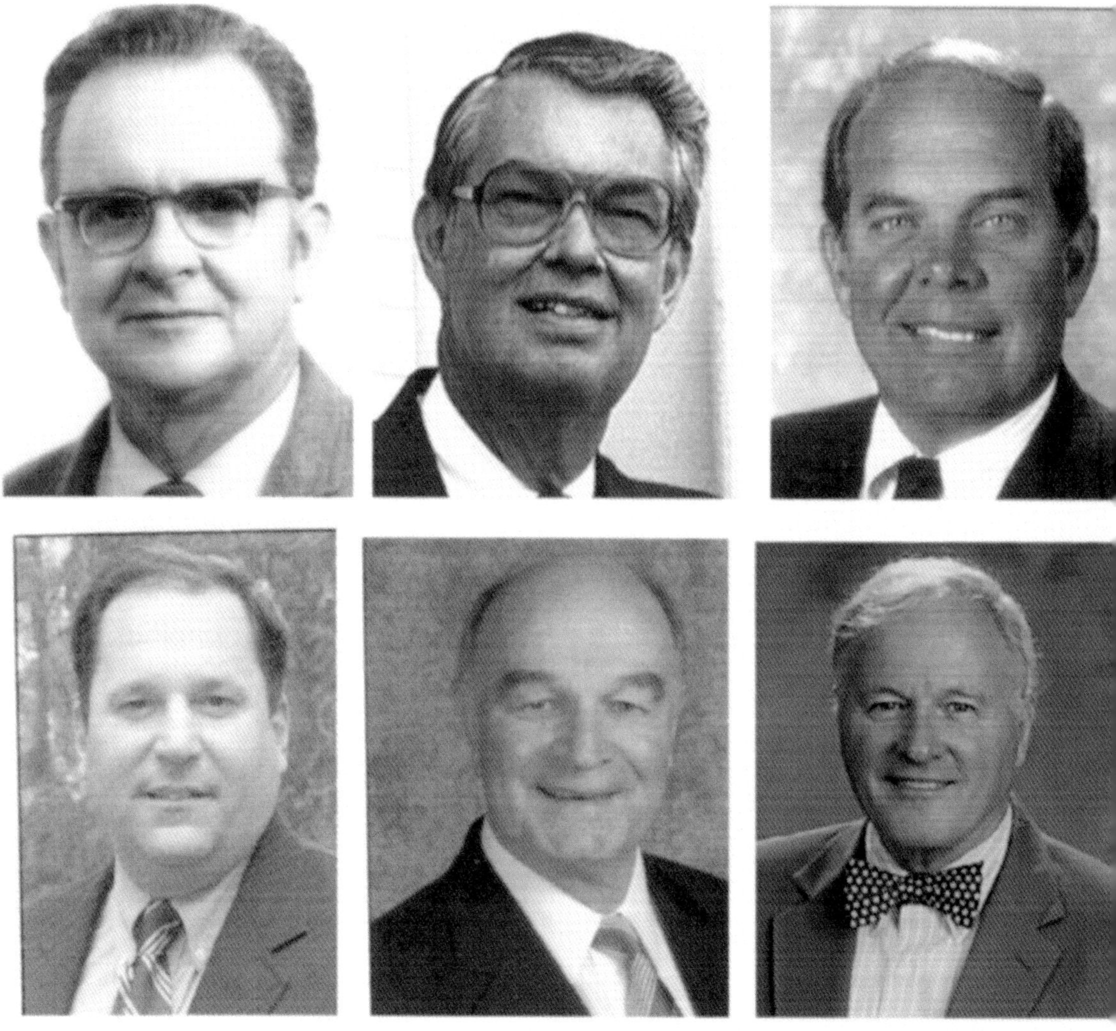

HEADMASTERS. From left to right are (top row) Dr. Gary Jones, who served Webb as president from 1973 to 1978; Jackson E. Heffner, who was headmaster between 1977 and 1989; and A. Jon Frere, who brought in the 21st century as headmaster from 1989 to 2005; (bottom row) Albert Cauz, who served as head of school from 2005 to 2009; Gordon E. Bondurant, who served as interim head of school for the 2009–2010 school year; and Raymond S. Broadhead, the current head of school beginning in 2010.

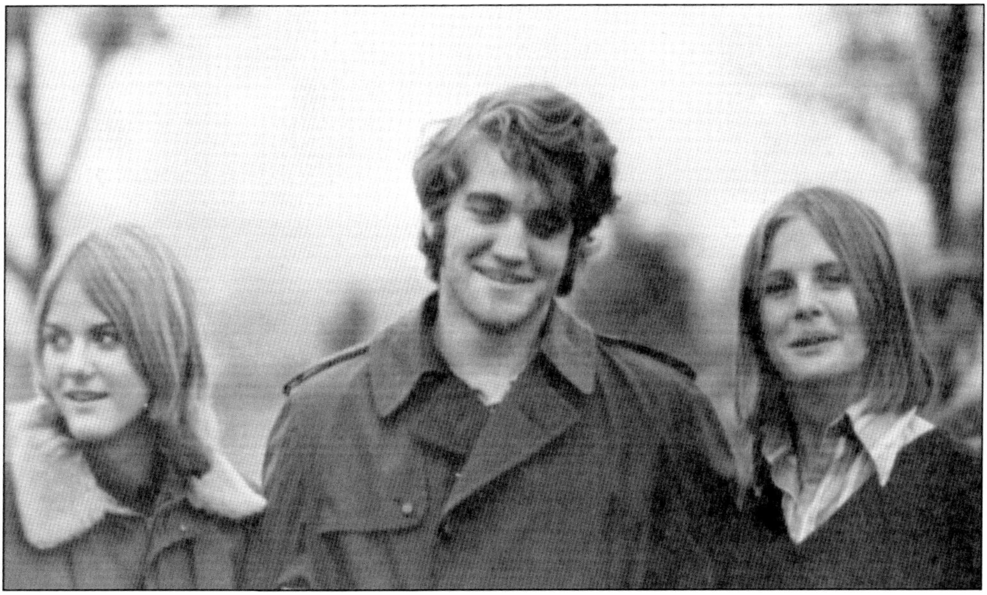

Female Students Return. After 24 years as a single-sex institution, Webb welcomed female students back in 1970. In 1972, the first female residential students attended Webb.

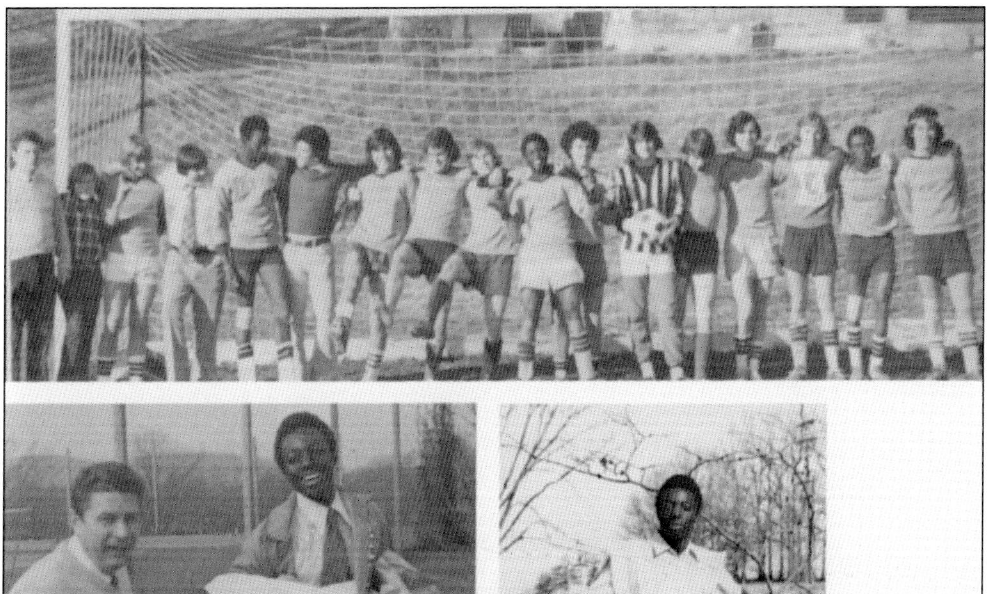

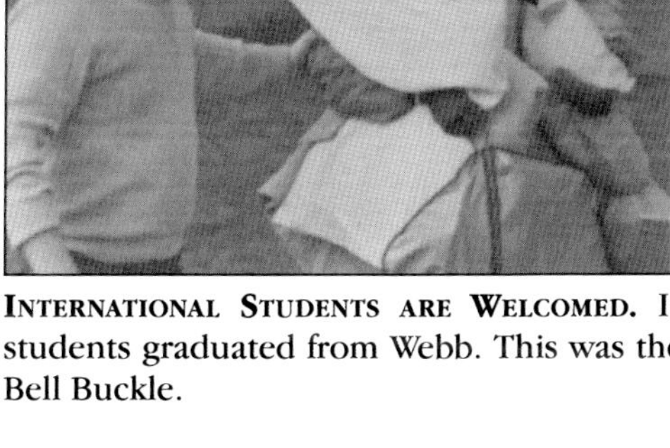

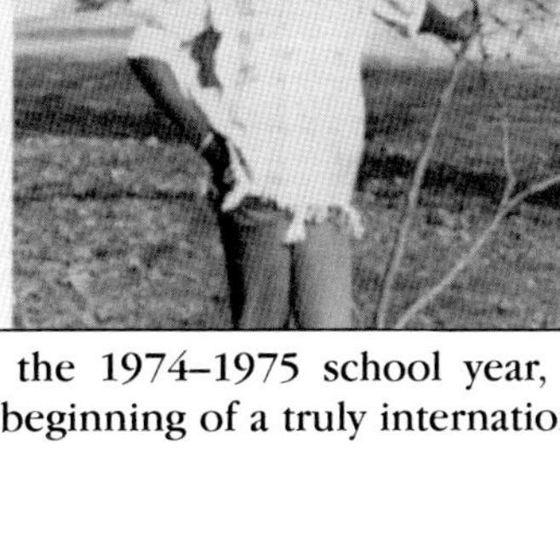

International Students are Welcomed. In the 1974–1975 school year, four Gambian students graduated from Webb. This was the beginning of a truly international program in Bell Buckle.

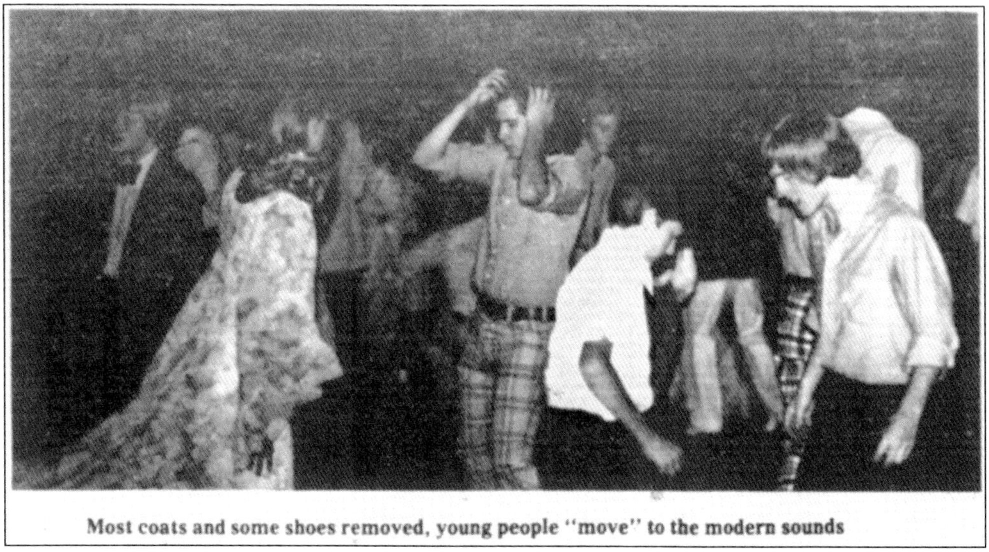

Senior Prom, 1975. These students danced the night away and had breakfast the next morning, cooked by Dr. Gary Jones, Luke Boyd, Joan Jones, and Sue Johnson. This image was published in the *Alumni Bulletin* in July 1975.

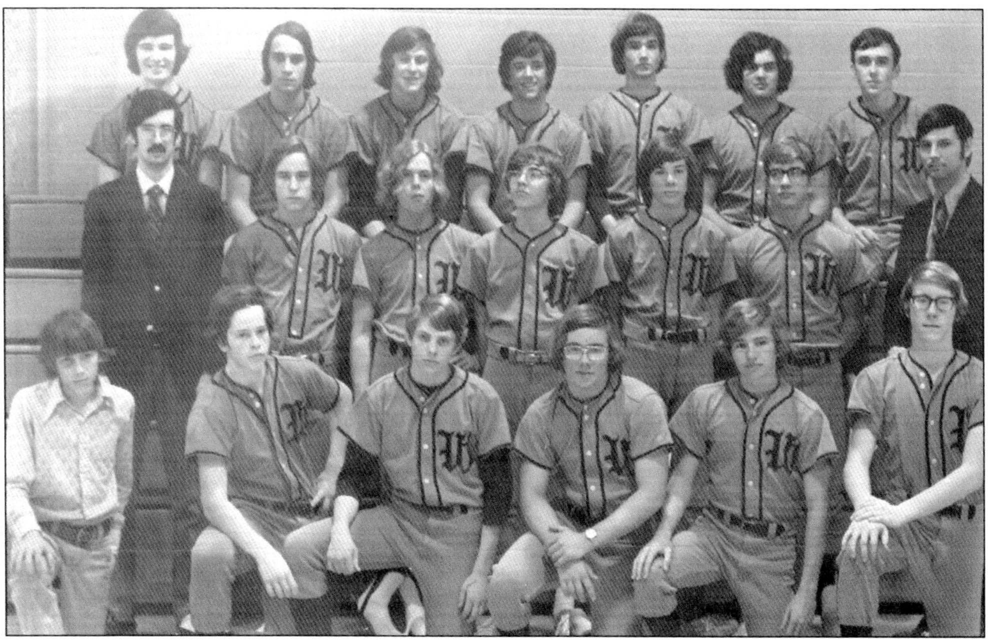

Baseball Team, 1973. At far left in the second row is Webb's own Charles Alexander, a 1968 Webb graduate and the team's assistant coach.

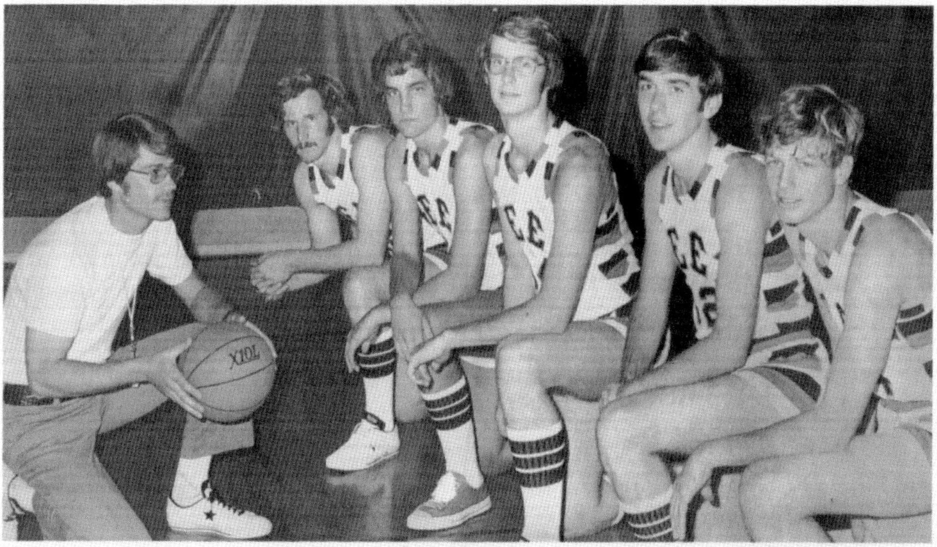

Pictured above are players from the 1974-1975 varsity boys basketball team: Coach Roy Johnson, Keith Barton '75, Dan Andrews '75, Cannon Tilford '75, John Johnson '75, and Gilbert Gordon '75. This team holds one of the most successful records in Webb's sports history.

BASKETBALL, 1974–1975. Seen here are the starting five of the 1974–1975 varsity basketball team with coach Roy Johnson; from left to right are Keith Barton, Dan Andrews, Cannon Tilford, John Johnson, and Gilbert Gordon.

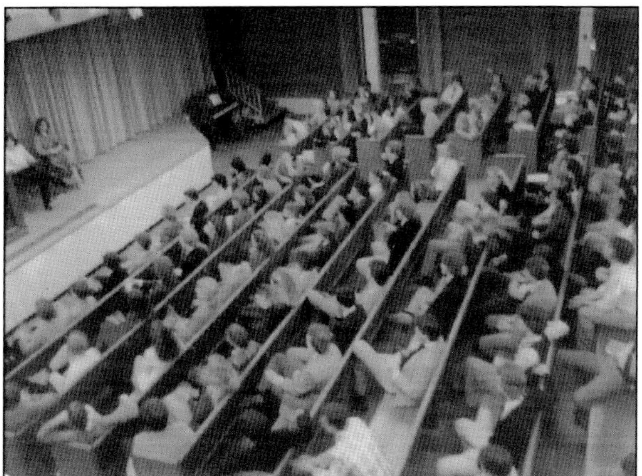

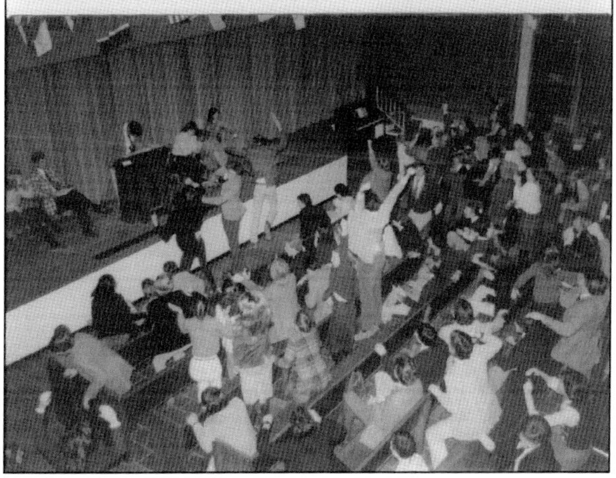

YOU MAY HAVE THE DAY. These photographs from 1982 show scenes before and after headmaster Jack Heffner declared that day a "holiday." Headmasters throughout the school's history dating back to Sawney have uttered the phrase "You may have the day!"

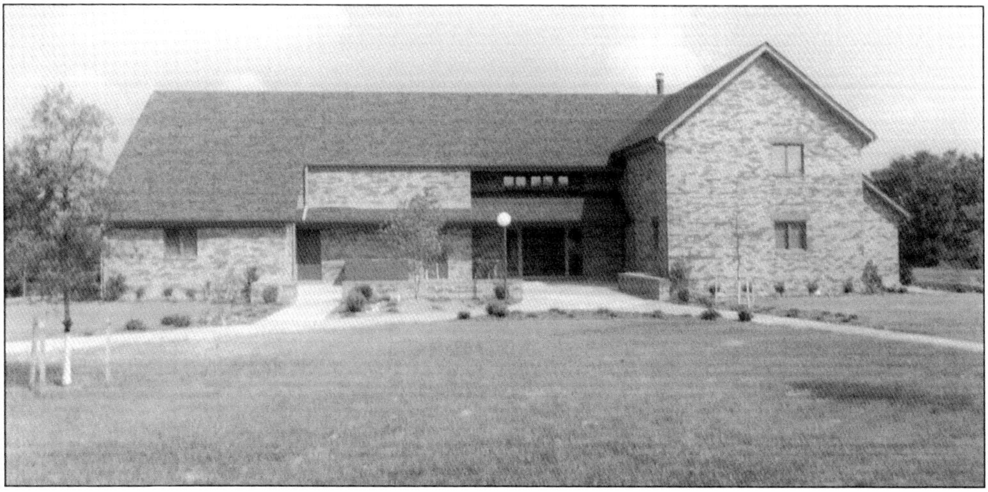

DORMS FOR BOTH MALE AND FEMALE STUDENTS. Austin Davis Dormitory was built and dedicated in 1980. Austin Davis was a longtime supporter of The Webb School. It was the first dormitory built to house girls. Cooper-Farris Dormitory was built in the spring of 1981 and dedicated in October of the same year. This dormitory was named for the late Thomas A. Cooper Sr. (class of 1930 and father of Thomas A. Cooper Jr., class of 1966), who was a trustee from 1952 to 1979, and the late Mary Penick Farris (mother of Bill Farris, class of 1966), who served as a trustee from 1974 to 1996.

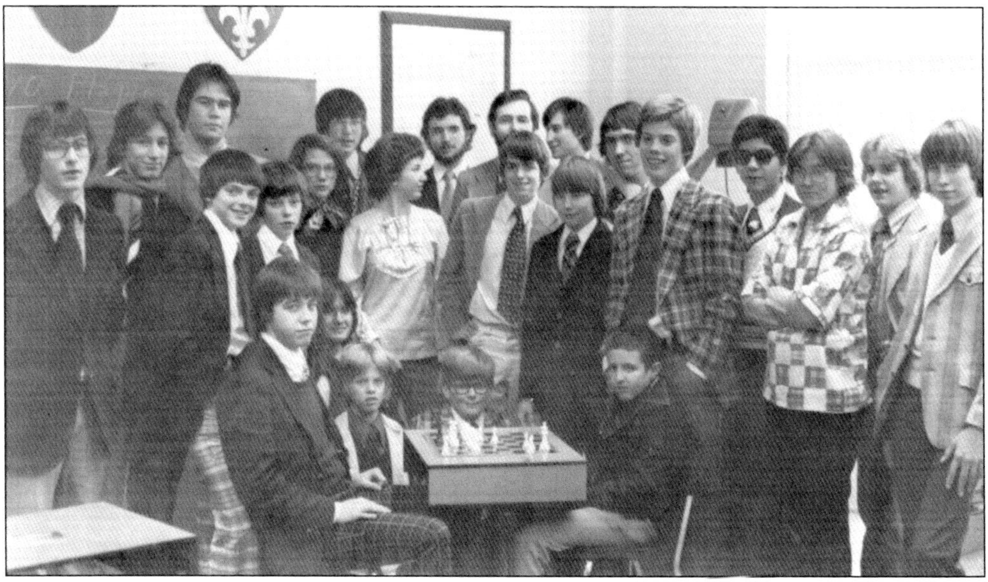

WEBB CHESS CLUB. Pictured is the 1977 Webb Chess Club, led by teacher Marion Marks (class of 1967). This club provided intramural competition among the students. From left to right are (first row, seated) Billy Ring, Tim Mankin, Sydney Phillips, Richard Smith, and Robert Kalteouns Kaltsounis; (second row, standing) Randy Richards, John Schippers, Chris Ditto, James Potts, Randy Tremaine, Ginger Marks, Proby Dulaney, Carolyn Ownby, Jack Ownby, Marion Marks, Lee Mountcastle, Hamilton Woods, Robert Brown, Mike Deitschmann, Jeff Whorley, Vahid Ordoubadian, Patricia Perry, Bret McKinney, and Nicky Nichols. Not pictured are Billy Hardin, Bruno Censori, Mark Hall, John Carr, John Cushing, Tom Cushing, Scott Friedland, Joe Wilhite, Jason Ditto, Rafe Smith, Trent Tolbert, and Jay Slatton.

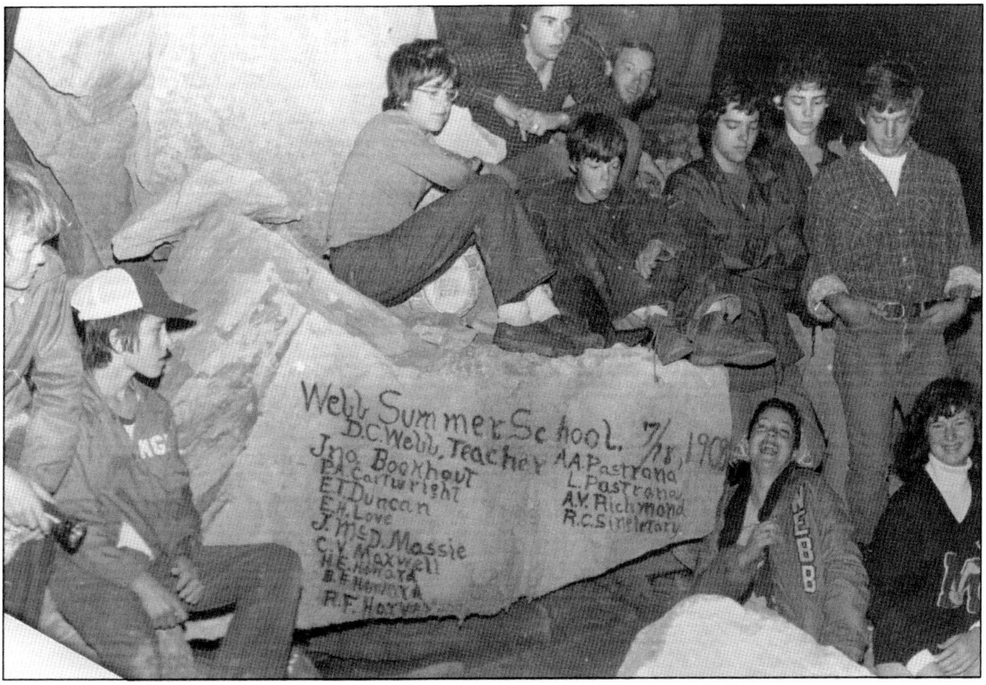

Cumberland Caverns. In 1903, Daniel Clary Webb took a group to Cumberland Caverns, where they left their names engraved in this stone. Pictured is a group from the 1970s hiking in the same area. Alumni still run across this carving. Tabetha Newport Sullens, class of 1994, tweeted a photograph from Brad Bolding of the same spot in 2016.

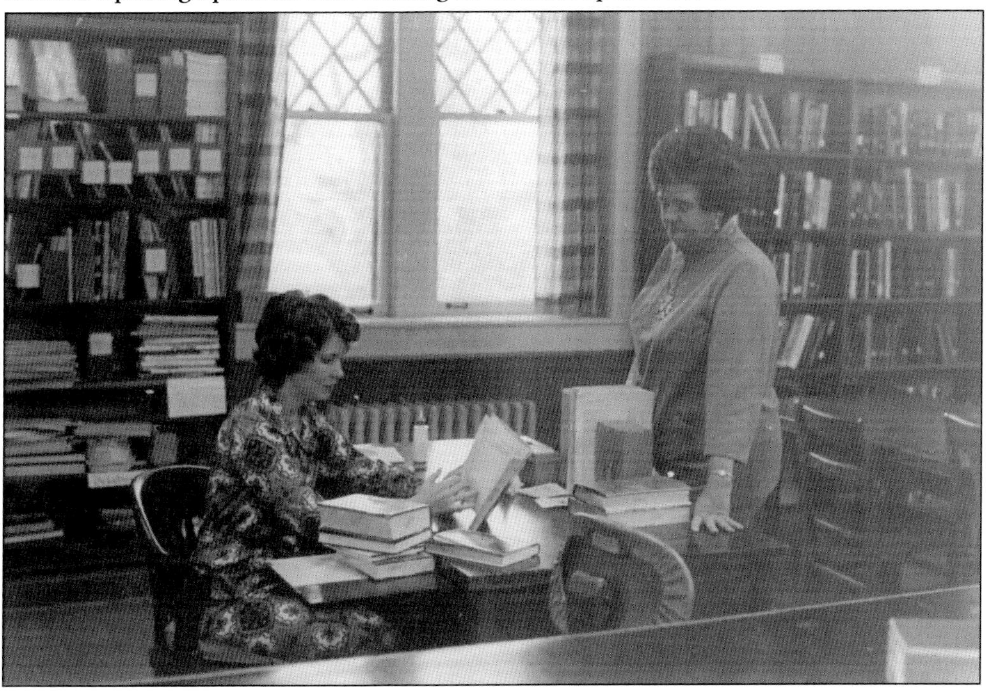

Librarians, 1970s. Prior to the William Bond Library being built, these are the people who kept the library in shape in the late 1970s: Lynn Holliman (left) and Joyce Atterholt.

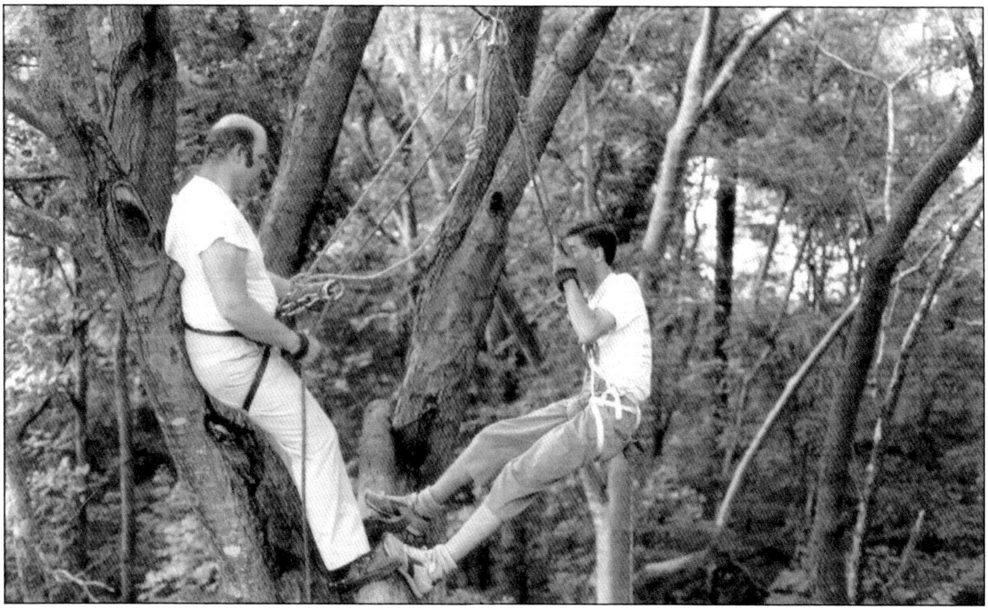

WILD Ropes Course. Wilderness Instruction and Leadership Development (WILD) is an exciting program that combines the classroom with the outdoors. WILD is an academic class that includes book discussions about camping and leadership. The class also uses experience gained from the outdoors and Outerlimits activities such as camping, canoeing, backpacking, rock climbing, and others to teach the skills needed to attend and lead trips into the wilderness.

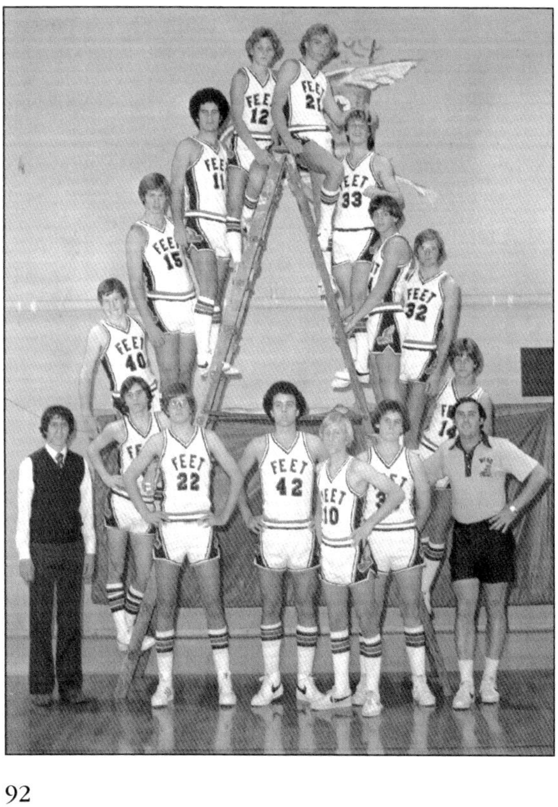

Boys' Varsity Basketball Team, 1980. Pictured is the 1980 boys' varsity basketball team, with the foot emblem in the background. They were a very successful team that year. The Feet had an overall record of 15-3 and placed second in the district tournament. The team was coached by Tom Radford and assisted by Joe Barnes. Pictured from left to right are (first row) manager Paul Spencer, Jim Whorley, Jay Slatton, Bill Huddleston, John Gray Burns, and coach Tom Radford; (second row) Mark Harrison, Trent Tolbert, John Cushing, Hossein Ordoubadian, Bobby Turner, Dave Smith, Bryan McElroy, Will Coble, Tim Hill, and Tom Cushing. Not pictured is Ron Hirsch.

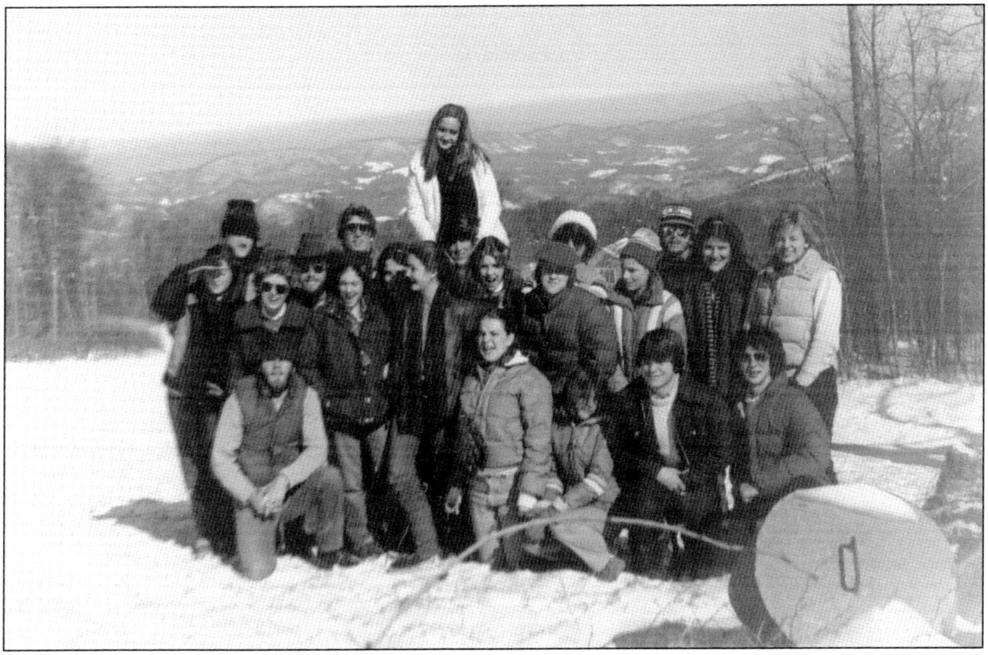

OUTERLIMITS. The Outerlimits program takes several trips throughout the school year. This picture shows a trip to Beech Mountain, North Carolina, on January 31–February 3, 1980.

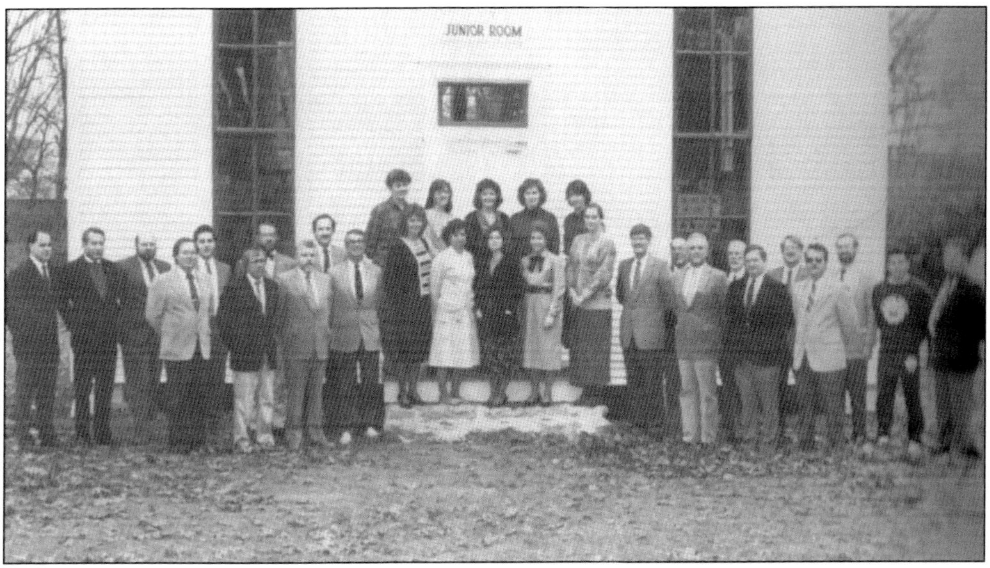

WEBB SCHOOL FACULTY, 1988–1989. Pictured is the 1988–1989 Webb School faculty in front of the Junior Room. From left to right are (first row) Jim Bruton, Gar Maunula, Imre Lagler, Jackson E. Heffner, Linda Williams, Sandra Truitt, Gloria Wilhite, Sandra Sanders, Louisa Heffner, Delbert Coggins, Tom Gorry, L.R. Smith, and Lester Dufford; (second row) Chris Heying, Larry Nichols, Brian Wofford, Ron Smith, Thomas E. Haynes, Stan Rupley, Debbi Gilmore, Donna Jensen, Carol Burnau, Marilyn Morgan, Loula Heffner, Ralph Nollenberger, James James, Phil Martin, Ralph Jones, David Russo, and Richard Miller. Not pictured is Bill Rice.

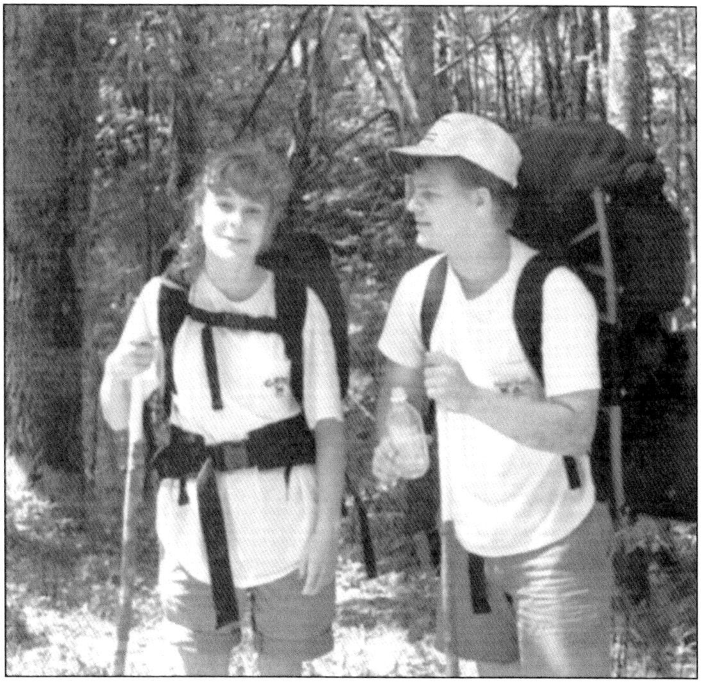

Senior Survival, 1989. Senior Survival is a Webb tradition that began in 1977. Along with weekend group trips throughout the year, Winter Freeze and Spring Break adventures test students' skills. Senior Survival, a weeklong backpacking trip ending the day before graduation, is the final bonding experience for each class that makes lasting memories.

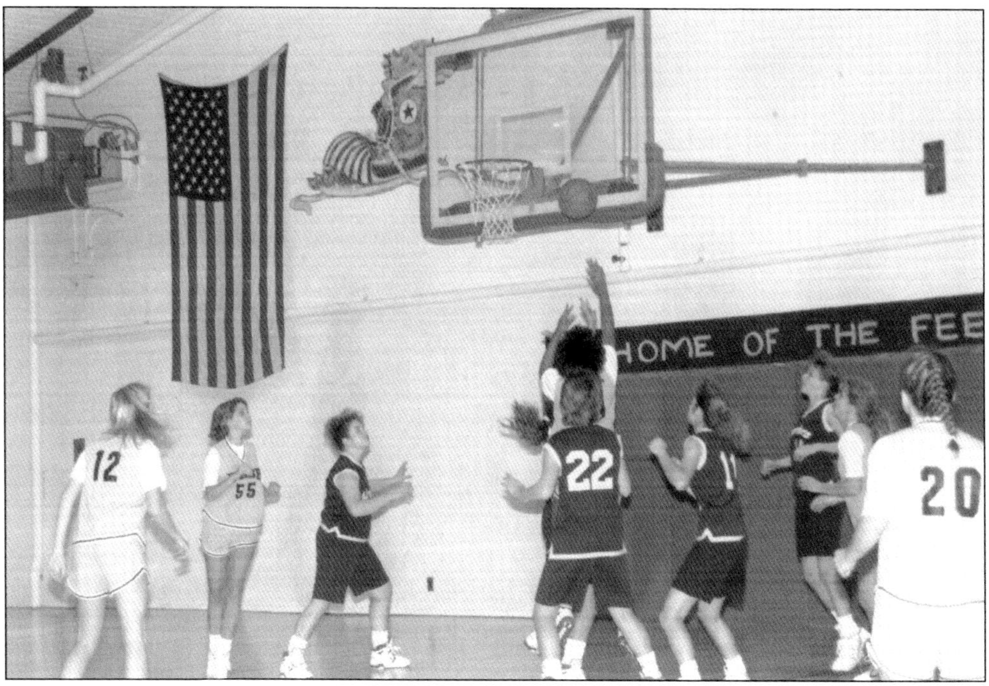

Girls' Basketball Team, 1988–1989. After female students returned to Webb in the 1970s, they began to build the Lady Feet brand. This action shot is of the 1988–1989 girls' basketball team. This team enjoyed a winning season.

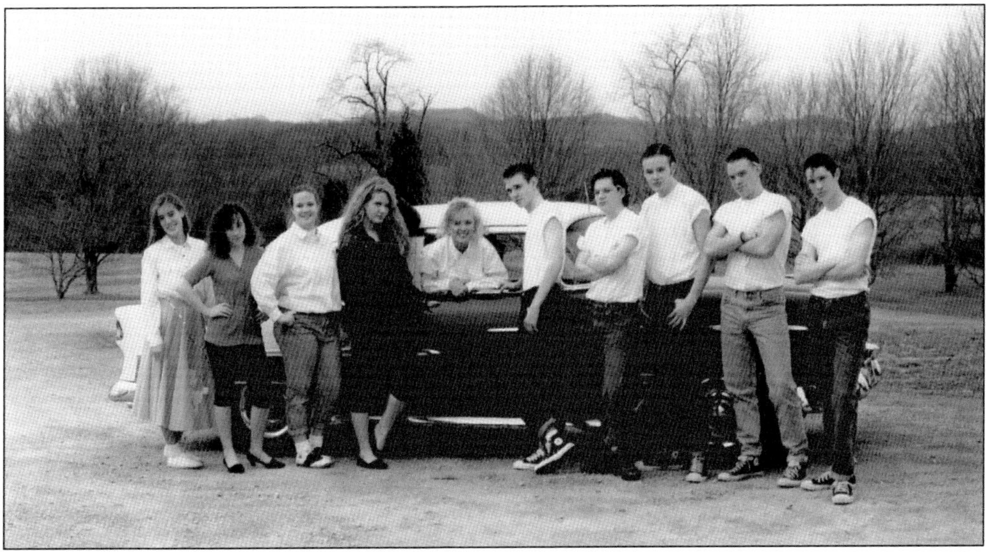

***Grease*, 1994.** This picture is from Webb's production of *Grease* in 1994. At center in the car is Webb's current middle school head, Tabetha Newport Sullens, a 1994 Webb graduate. From left to right are Erin Craig, Marcie Beasley, Jessica Callow, Amber Edwards, Tabetha Newport, Michael Morgan, David Wilhite, Matt Hornsby, Chris Ireson, and Louis Hamric.

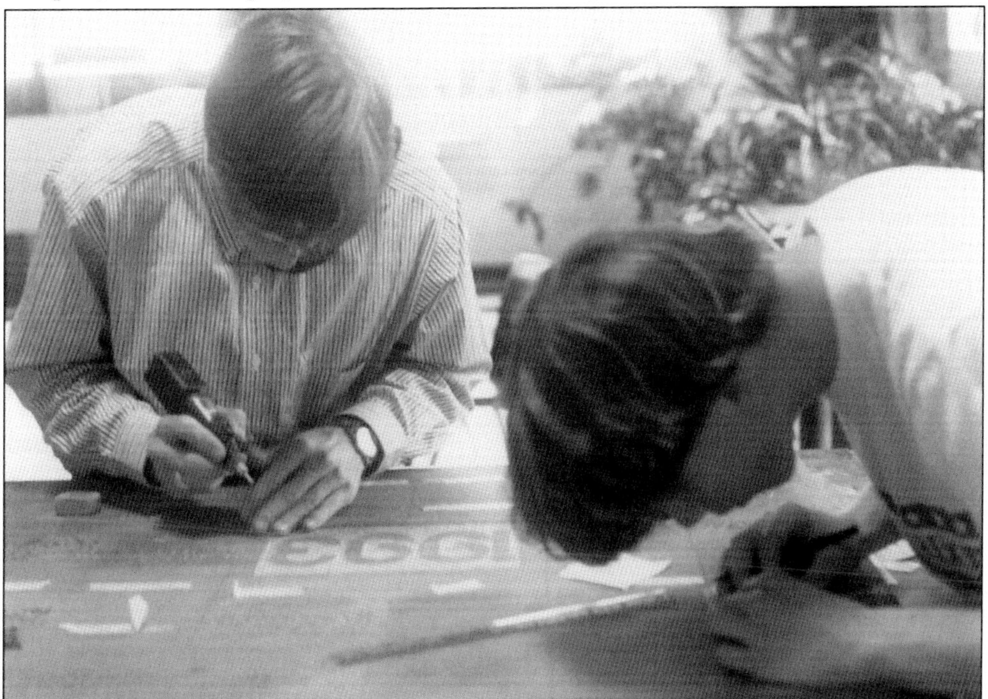

Senior Boards, 1993. The tradition of senior boards is an outgrowth of a stipulation Sawney made—that students would not carve on the wooden desks. To this day, each member of the graduating class carves a section of their senior board. Boards in recent years have included sections that have been carved and painted. The boards are displayed and are main attractions for alumni at each reunion.

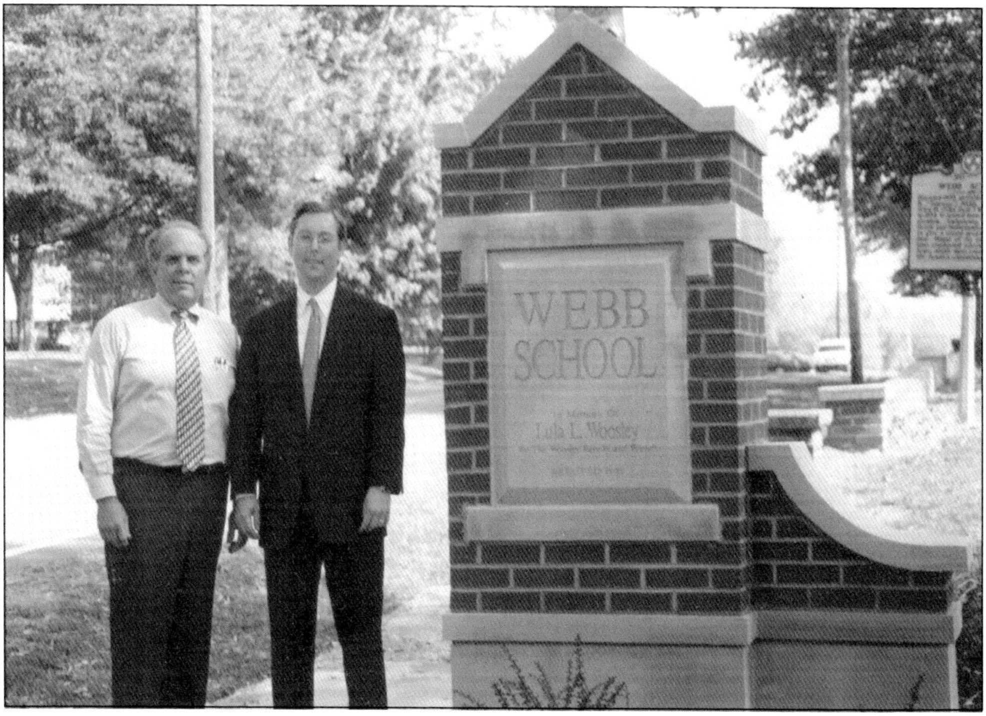

Frere with Woosley. The Laura Woosley Poston Memorial Plaza was installed in 1997. It was created as a memorial to the late Laura Woosley Poston, a 1980 Webb graduate who passed away. Pictured here is headmaster Jon Frere (left) with H. Lee Woosley III (class of 1978), brother of Laura, in front of the Woosley-Gilliland memorial gates.

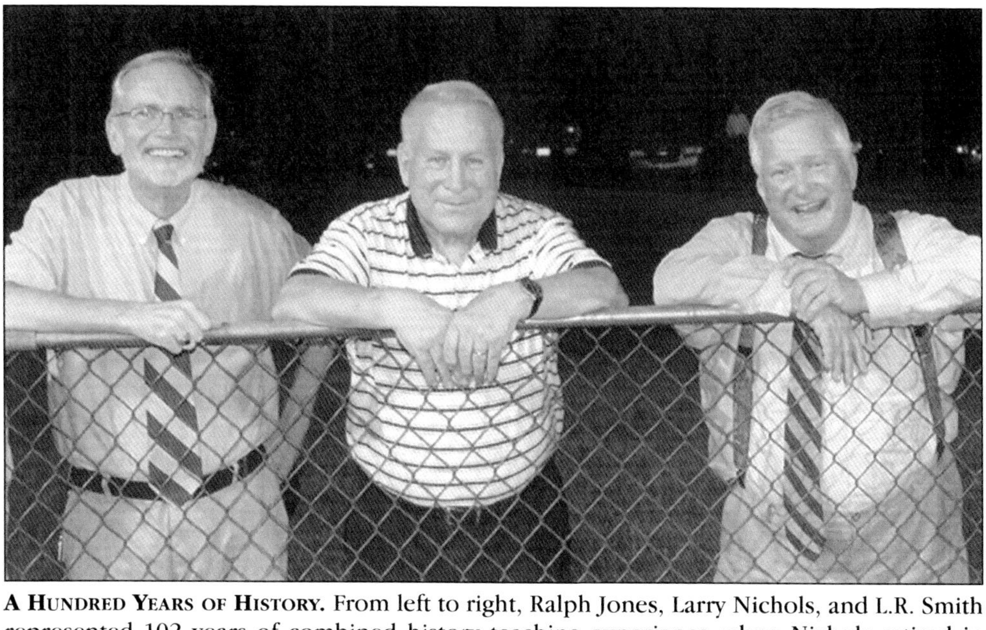

A Hundred Years of History. From left to right, Ralph Jones, Larry Nichols, and L.R. Smith represented 102 years of combined history teaching experience when Nichols retired in 2018. The three long-tenured history faculty members created a "history" of their own by attending a symposium at the Sayre School in Lexington, Kentucky, for nearly two decades.

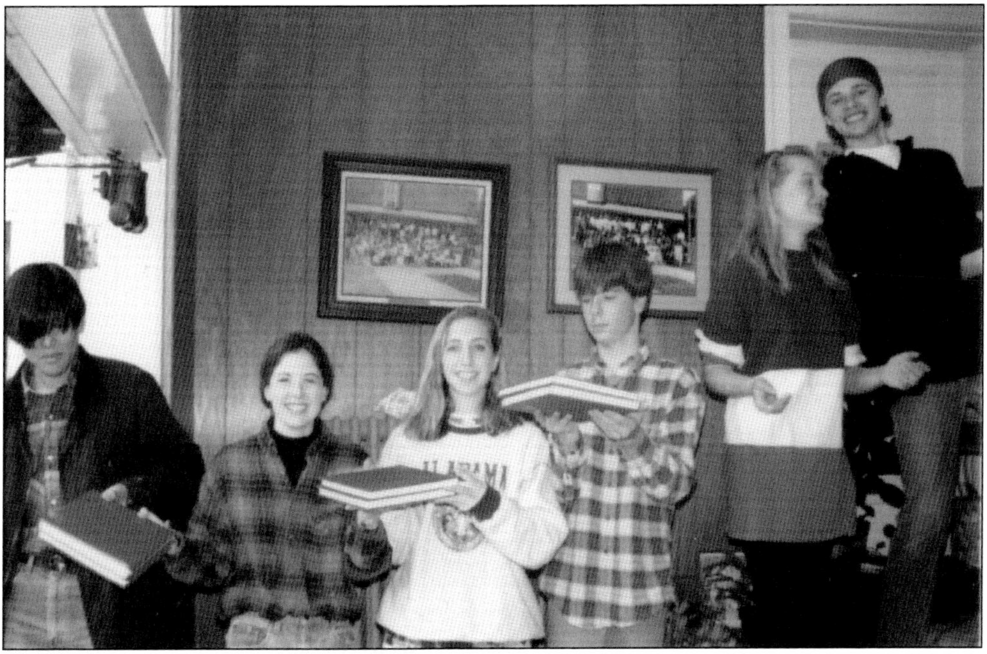

William Bond Library. When it was time to move into the new library, it took everyone's help to move the many volumes of books and other materials from the original building. Students and teachers alike formed lines passing books from person to person until all the books had been moved.

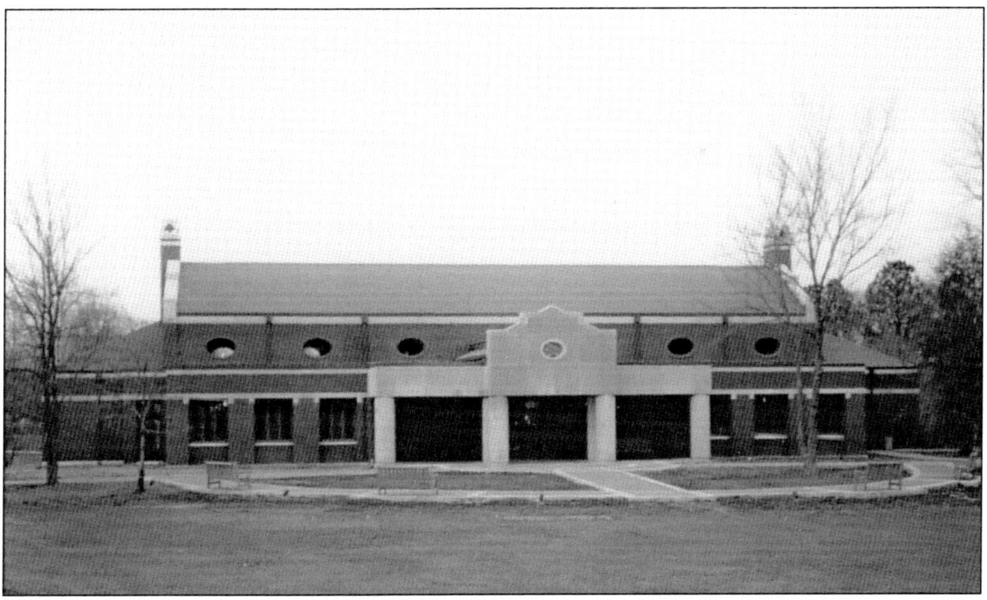

William Bond Library. The William Bond Library was built in 1992 and dedicated in February 1993. The family of William West Bond, a 1903 Webb graduate, donated the funds to construct this building. It is located next to the first library, which was built in 1927. The new library is named for prominent 1903 graduate William West Bond Sr. His son William West Bond Jr., class of 1938, was the architect and designer for Holiday Inn hotels.

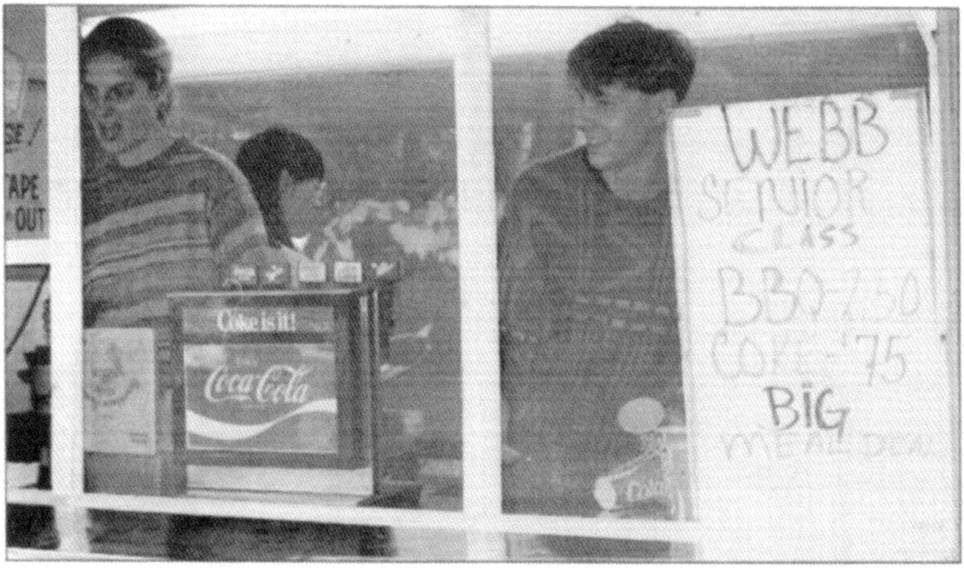

Sabine Wiedenmann, Elaine Yang and Louis Barbeau sell barbecue for the senior class at the Arts and Crafts Festival.

Webb School Craft Fair. The Webb School Craft Fair has been in existence for over 40 years. For many years, Webb students set up booths and sold food and drinks to raise money to benefit their classes or clubs.

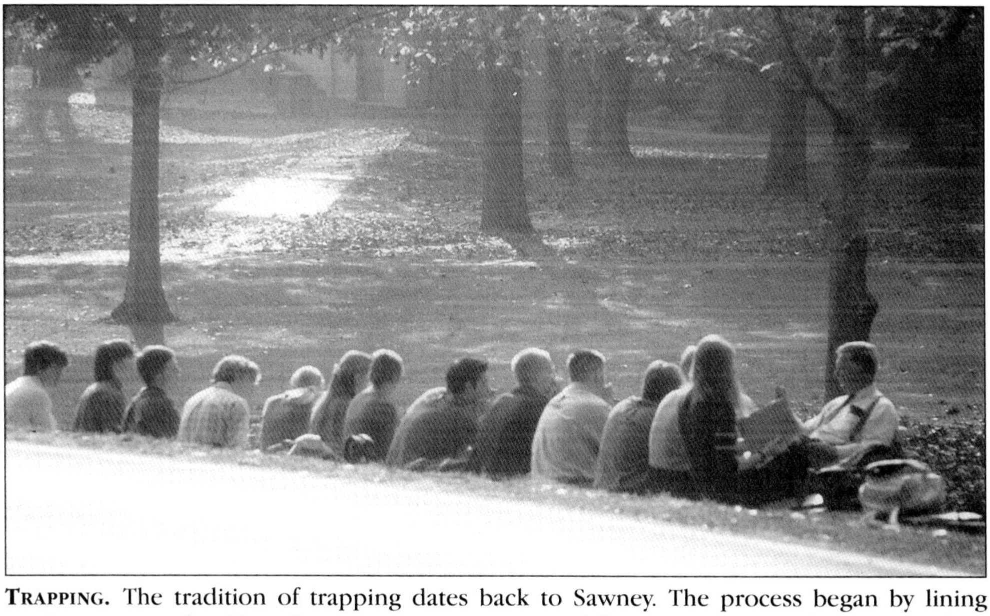

Trapping. The tradition of trapping dates back to Sawney. The process began by lining students up and asking them questions in a rapid-fire manner in order to test their knowledge. If a student did not know the answer and the boy next to him did, the boy with the correct answer would take the other's place in line, or "trap" him. This practice creates some competitiveness between the students. This picture shows longtime Webb teacher L.R. Smith trapping with his class outside.

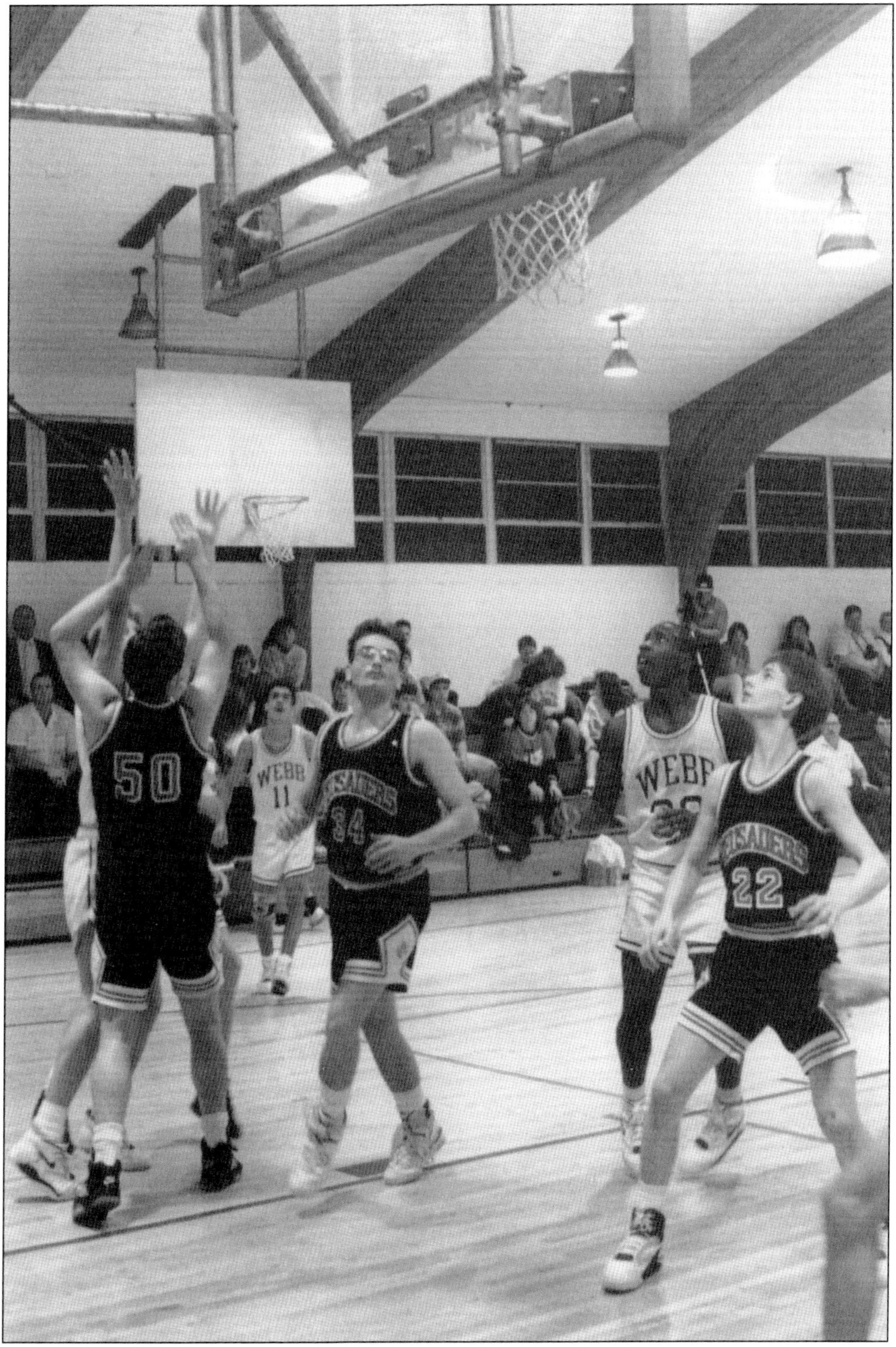

Basketball Game, 1991. Webb has a history of legacy students; pictured in this 1991 basketball game is Curtis Jenkins, whose son Jordan Jenkins plays on the 2018–2019 team.

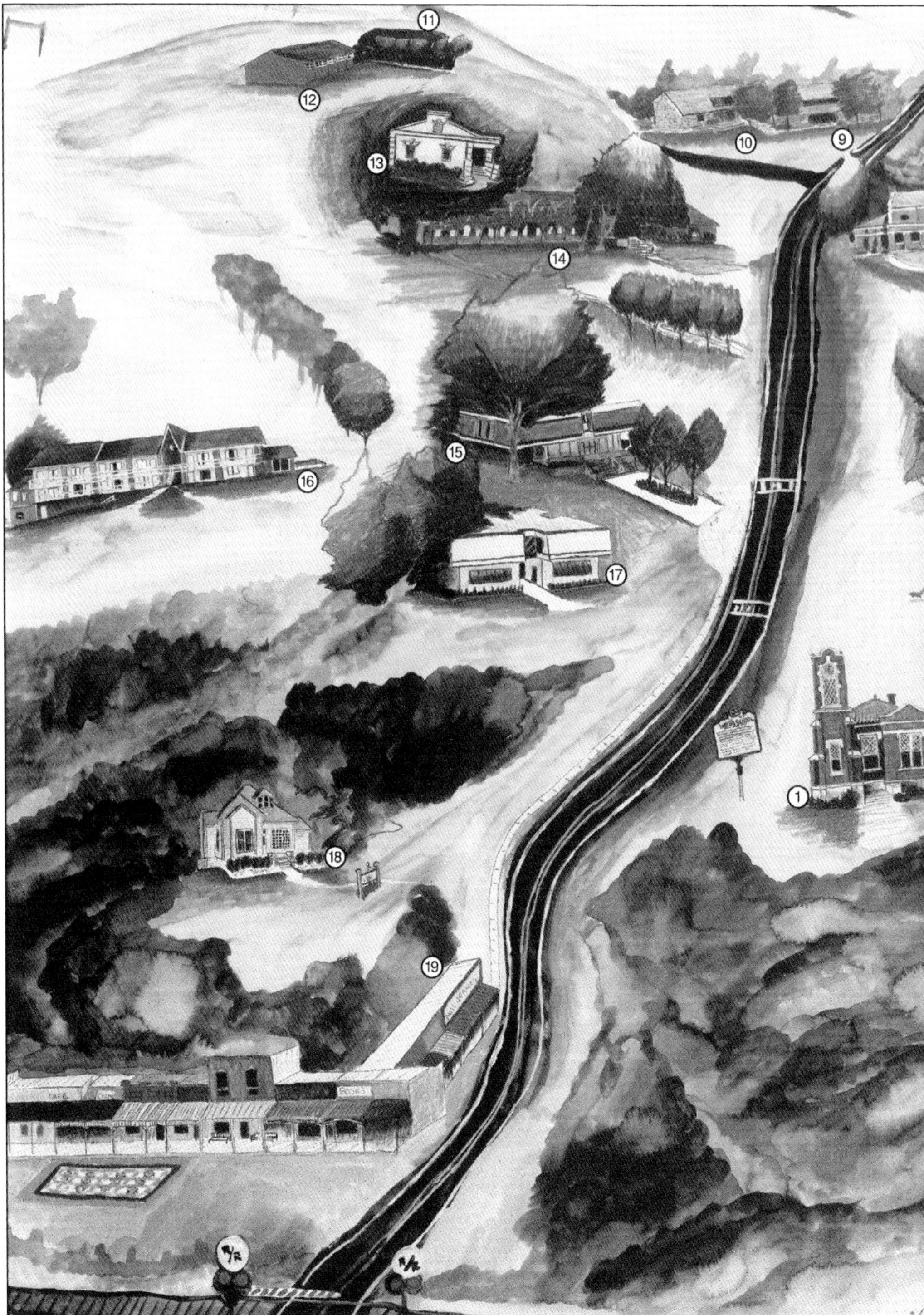

CAMPUS MAP. Sandi Jobe, class of 1995, created this map of the campus as it appeared in

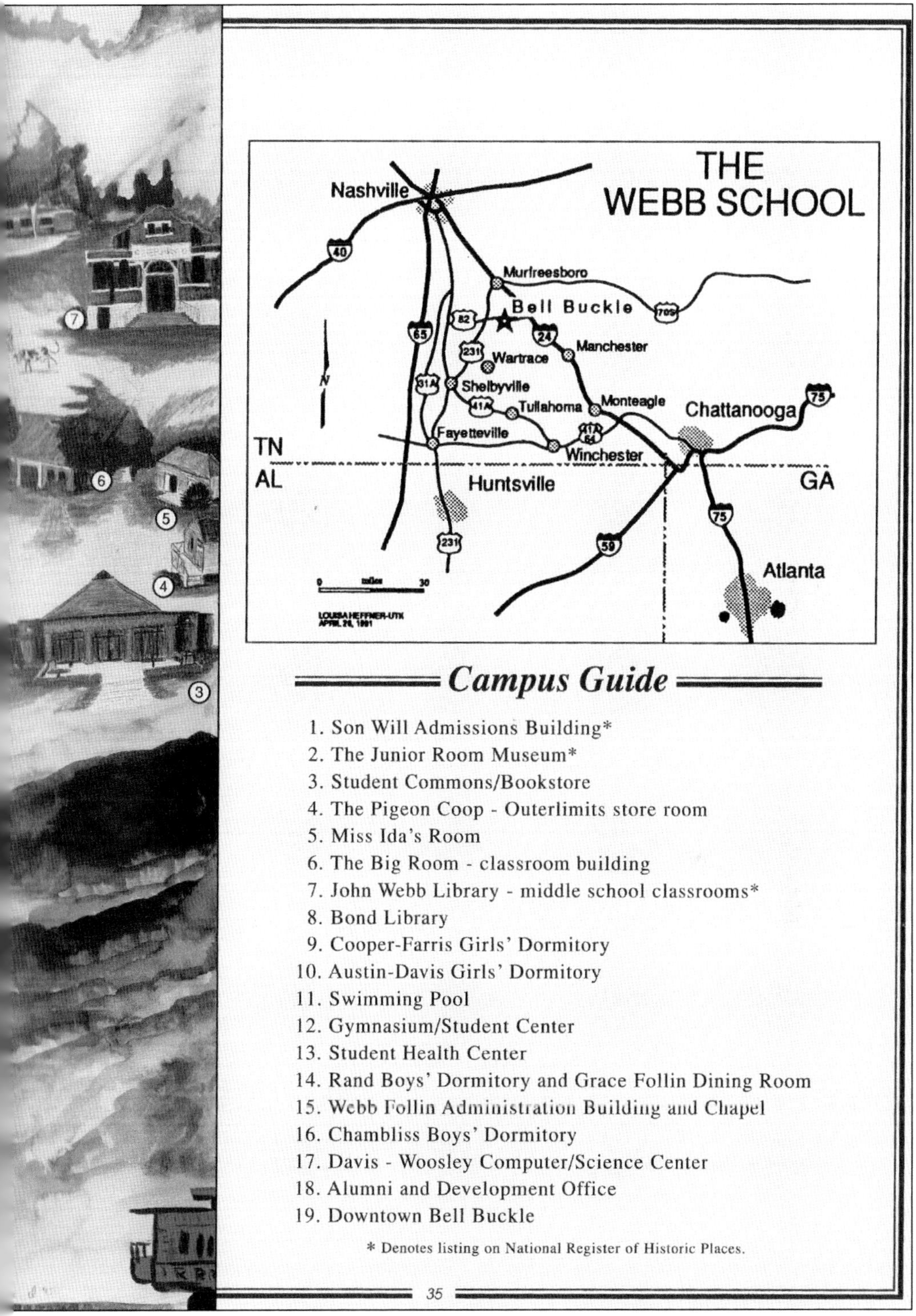

Campus Guide

1. Son Will Admissions Building*
2. The Junior Room Museum*
3. Student Commons/Bookstore
4. The Pigeon Coop - Outerlimits store room
5. Miss Ida's Room
6. The Big Room - classroom building
7. John Webb Library - middle school classrooms*
8. Bond Library
9. Cooper-Farris Girls' Dormitory
10. Austin-Davis Girls' Dormitory
11. Swimming Pool
12. Gymnasium/Student Center
13. Student Health Center
14. Rand Boys' Dormitory and Grace Follin Dining Room
15. Webb Follin Administration Building and Chapel
16. Chambliss Boys' Dormitory
17. Davis - Woosley Computer/Science Center
18. Alumni and Development Office
19. Downtown Bell Buckle

* Denotes listing on National Register of Historic Places.

35

1995. Jobe later joined the alumni and development staff between 2008 and 2012.

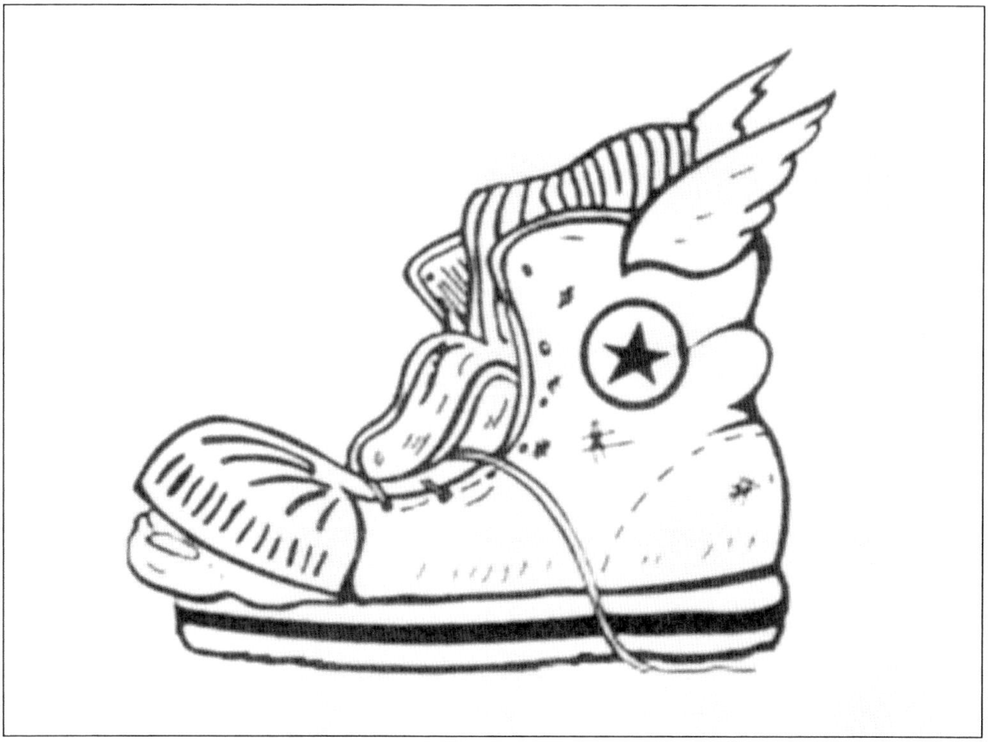

The Webb Feet Mascot. The Webb School's mascot has been a foot since the mid-1970s. Coach Roy Johnson, faculty member John Callow (class of 1966), and student Casey Jones (1975) were instrumental in bringing the foot to life. Jones was the original artist for the foot, and the 1970s students liked it.

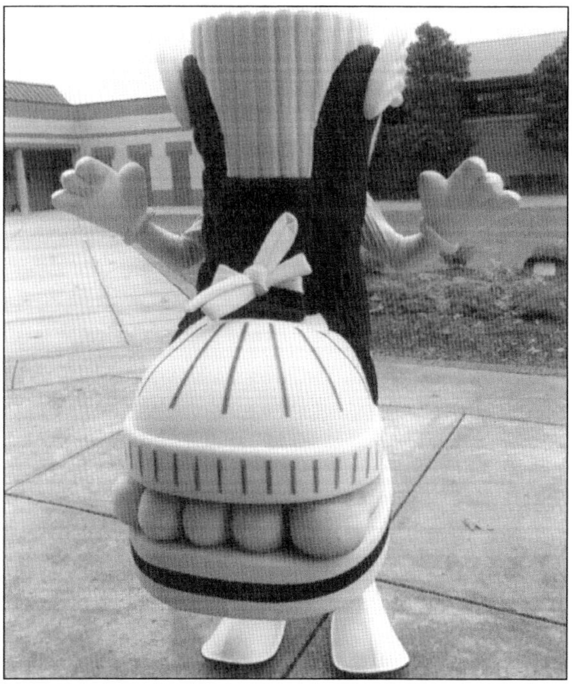

The Webb Feet Mascot. The Webb School class of 2013 decided they would like the school to have a full-size mascot costume to be worn at football and basketball games, so they made it their senior-class gift.

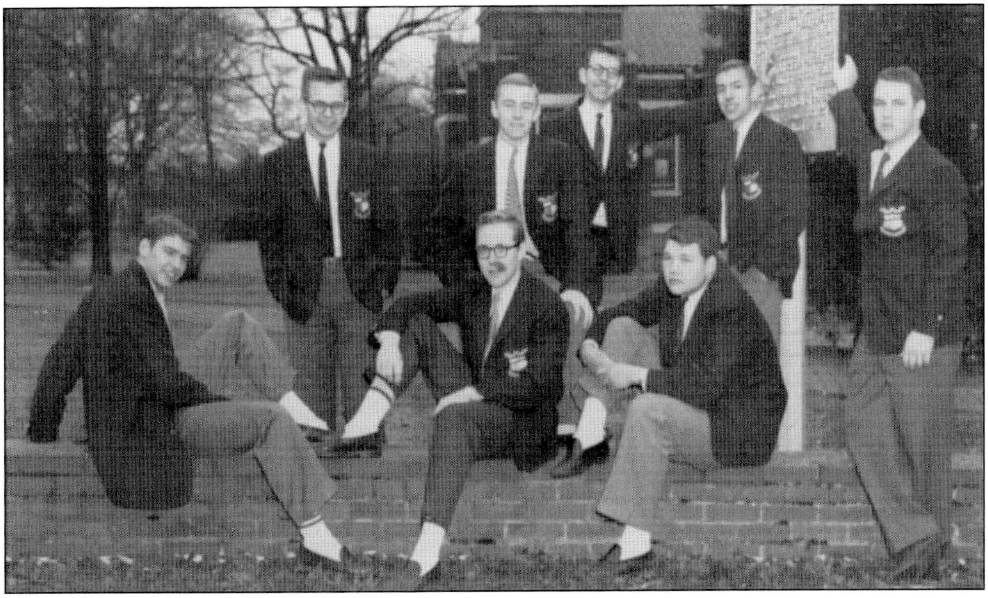

Senior Blazer Day, 1959. This tradition dates to 1959. At that time, seniors were looking for something to set them apart, and was only for graduating seniors. An embroidered patch was designed with the school colors (gold and purple at the time), the school motto, a coat of arms, and a torch with a flame. This patch was put on a blazer worn by each graduating senior. From left to right are (seated) Jim Morris, Charles Bass, and John King; (standing) John Faires, Pete Blanton, Pete Stevens, Noble Pace, and Cecil Gibson.

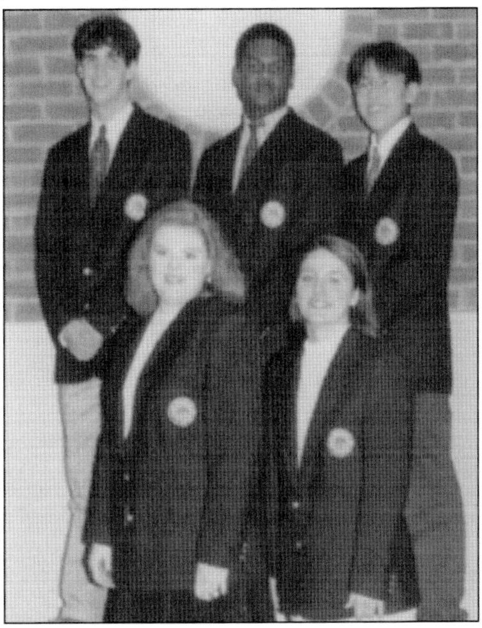

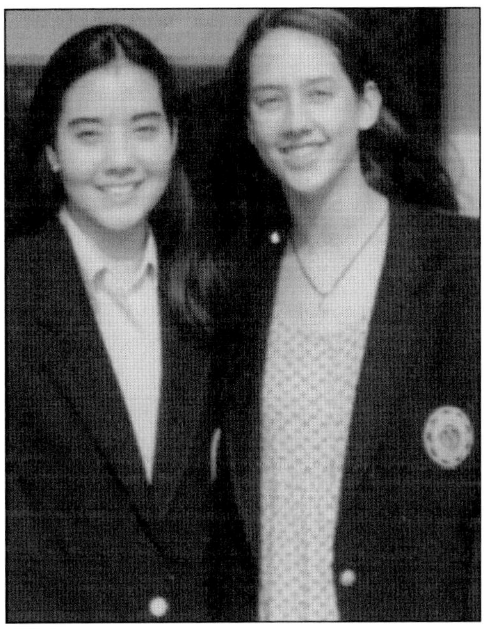

Senior Blazer Day, 1995. This special event ceased to exist beginning in the mid-1960s, but was revived in 1995. At that time, and today, the patch is The Webb School seal. The ceremony when blazers are presented to seniors is celebrated on or near November 11, Sawney's birthday. Pictured at right are 1995 graduates Julie Yamamoto Harris (left) and Megan Watson. Harris is the current director of enrollment management at Webb.

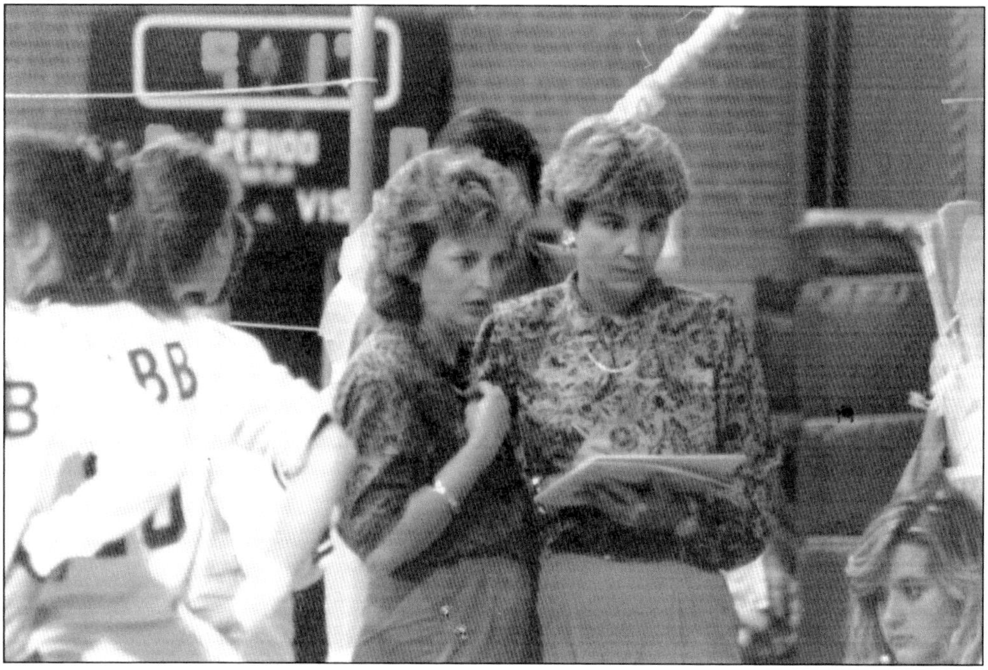

Linda Williams and Debbie Gilmore. Pictured are two multi-faceted teachers, Linda Williams (left) and Debbie Gilmore. Gilmore served Webb faithfully as a teacher and coach for 19 years and passed away suddenly in the summer of 2006. Williams served for 30 years in many roles, including a number of years as the head of the middle school.

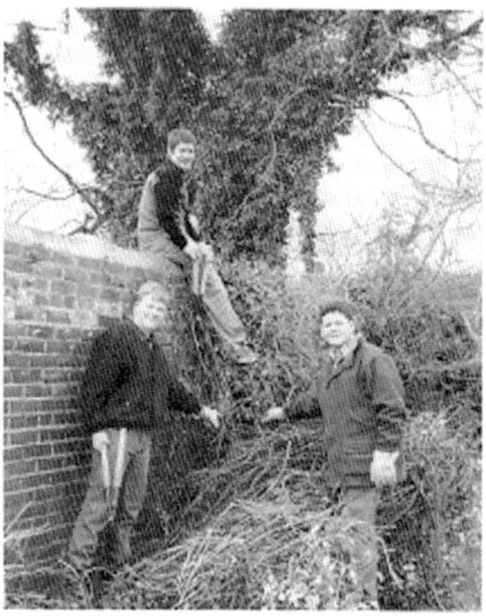

Kendall Butner '04, Parker Quinn '04, and Andrew Steele '04 removed a great deal of brush from a brick wall at the Children's Discovery Museum in Murfreesboro.

Community Service Day. Community Service Day has been incorporated into the curriculum and fabric of The Webb School for many years. This day also correlates with the principle that is taught to Webb students, which is to share the responsibility and honor of serving others. Students in these pictures are working to help in various areas of the community.

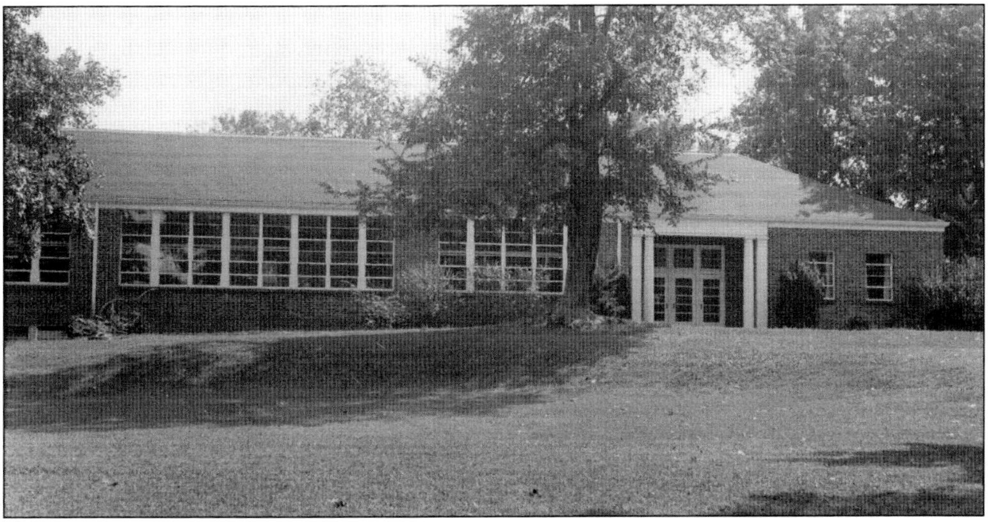

The Big Room. The new Big Room was built similar to the old one and was completed in late January 1952. It contained an auditorium with a stage and projection booth. Later, that auditorium, known as the W.P. Cooper Auditorium, was converted into three spacious classrooms and two offices in 1974, and it was ready for use in the 1974–1975 school year. It received some renovations during the 1977–1978 school year and a refurbishing during the late 1980s. By 1987, all of the English and history classes were held in this building, with the art department moving to the lower level. Finally, in the summer of 1999, the Sawney Webb Big Room received a complete renovation.

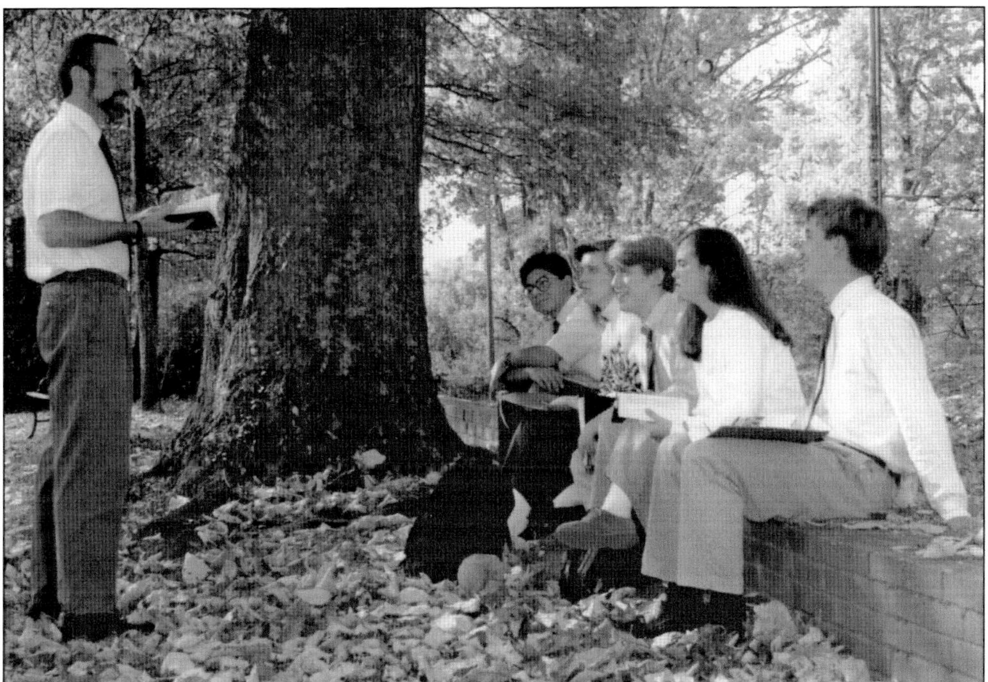

Outdoor Classroom. Teaching outdoors is a continuing tradition whether in an official outdoor classroom, seated in the grass, or trapping on the wall that lines Highway 82. Pictured is history teacher Ralph Jones, likely teaching US history.

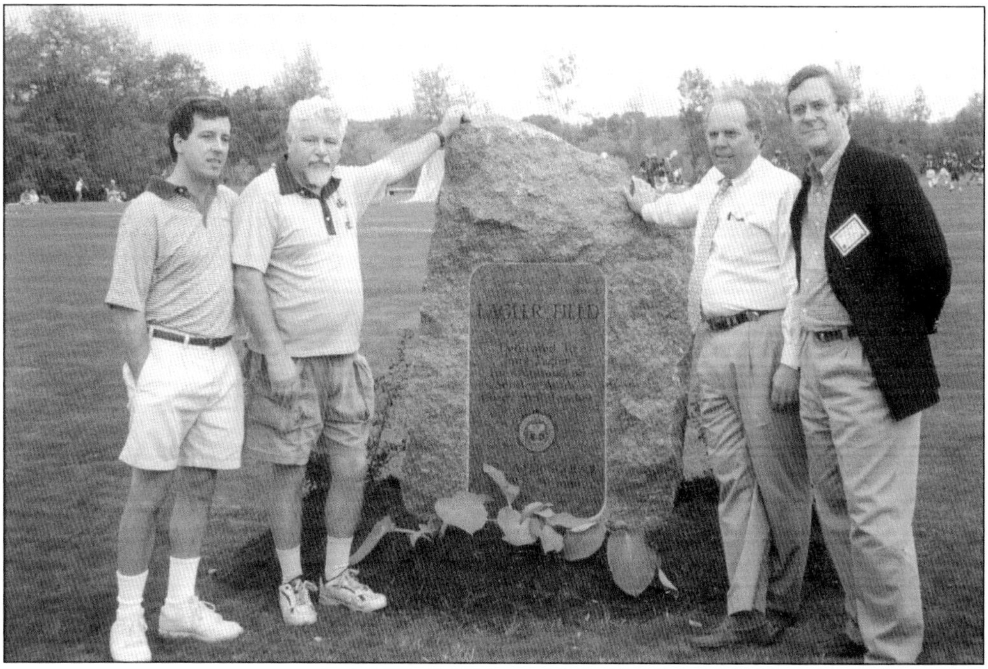

LAGLER FIELD. Dedicated in the spring of 1999, this athletic field has a special meaning. The field is marked with a large granite stone containing a plaque honoring Webb's beloved Latin teacher and soccer coach of 26 years, Imre Lagler (second from left). Lagler retired from Webb at the completion of the 2001–2002 school year after 30 years of dedicated service.

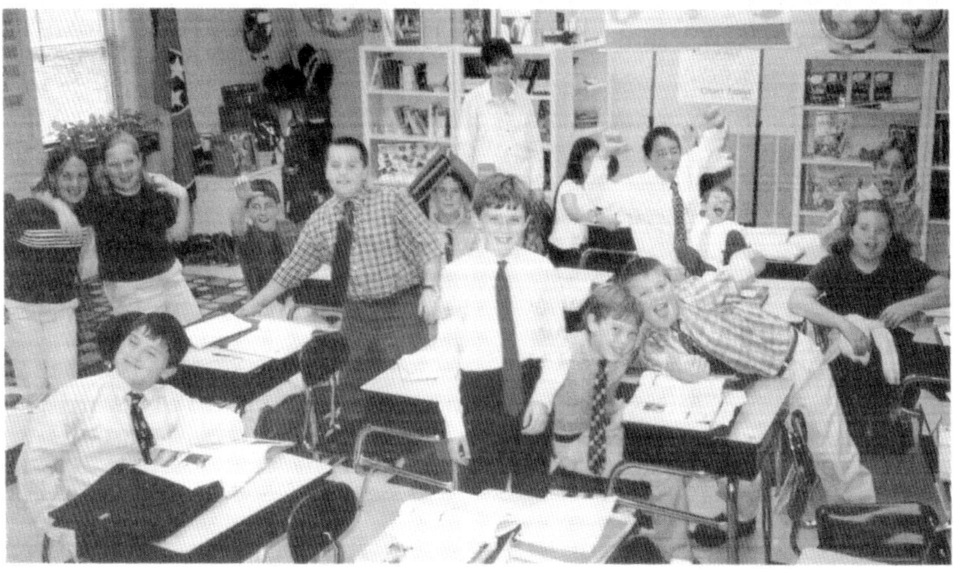

The sixth grade takes a break from class to show their wild side. Jacquelyn Boyanton, their teacher, stands in the back.

SIXTH GRADE. The sixth grade was added to the Webb student population in the fall of 2000. Jacquelyn Boyanton was their primary teacher. Pictured here is Webb's first sixth-grade class with Boyanton.

Webbstock. Student-led music has been around since 1873 with composer and choir leader Ned Carmack. In the modern era, a student-led festival called Webbstock became an annual fall event. This image captures a band in 2001 playing at Webbstock. A similar event called Springfest has become a favorite as well.

Webbstock 2001

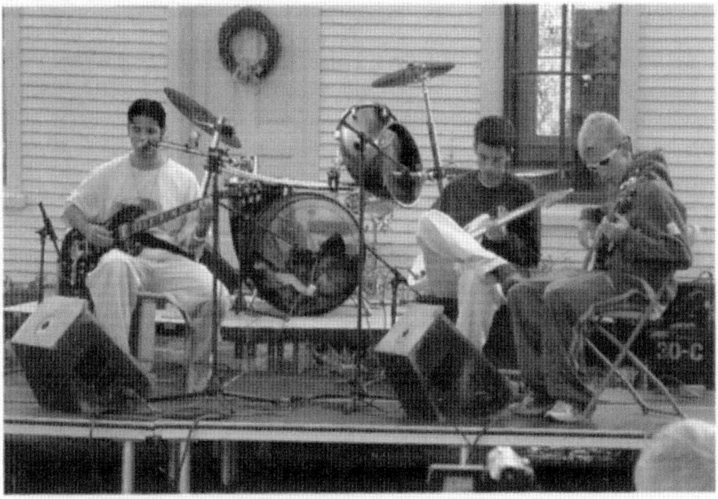

Lance Lormand '02, Jonathan Waldrop '02 and Hap Collier '05 perform a set during the afternoon concert.

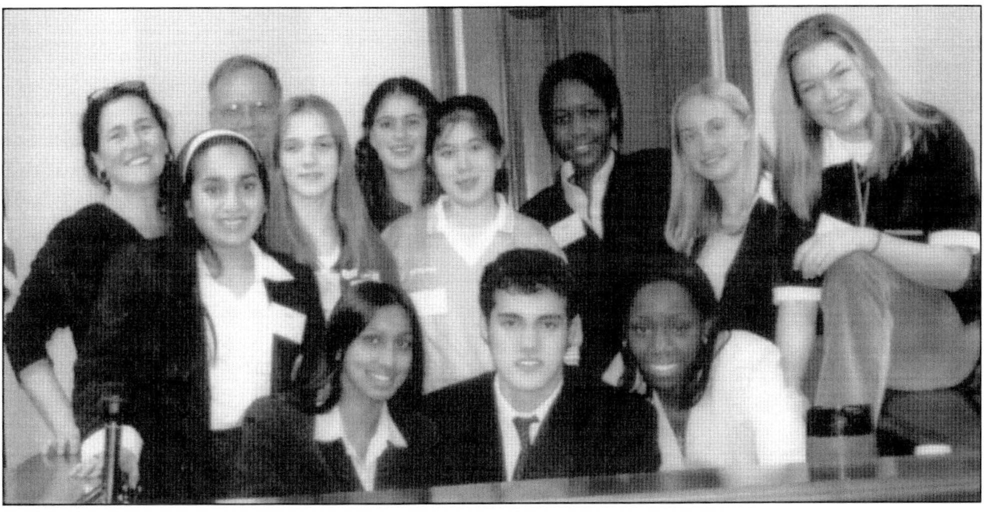

Mock Trial. Mock Trial has been available to Webb students as an extracurricular activity for many years. In the 2003–2004 school year, Webb's team defeated nine schools, winning the district championship. This win also gave them a chance to compete for the state championship. Two of Webb's team members were chosen as Best Attorney, and one member was chosen as Best Witness. Bill Abernathy, a 1972 Webb graduate and attorney, coached the team. Kimi Abernathy, his wife and Webb's college counselor, was the team sponsor. Pictured from left to right are (first row) Swapna Reddy, Havan Tucker, and Effie Johnson; (second row) Dee Dee Banerjee, Jeanne Humphrey, Elissa Jennings, Nandi Quao, Kelsey Lewis, and Hallie Dyer; (third row) sponsor Kimi Abernathy, coach Bill Abernathy, and Shirin Ahlhauser. In 2014, Webb sent two teams to the district competition at Maury County Courthouse in Columbia and claimed both first and second place under the direction of Kathleen Camp.

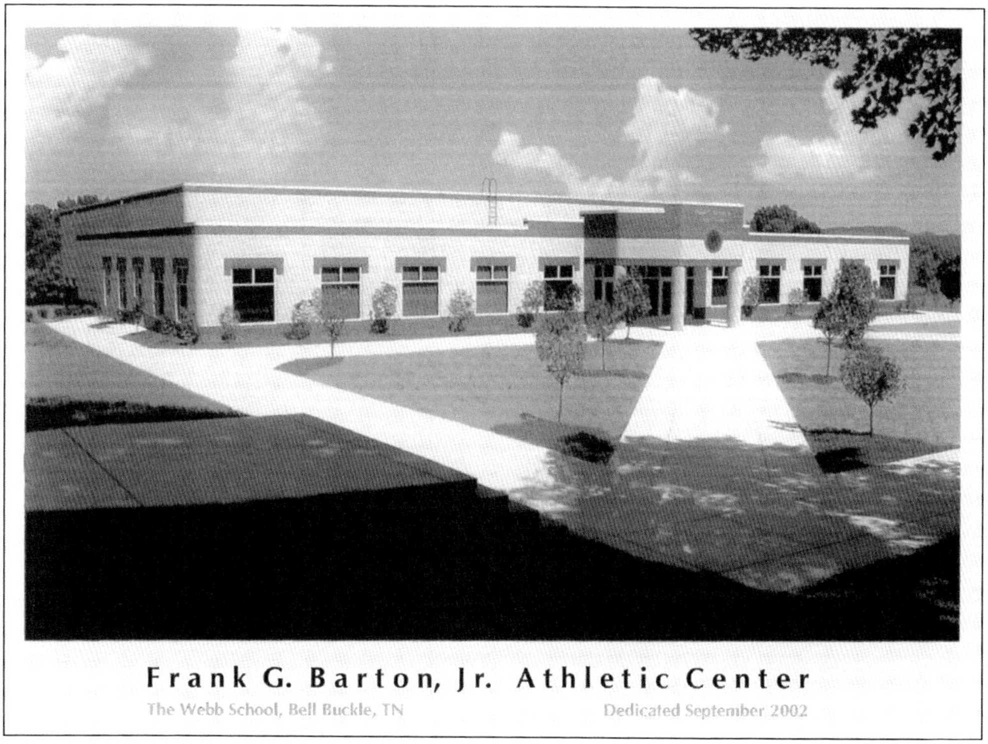

FRANK G. BARTON JR. ATHLETIC CENTER. Ground was broken for this facility in April 2001. Frank G. Barton Jr. (class of 1950) made a large donation to the school specifically for this purpose. The building consists of a weight room, multipurpose room, lecture room, a climbing wall, basketball and volleyball courts, and coaches' offices and is also used as a polling place. The athletic center was dedicated in September 2003. At a later date, Webb held Barton Family Appreciation Day with a reception recognizing and thanking the Barton family for their generosity.

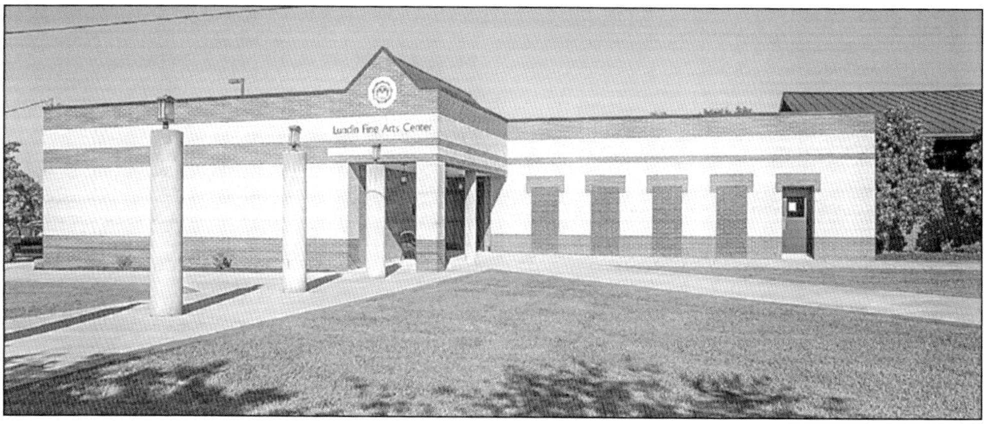

LUNDIN FINE ARTS CENTER. The Lundin Fine Arts Center was the result of the Haun-Ragland Gym renovation that took place in 2006. It includes an exhibition space, a piano lab with 12 pianos, individual practice rooms, a choir room, a black box theater, and a large studio for pottery, painting, and drawing. These improvements were made possible through the support and giving of Lukas Lundin, father of 2005 Webb graduate Adam Lundin. It opened in the 2007–2008 academic school year.

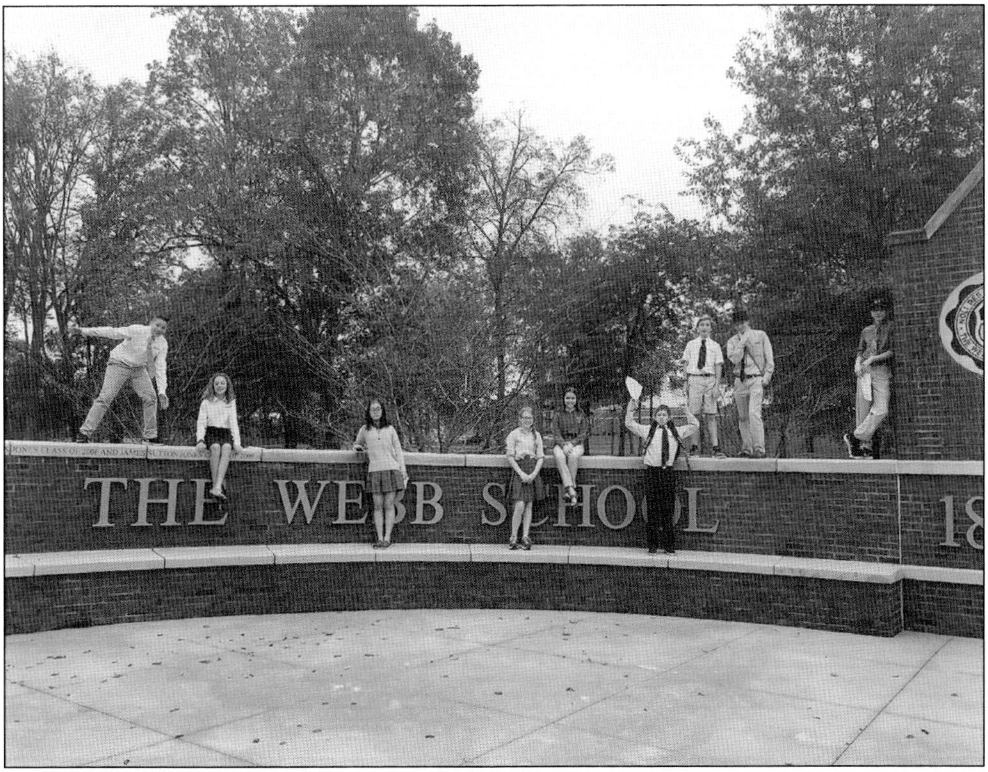

New Webb School Entrance. When an old home occupied by the school's alumni and development office was torn down in the fall of 2008, The Webb School board of trustees began discussing ideas for the property. A donation from former Webb trustee and parent of Webb alumni Kathy Jones made the plaza a reality. Construction of a plaza in the 300 block of Webb Road East (Highway 82) that features a brick and cast concrete sign and a bench that marks the westernmost boundary of the school was completed in April 2010.

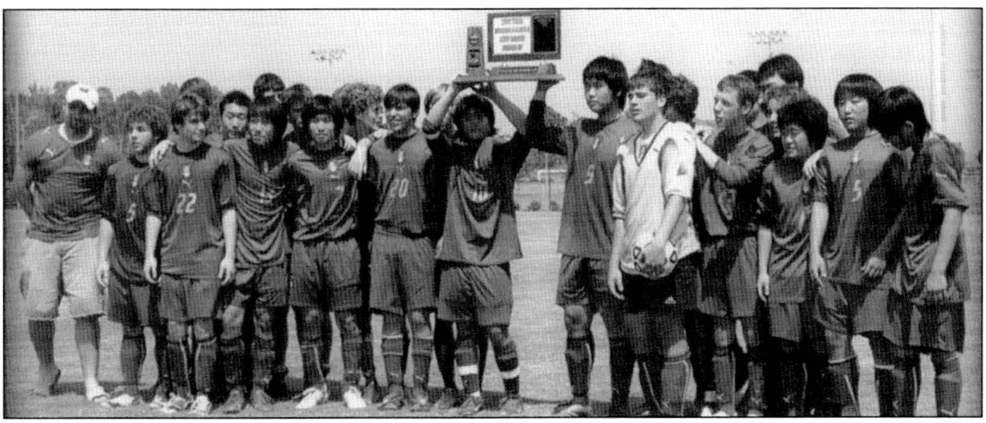

State Soccer Finals. The Webb School's boys' varsity soccer team made it to the state tournament finals for the first time in school history in 2008. Webb had joined the Tennessee Secondary School Athletic Association in 2004. Their dedicated coach, Adrian Anderson, pushed the boys to reach their potential.

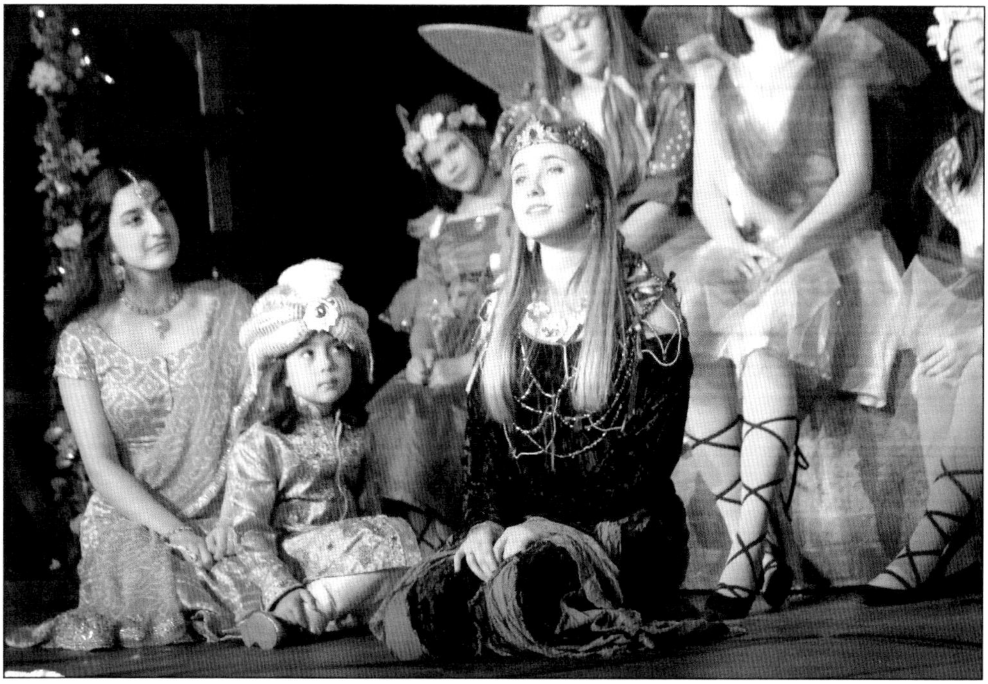

The Webb Players. Shakespeare is performed regularly at Webb. *A Midsummer Night's Dream* was presented by the Webb Company Players in April 2017, and both middle school and high school students were featured.

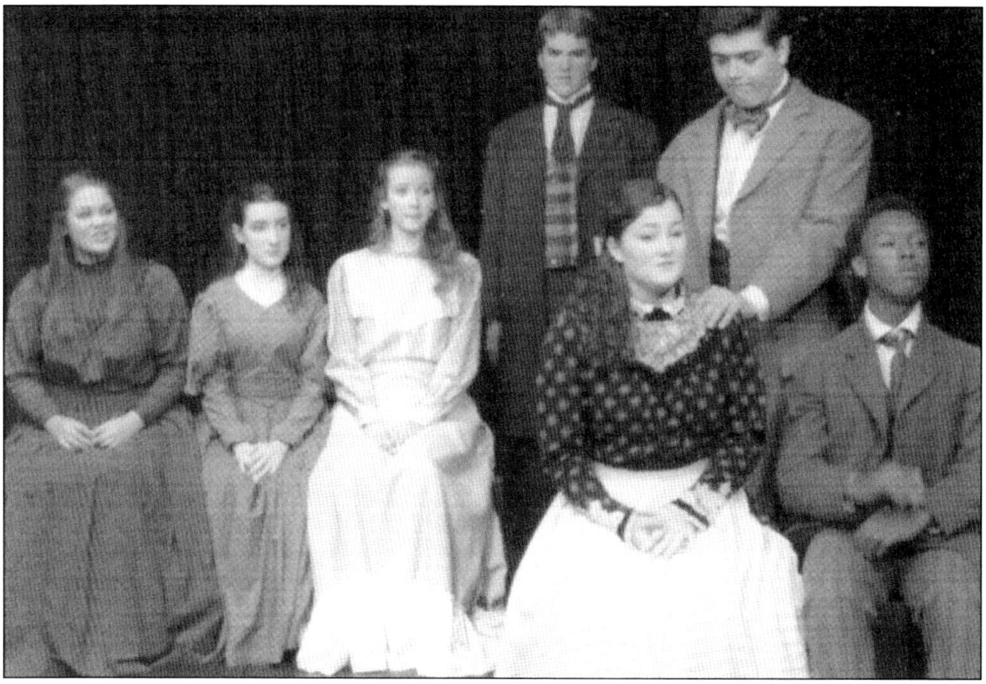

Players in the Black Box. The Webb School Black Box Theater is the venue for many of the Webb Players' productions, including *The Schoolmaker*, an original play written and directed by Carol Ponder and Robert Kiefer.

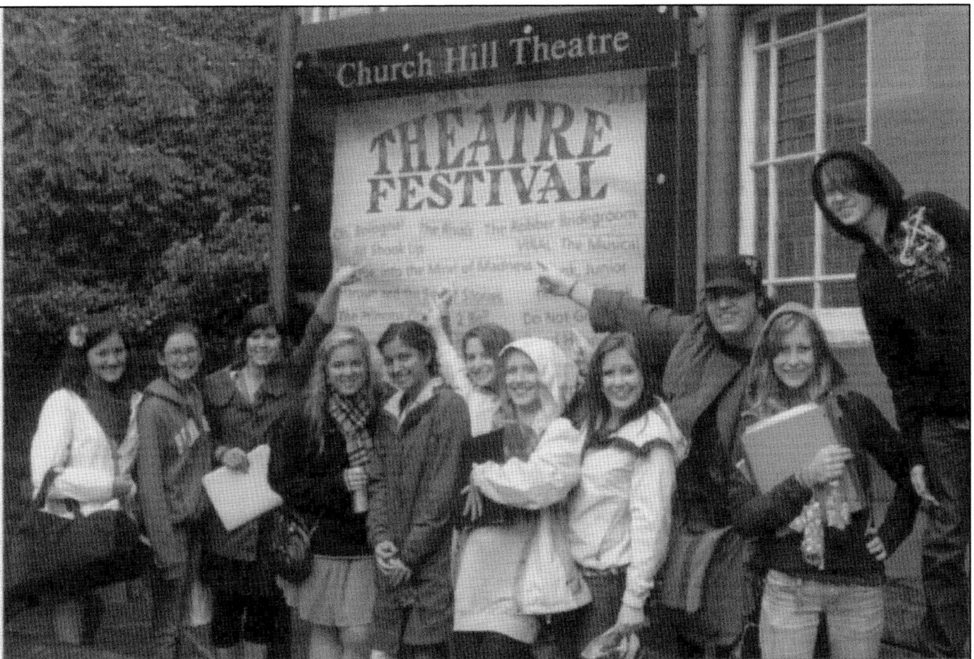

Jami Averwater, Mary Kathryn Menck, Callie Kerbo,Scout Turner, Sarada Kolli, Kayetlyn Jones, Helen Bartlett, Harley Walker, William Fahrnbach, Tea Phillips and Coleman Walker

FRINGE FEST. Less than 50 high schools are selected to attend Fringe each year. Invitations are extended based on a competitive nomination and application process that involves an assessment of the programs' most recent work, awards, community involvement, philosophies, and recommendations. The 2010–2011 Webb theater team included student actors, technical assistants, and director Ruth Cordell. The team performed four times while they were in Scotland.

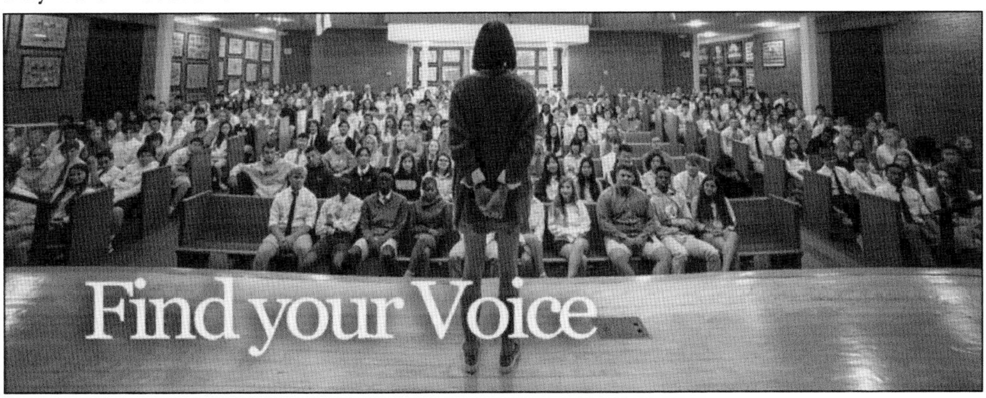

PUBLIC PERFORMANCE. Writing and public speaking are major emphases at The Webb School. Through the Emerging Voices program, students learn to create original ideas, assemble research, and communicate those ideas effectively through writing and public speaking. Students showcase their skills each year by performing declamations, orations, performance creations, and senior paper presentations. These exhibitions are developed and completed under the mentorship of the students' advisors and other members of the community. The goal is to create confident contributors in the classroom and beyond.

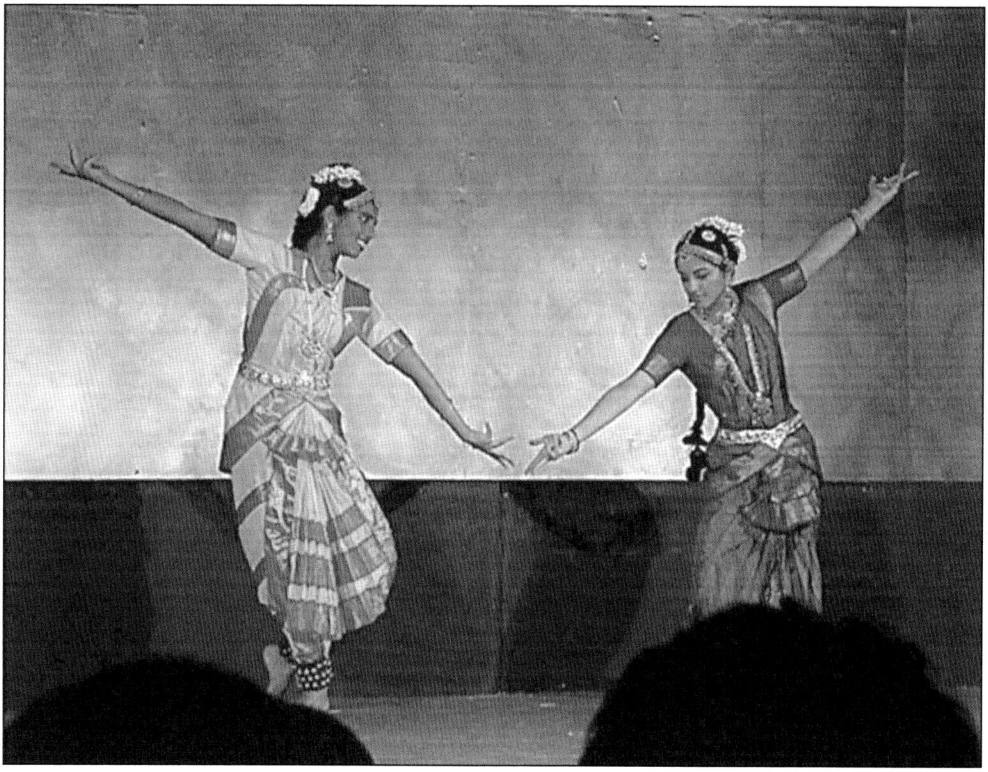

INDIAN CLASSICAL DANCERS. With Webb having so many international students, former librarian Sandra Sanders had a desire for the students to learn about and celebrate this diversity of cultures. Here, two Indian students perform a traditional Indian dance during Diversity Day 2009.

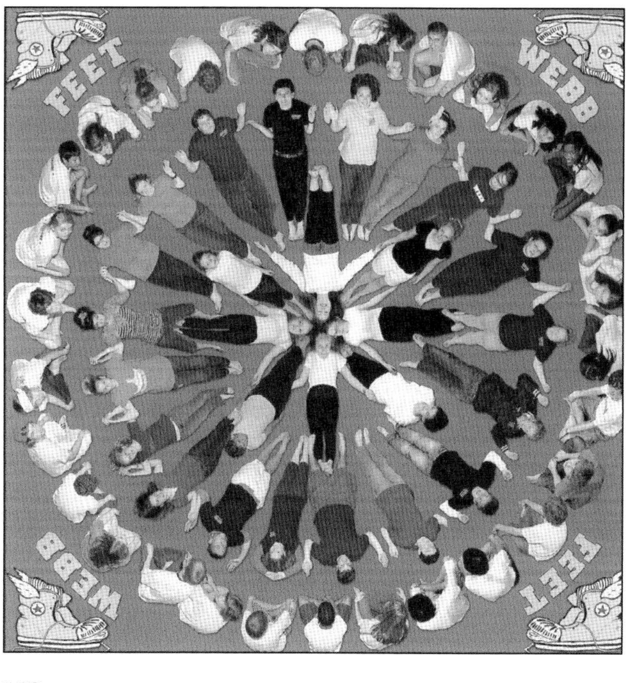

A HUMAN MANDALA. This image was captured during Diversity Day in 2009. Many Webb students of all ethnicities came together to form a human mandala. They were assembled and photographed by artist Laura Brookhart.

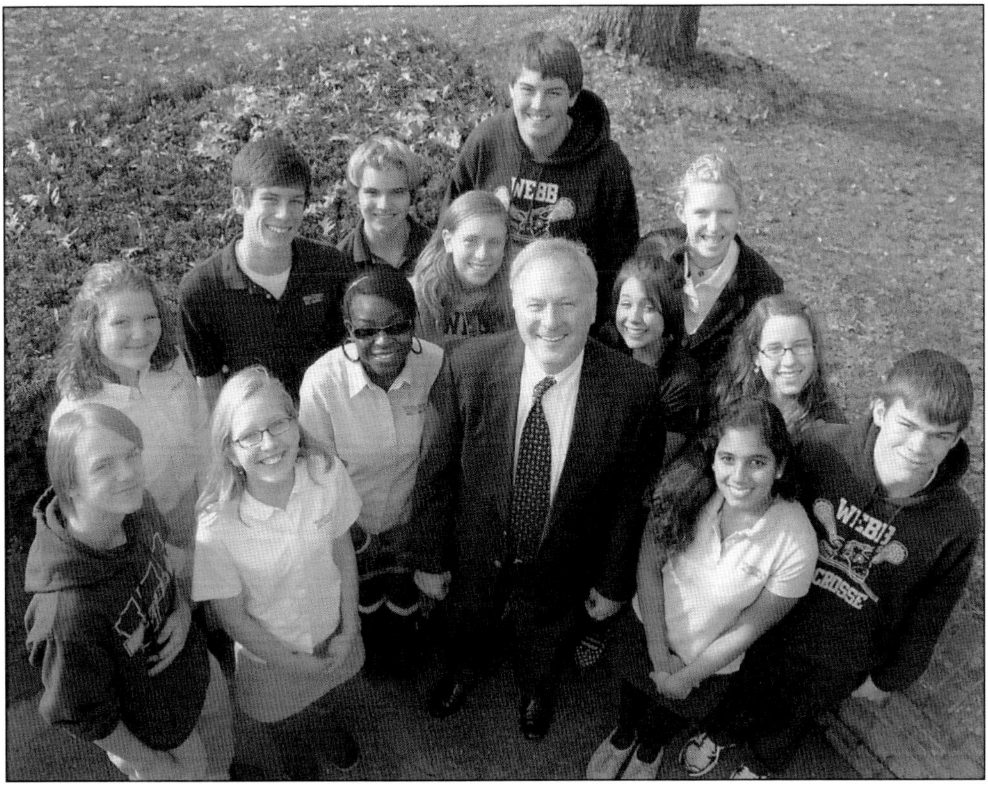

A New Head of School. Raymond S. Broadhead was named The Webb School's current head of school in November 2009. Prior to making his move to Bell Buckle in July 2010, he made many visits to the Webb campus. During these visits, he met with various departments and attended a few events. This picture shows him with several Webb students during his visit in December 2009.

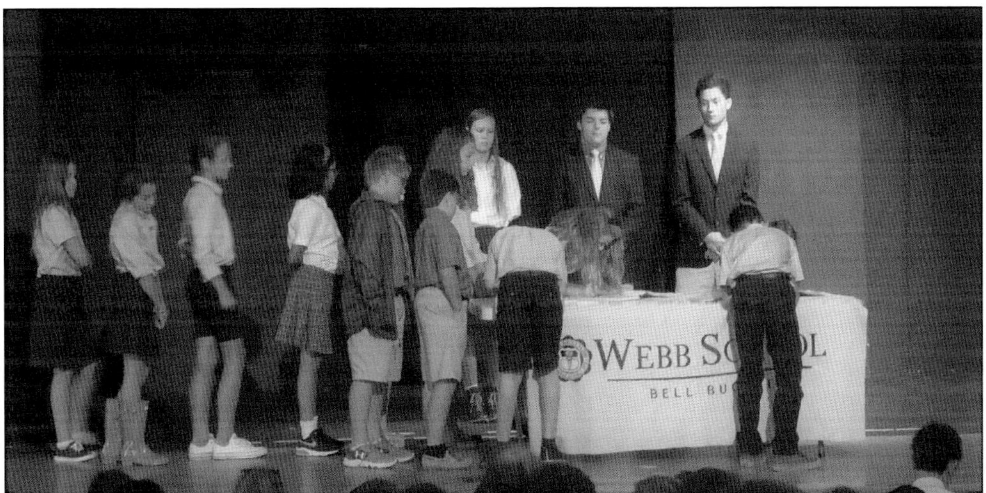

Signing Honor Books. At the beginning of each school year, students line up to sign two pledges. One pledge is that they will not lie, cheat, or steal, and the other is to be on premise. Faculty members are also invited to sign the pledge.

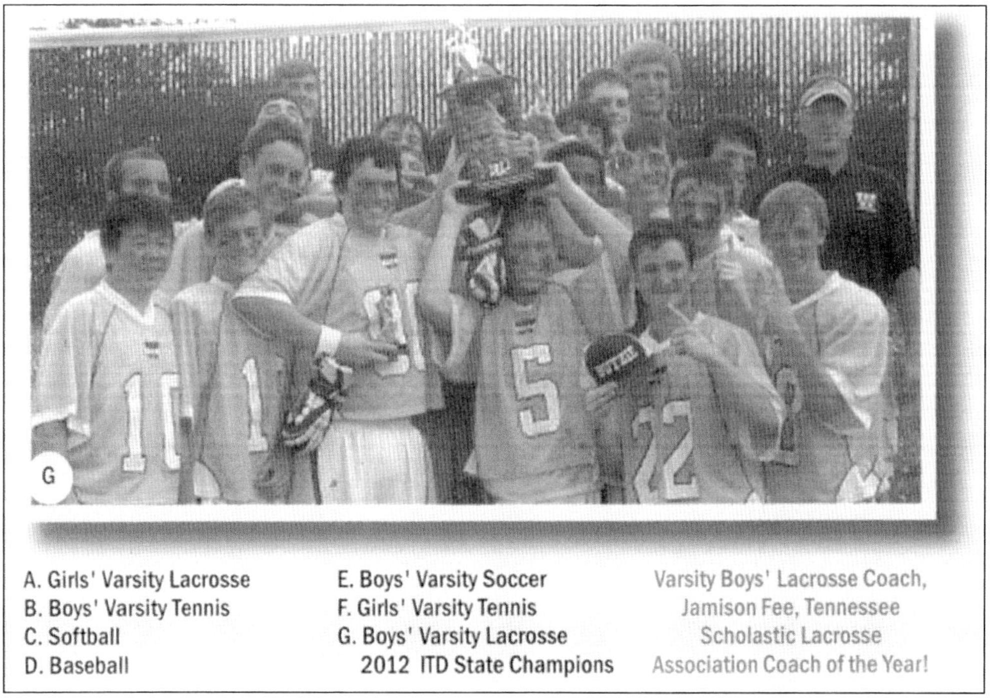

Lacrosse State Champions, 2012. Webb's varsity boys' lacrosse team won the Invitational Tournament Division state championship in the spring of 2012. It was their first time at the state championship, and they beat St. Benedict's of Memphis 4-0. Their coach, Jamison Fee, also was selected as Tennessee Scholastic Lacrosse Association Coach of the Year. This image is from the summer 2012 *Webb School Magazine*.

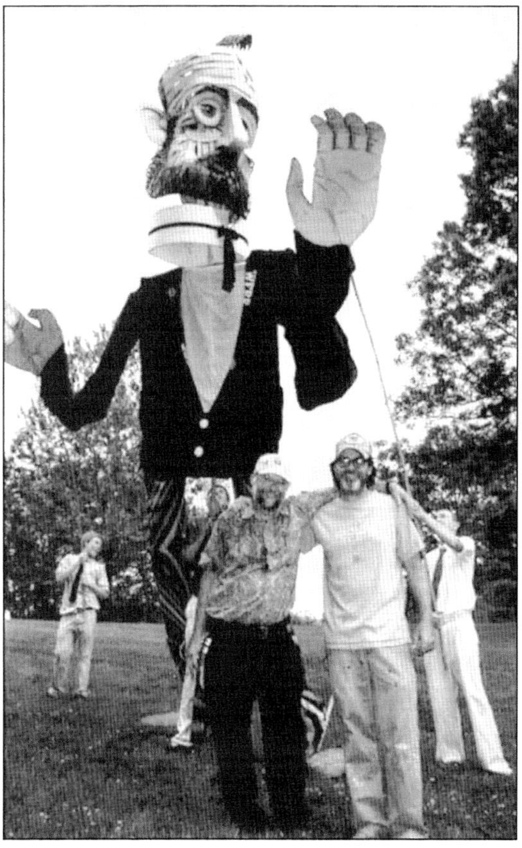

Sawney Puppet. Art instructor Mike Quinn reunited with his longtime friend Wayne White to create living art at The Webb School's Bell Buckle campus. White and Quinn created this Sawney puppet with legs, arms, hands, and feet—all in just two and a half days. The 40-pound puppet was fashioned entirely from cardboard, foam core, bamboo, paint, and wire.

EMPTY BOWLS. Sue Wood partnered with Bedford County Schools to organize Empty Bowls, a fundraising project. For the price of a ticket, those attending were served soup in a handmade pottery bowl that they were able to keep. As many as 400 bowls were handcrafted by Webb and Bedford County students for the annual occasion.

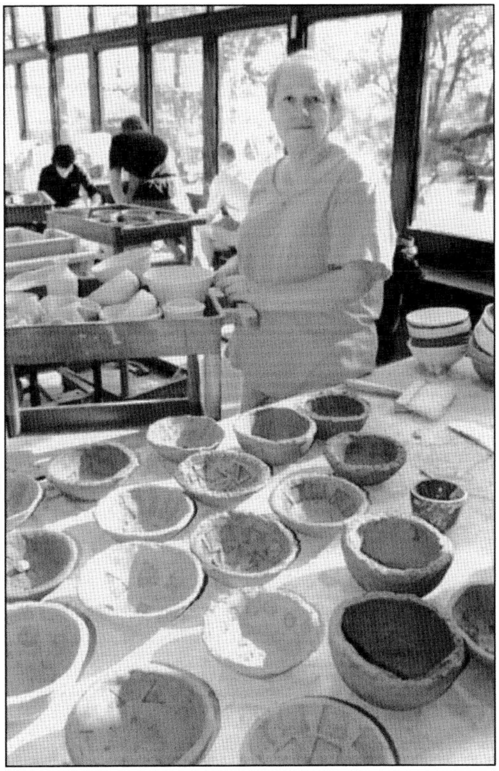

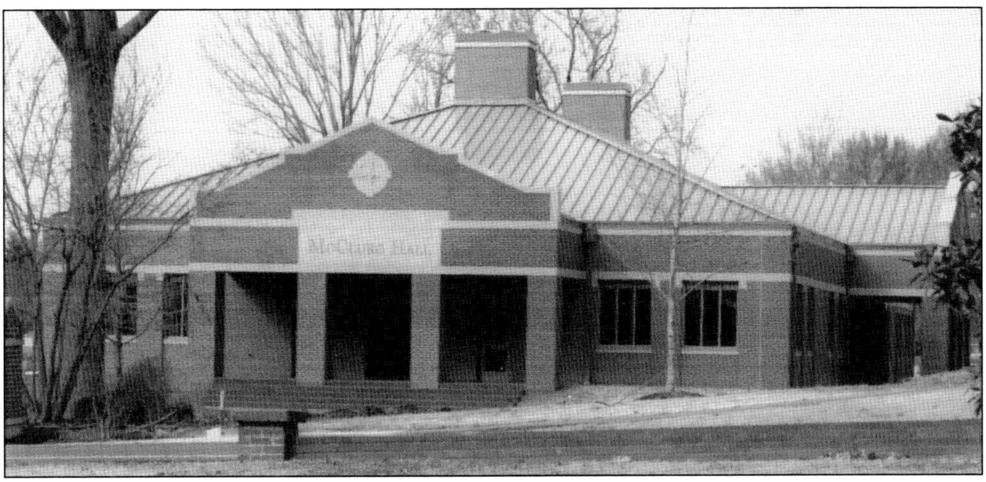

MCCLURG HALL. McClurg Hall, a new science-math building, was opened and dedicated in early 2014. Containing three labs with fifteen lab stations, two classrooms, and two prep rooms, it accommodates STEM-related classes. E. Vane McClurg, a 1960 graduate, and his son Hayden, a 1988 graduate, were two of the major donors for this building, giving it its name. Some other rooms that are named are the Kelton Tidwell Lab; the Sandy Truitt Classroom; the front portico, named by Pick Stephens (class of 1956) and his brother Blair (1953) in memory of their father, Bob (1920); an office named for Craig Ferrell; and lab stations named by Dr. Hunter and Amy Norris in honor of their two children at Webb, and by Forrest Shoaf (1968) in honor of his mother, in addition to others.

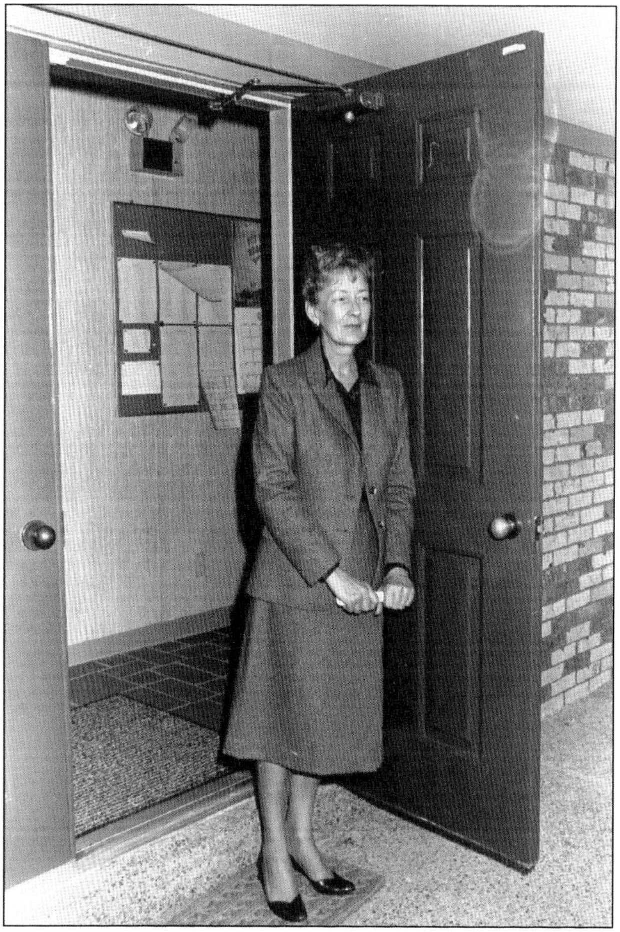

Margaret G. Turner House. April 26, 2013, was the date of the dedication of the Margaret G. Turner House, the new faculty house attached to Cooper-Farris, named for Margaret G. Turner, the first residential advisor of Cooper-Farris Dormitory. Members of the Turner family attended; speaking was Louisa Heffner Self (class of 1983) and longtime Webb teacher L.R. Smith. This was the first time that Webb added a faculty house to a dormitory that would accommodate a family.

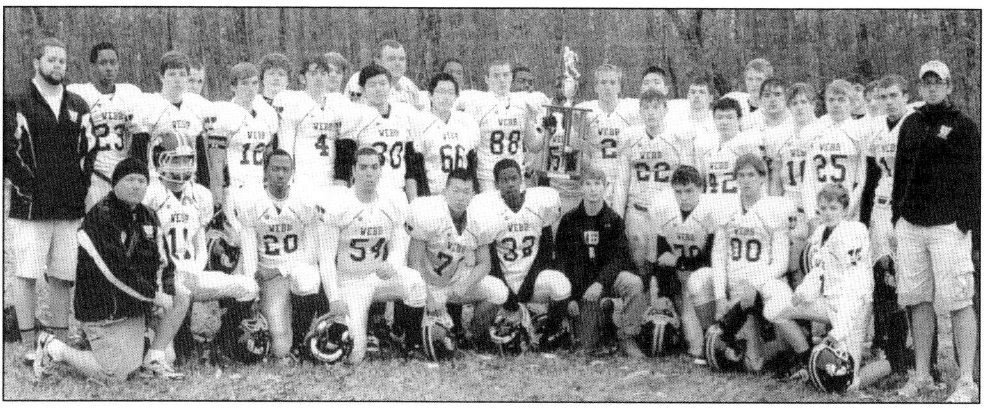

Interscholastic Football. The Webb School announced its plans to bring back an all-American tradition that had been absent for nearly 50 years. Head of School Ray Broadhead received applause from the student body when he announced Webb would be adding an eight-man football program to its lineup of interscholastic sports. In the 2013–2014 season, Webb went undefeated, winning the Middle Tennessee Athletic Championship and taking second place in the National Association of Christian Athletes Tournament. Pictured is the Webb 2013 football team.

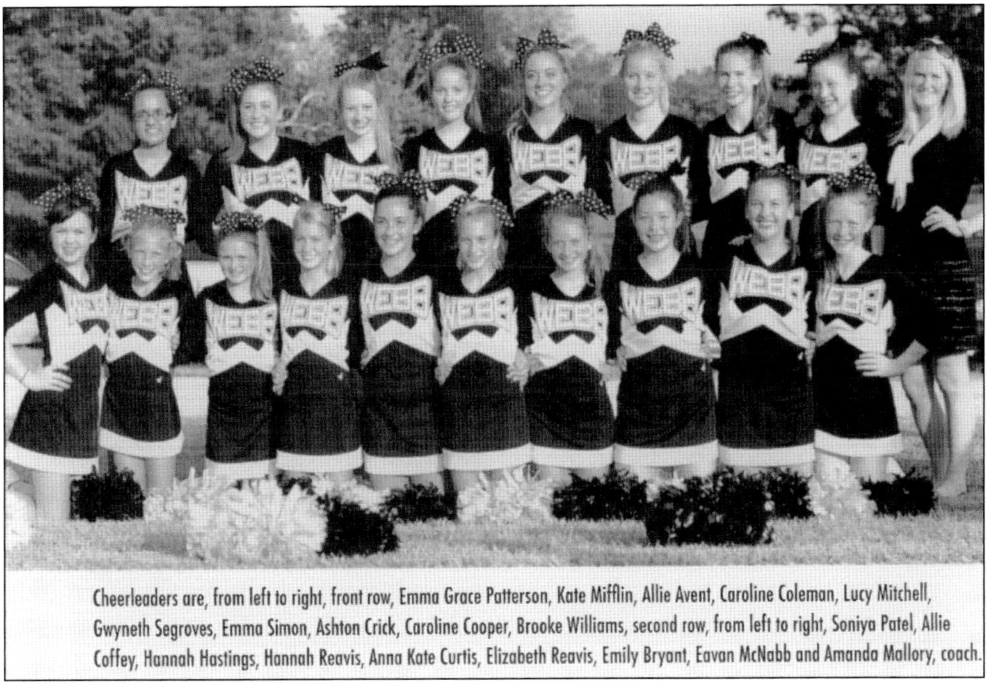

Cheerleading. The Webb School debuted its first cheerleading squad in September 2013. From left to right are (first row) Emma Grace Patterson, Kate Mifflin, Allie Avent, Caroline Coleman, Lucy Mitchell, Gwyneth Segroves, Emma Simons, Ashton Crick, Caroline Cooper, and Brooke Williams; (second row) Soniya Patel, Allie Coffey, Hannah Hastings, Hannah Reavis, Anna Kate Curtis, Elizabeth Reavis, Emily Bryant, Eavan McNabb, and coach Amanda Mallory. This image was in the fall/winter 2013–2014 *Webb School Magazine*.

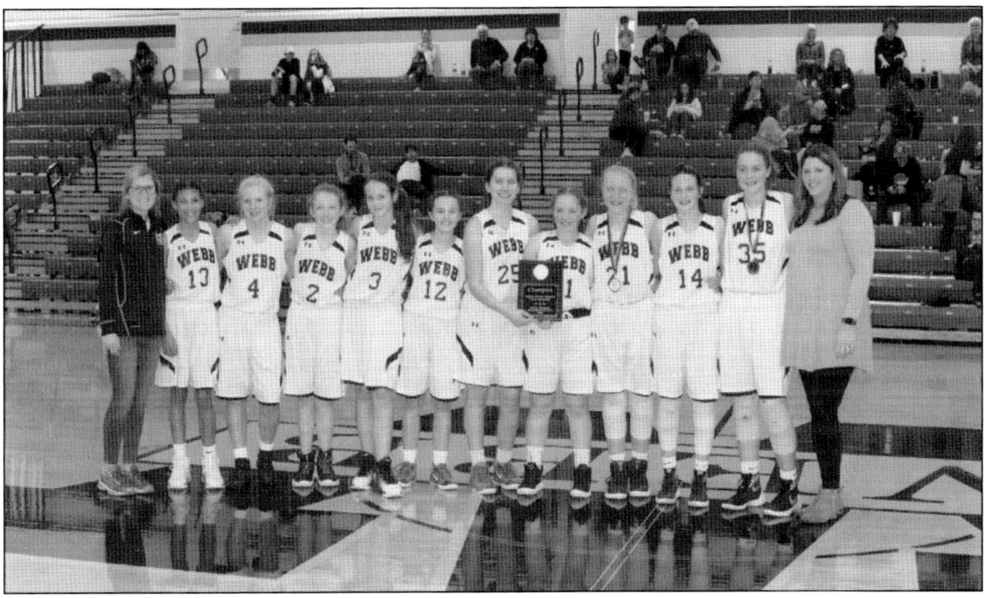

Girls' Basketball, 2018. The 2018 middle school girls' basketball team were Middle Tennessee Athletic Conference champions. The team is pictured in February 2018 with coaches Kat Coffey (left, class of 2013) and Jennifer Insell, Webb parent.

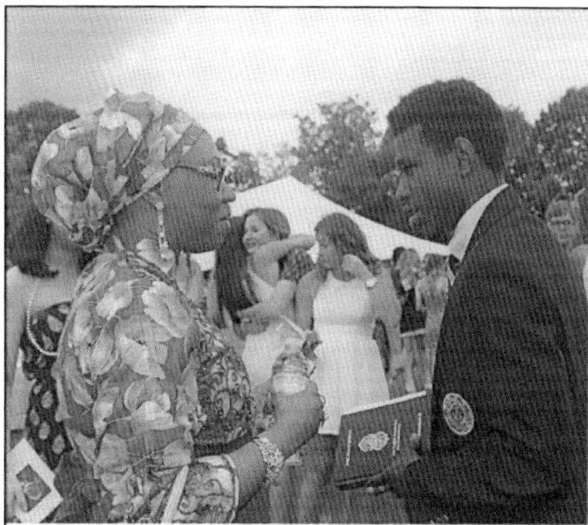

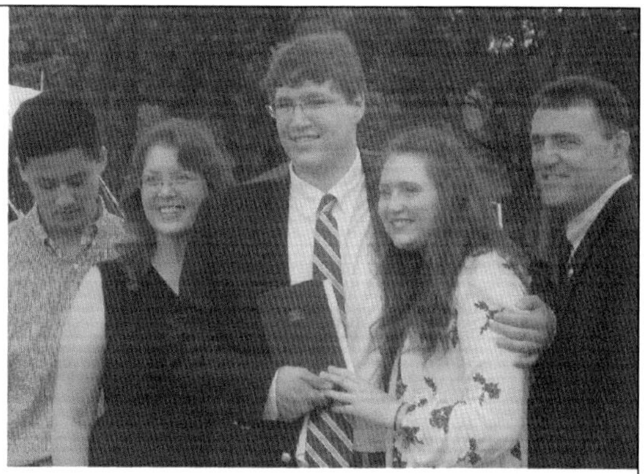

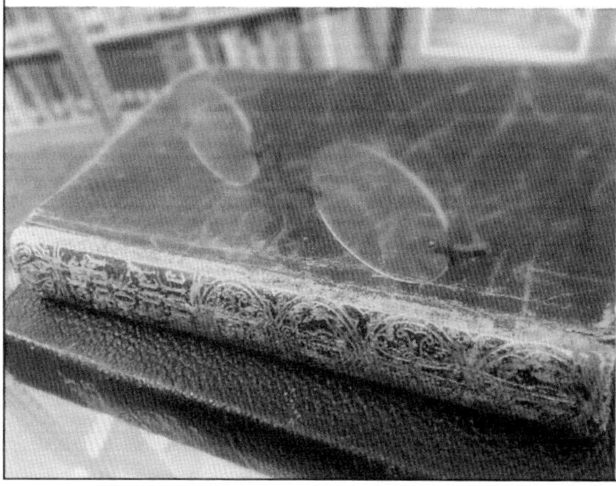

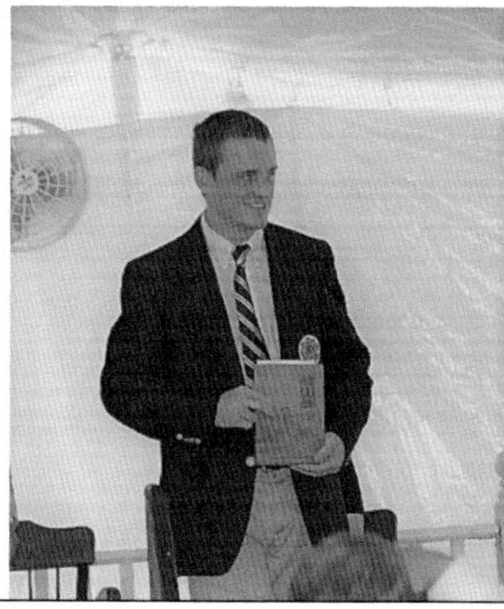

GRADUATION BIBLES AND HOLY BOOKS. Instead of a traditional diploma, Webb grants students a Bible or other religious book at commencement. Pictured clockwise from upper left are students receiving a Quran, a Bible, and a Buddhist holy book. At lower left is Jac Chambliss's Bible from 1927 on display in the library.

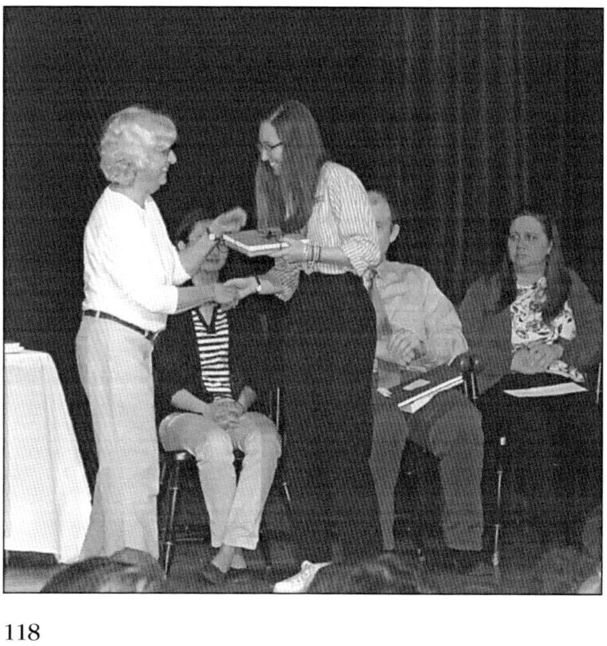

BOOK AWARDS. Instead of trophies and certificates for the highest average, students receive books carefully chosen by their teachers as awards. Long-serving mathematics faculty member Sandra Truitt is presenting an award to Siree McRady (class of 2018), one of her second-generation students.

Residential Village. Webb School broke ground on the Residential Village on November 7, 2014. This project consisted of two dorms and a student center. It was completed and dedicated in 2016.

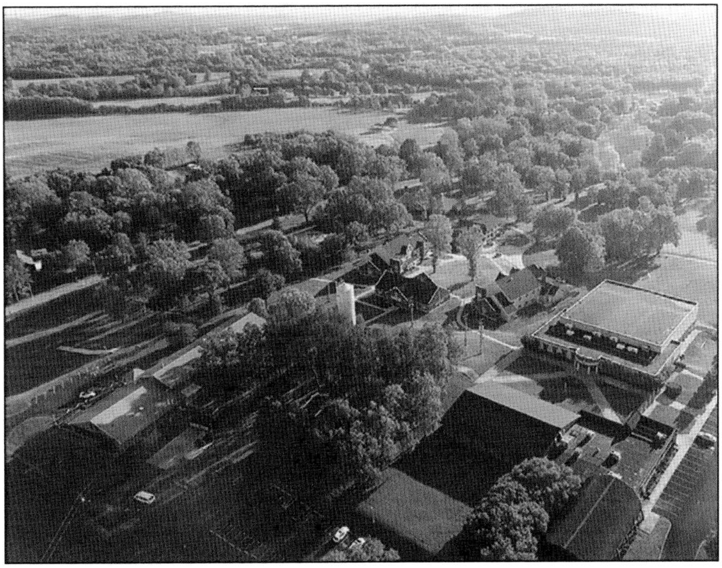

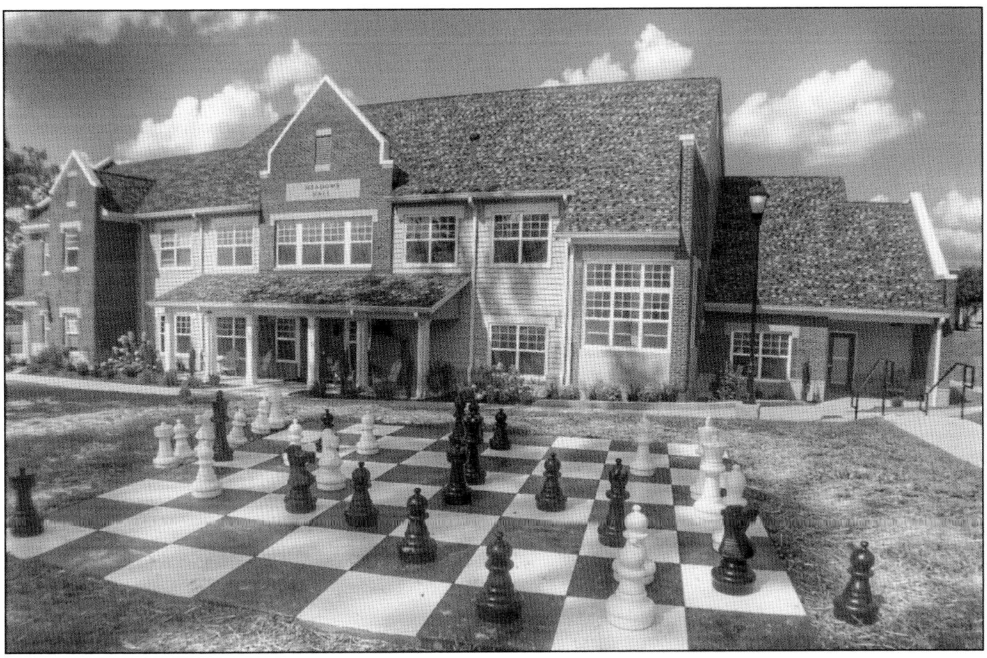

Meadows Hall. Meadows Hall is one of the dorms in the Residential Village. This dormitory received its name from the foundation of James R. Meadows Jr., a 1952 Webb School graduate and a former board of trustees chair. He played an active role in contributing to The Webb School and its growth and expansion. Haynes Hall is the second dorm in the Residential Village. This dormitory is named in memory of Wendel Haynes, a 1968 Webb School graduate.

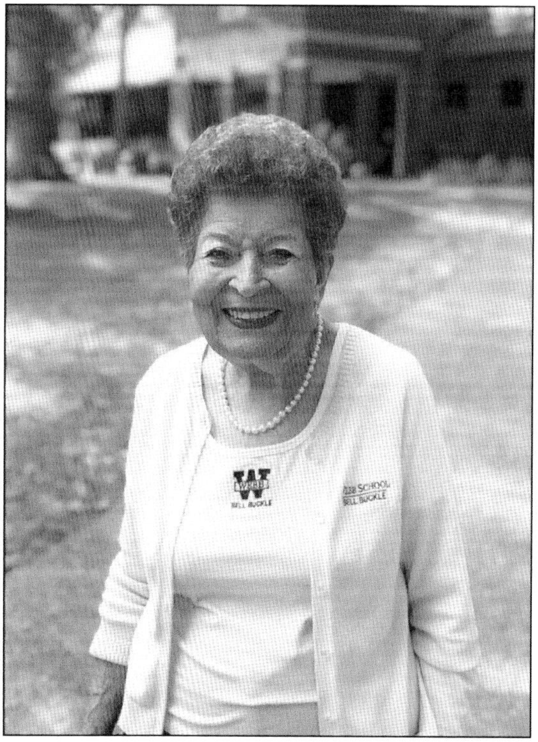

Dorothy Powell Elkins Student Center. As part of the Residential Village, a new student center was built. It was named in honor of Dorothy Powell Elkins, who has worked for the school for over 60 years and continues to do so today. Its dedication ceremony took place on April 29, 2016.

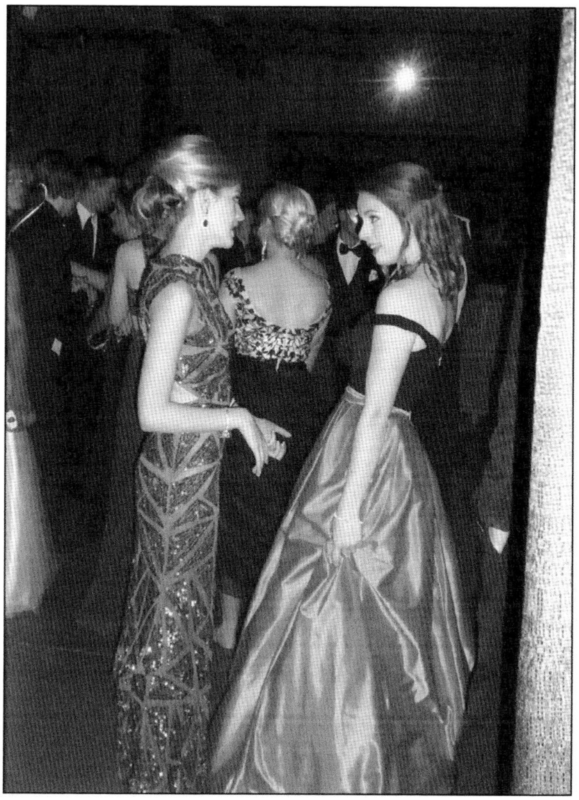

Prom Pictures. Webb juniors and seniors enjoy a night off campus at the junior-senior promenade. Each spring, the event features seniors in a presentation at the beginning of the dance. Hannah Reavis and Kennady Peak are chatting at the 2016 prom in Murfreesboro.

Diversity Week, 2018. Diversity Week is a new iteration of Diversity Day. Food, fashion, culture, and talent are on display for a whole week instead of just one day. The first year for Diversity week was 2018. This event is primarily student-led. At right, students line up in traditional clothing from Thailand, Iran, and Lithuania for the fashion show. Below, student Kojo Kufour hosts a booth displaying cultural items that help to educate fellow students about his country, Ghana.

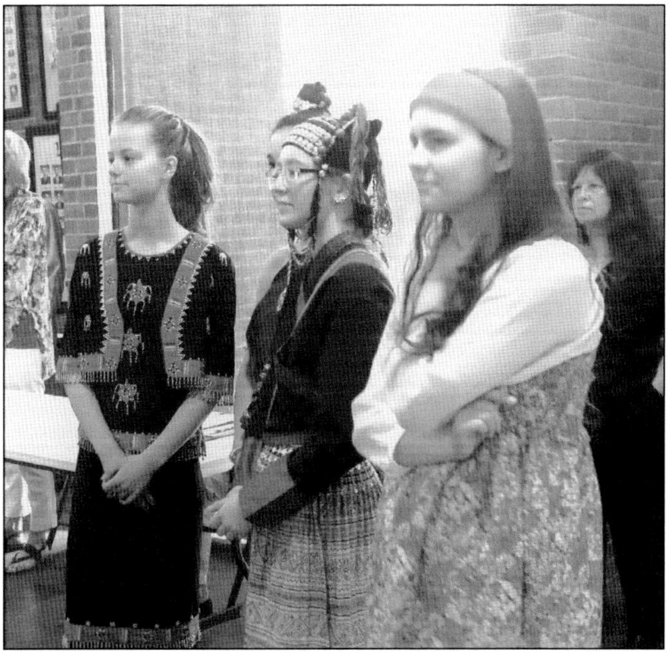

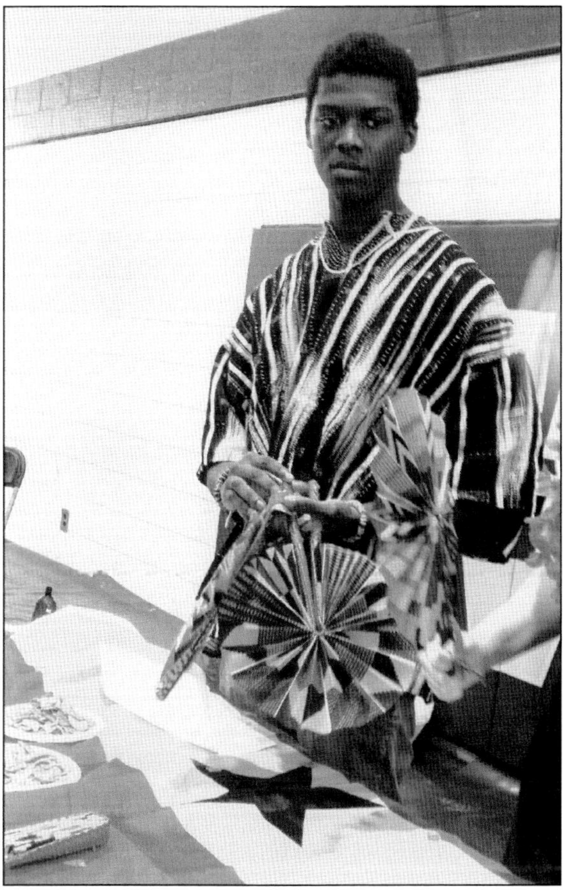

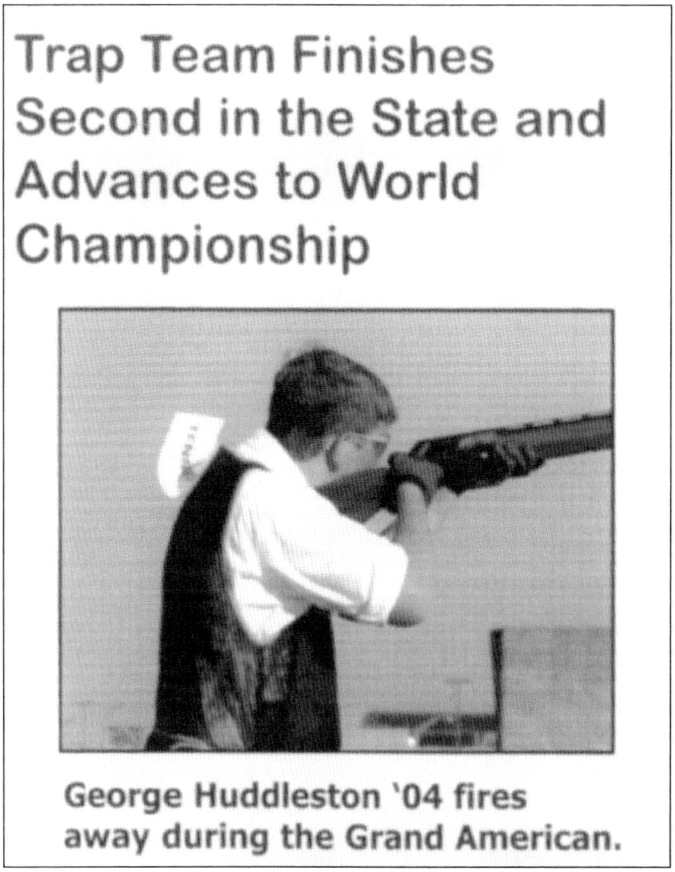

Trap Team Finishes Second in the State and Advances to World Championship

George Huddleston '04 fires away during the Grand American.

Trap and Skeet, 2004. A new trap field was opened on Webb's campus in 2003. In the 2003–2004 school year, Webb's team shot a school record, placing them in the senior experienced division of the Scholastic Clay Target Program state trap shooting championship. This second-place award advanced them to the Grand American World Trapshooting Championship in Vandalia, Ohio. Pictured here is George Huddleston, a 2004 Webb graduate, competing at the Grand American Championship.

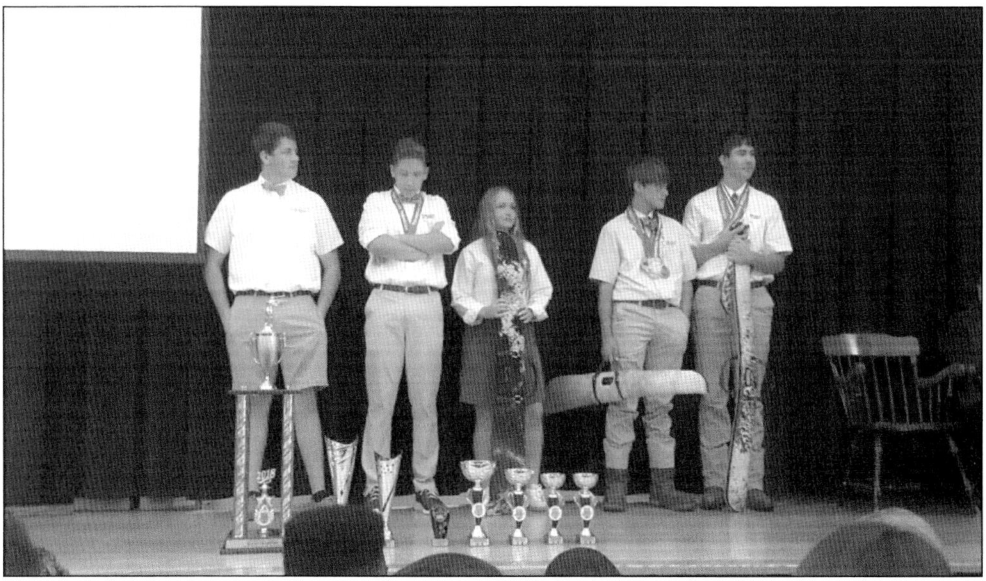

Trap and Skeet, 2018. The 2018 state sporting clay and skeet teams walked away with big awards. These include Jonathan Savage earning second overall in Junior Level 3 World Skeet at the Junior World Skeet Championships.

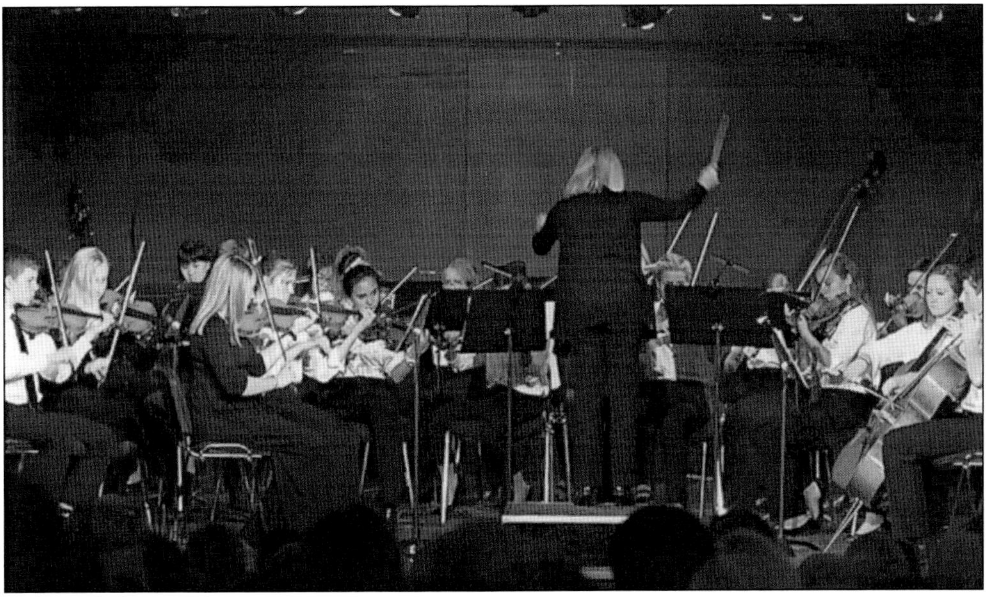

STRINGS. The Webb School's string instrumental program was established in 2008 under the direction of Susan Mullen. There are three levels of classes: beginner, intermediate, and advanced. There is also a string orchestra ensemble. Members of the string program have several concerts each year and also perform at Webb's annual Lessons and Carols service and Webb's commencement exercises.

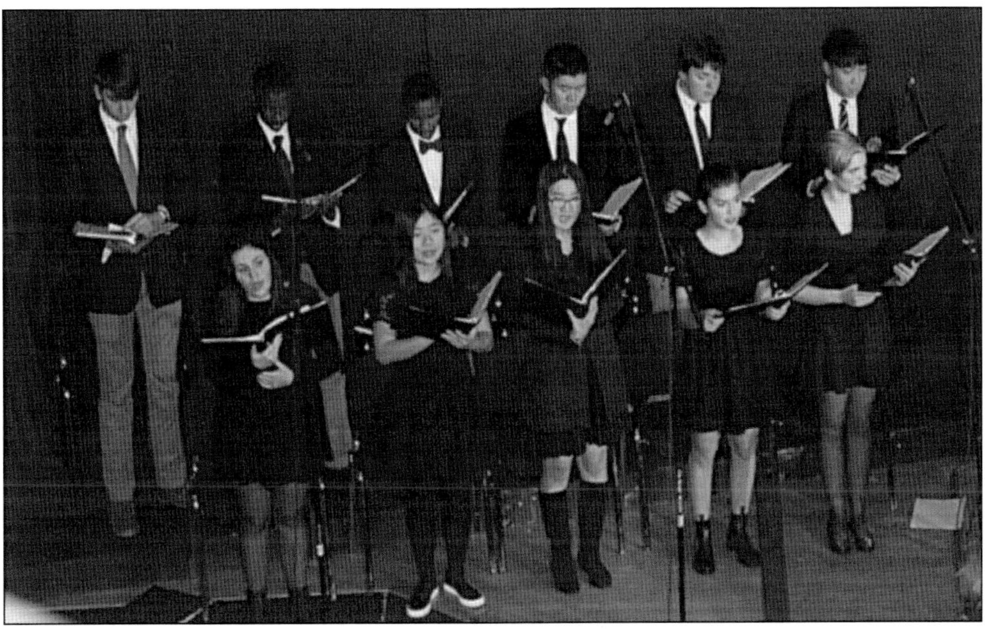

LESSONS AND CAROLS. A service held each year near Christmastime, Lessons and Carols has been a part of Webb for many years. It consists of performances by The Webb School Choir and String Orchestra, in addition to the traditional reading of several Bible passages by select members of the Webb faculty and student body. The Lessons and Carols production is based on the 1880 service first designed by Archbishop E.W. Benson for use on Christmas Eve in the cathedral at Truro, England.

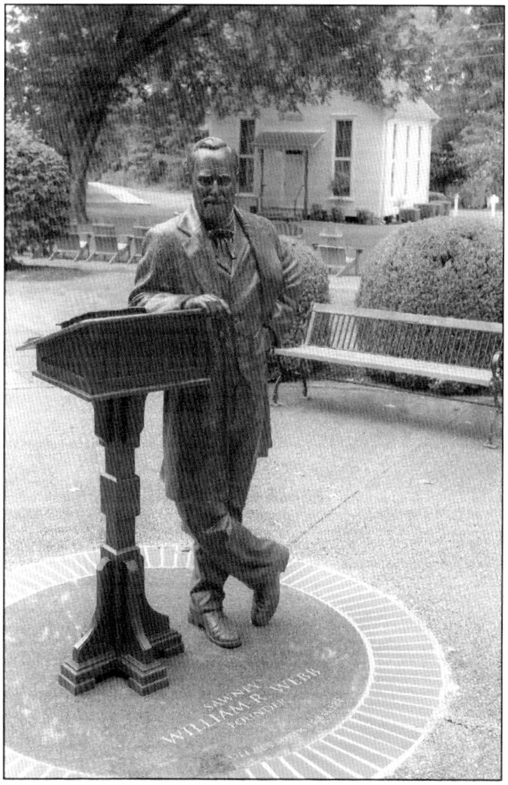

Sawney Sculpture. A sculpture of Sawney was placed in the center of the Laura Woosley Poston Plaza in February 2017 and dedicated in April. The generosity of David and Claudia Hazelwood helped provide Webb with this sculpture. It was given in honor of their daughter, Whitney Hazelwood Brough, a 1999 Webb graduate. The sculpture was created by Russ Faxon of Bell Buckle, who is also a former Webb artist-in-residence. The sculpture shows Sawney standing at his lectern with his Bible.

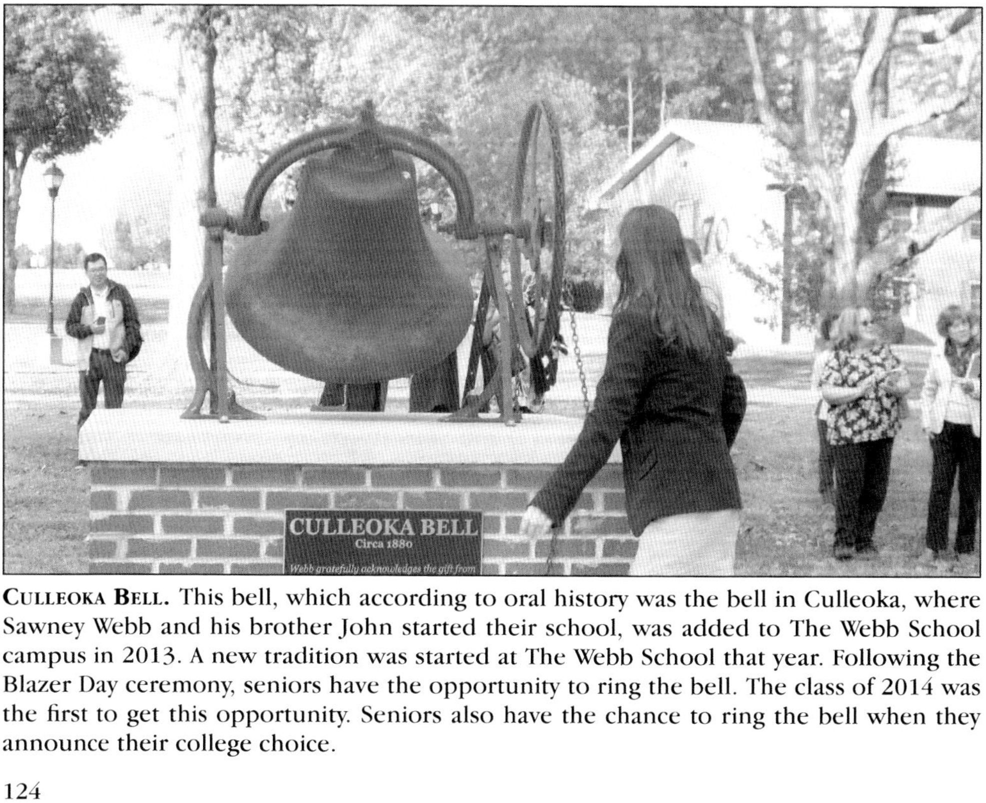

Culleoka Bell. This bell, which according to oral history was the bell in Culleoka, where Sawney Webb and his brother John started their school, was added to The Webb School campus in 2013. A new tradition was started at The Webb School that year. Following the Blazer Day ceremony, seniors have the opportunity to ring the bell. The class of 2014 was the first to get this opportunity. Seniors also have the chance to ring the bell when they announce their college choice.

World War I Centennial Anniversary. Webb has many archival treasures, but in the past year, these pieces of history have captured the attention and renewed interest of history teacher L.R. Smith. Smith learned of the slide collection in about 1978 from the late Lane Abernathy, former alumni and development director. Through the years, Smith would set up a projector and show slides during the study of World War I in his classes. He dressed in period attire and took Son Will's "Four-Minute Man" script, slideshow, and the balopticon to the annual Tennessee Parks Service Living History Weekend at the Sgt. Alvin York State Park in Fentress County for the centennial anniversary of World War I.

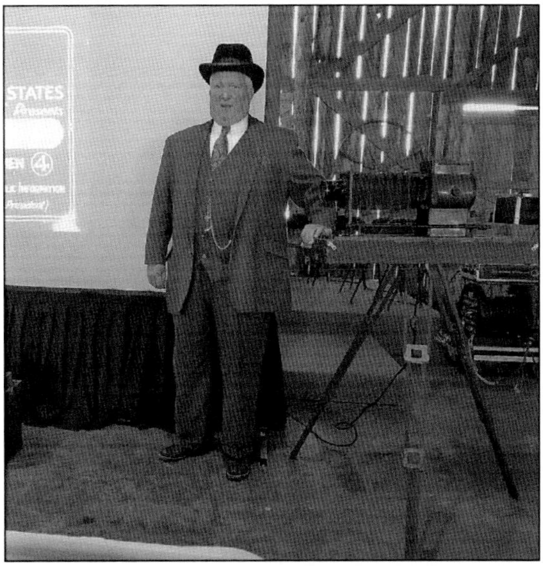

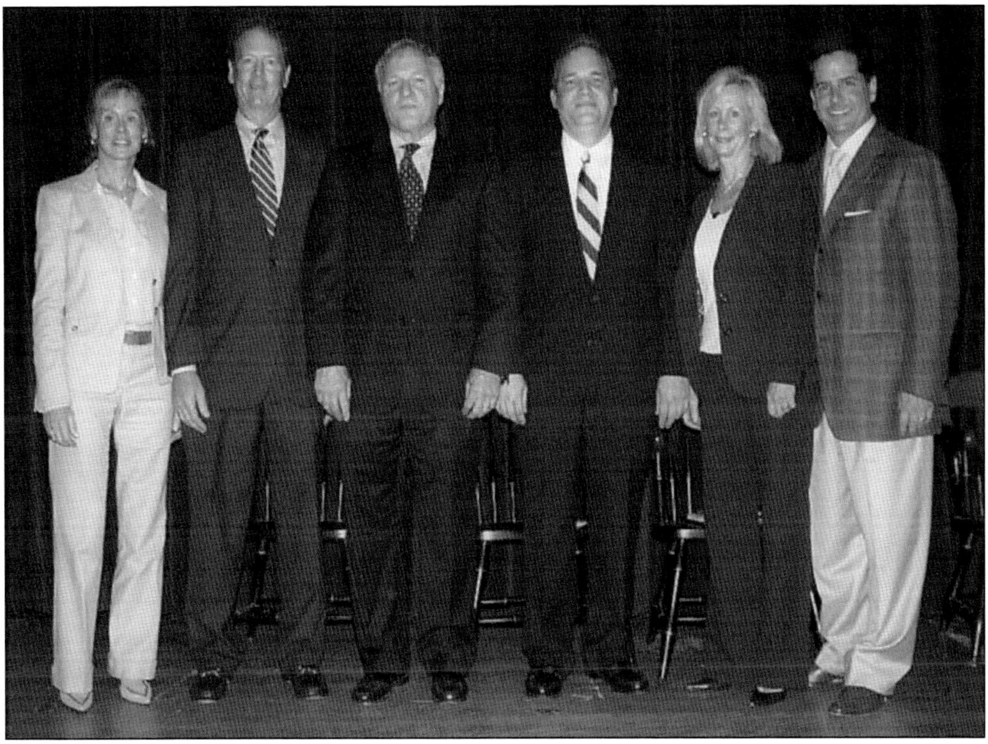

Chair of English. The Follin Chair was created to honor the late G. Webb Follin Jr. for a lifetime of service to the school and his contributions to further education in Tennessee. The proceeds from this permanent endowment are used to fund in perpetuity a member of the faculty chosen by the administration to lead teaching and research in this discipline. Ron Smith, an English teacher at The Webb School, was presented the G. Webb Follin Jr. Chair of English. "This is a special day in the rich history of The Webb School," said Ray Broadhead, head of school. "It is a day when we thank a family for working with The Webb School to honor a beloved family member and a Webb faculty member at the same time."

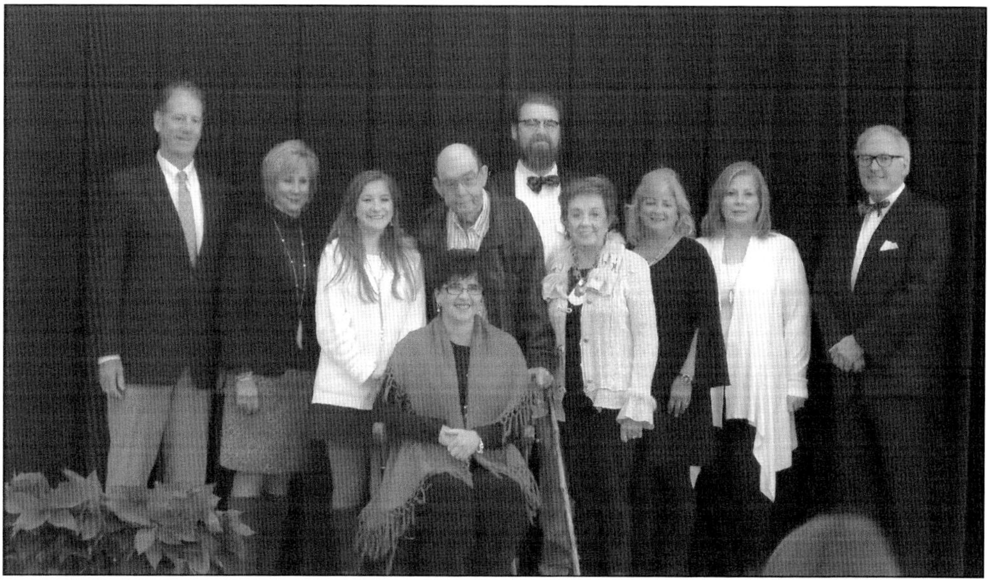

Second Chair of English. Jacquelyn Boyanton, English department chair, was presented the G. Webb Follin Jr. Chair of English. She was named English chair after the first chair, Ron Smith, retired. In making the presentation to Boyanton, Broadhead noted that she has served primarily as a middle school English teacher, where she has a unique skill set to teach the sixth grade: "Teaching sixth grade involves a remarkable blend of instruction, discipline, humor, and a strong love for students which allows the students to move forward, often without them really knowing it. Mrs. Boyanton has that gift." He added that as chair of the English department, she has helped the department create a vertical curriculum that makes sense for students from grades six through twelve.

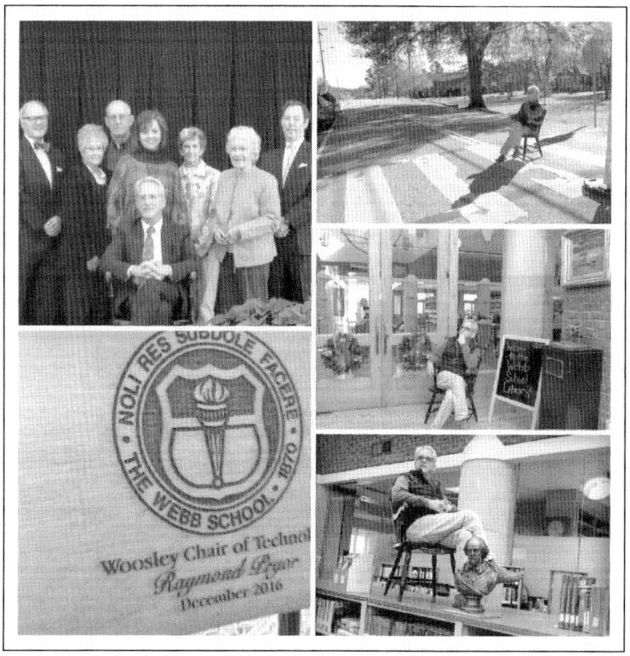

Chair of Science and Technology. Raymond Pryor was presented the W. Bryant Woosley Sr. Chair of Technology. Bryant Woosley Sr., class of 1922, and wife Lula Woosley's philanthropy established the W.B. Woosley Sr. Chair of Private Enterprise in 1984 as the first of Webb's academic chairs. The name and focus were changed in 1996 to technology. The intent was to advance the school's ability to use technology for educational as well as administrative purposes, keep hardware and software current, train teachers and staff, and partially fund the technology coordinator position.

Chair of Foreign Languages. The Webb School recently honored faculty member Moira Judas Smith with the Wilson "Woody" Sims Sr. Endowed Chair in Foreign Language in the spring of 2017. Members of the Sims and Smith families and other guests joined Webb faculty, staff, and students at the presentation. Sadly, Madame Smith passed in the fall of 2018. "Endowed chairs are living, perpetual symbols to honor great teachers—teachers who have served their students well, and who live and share the values of the school. This is now the third endowed chair for The Webb School faculty," said Head of School Ray Broadhead.

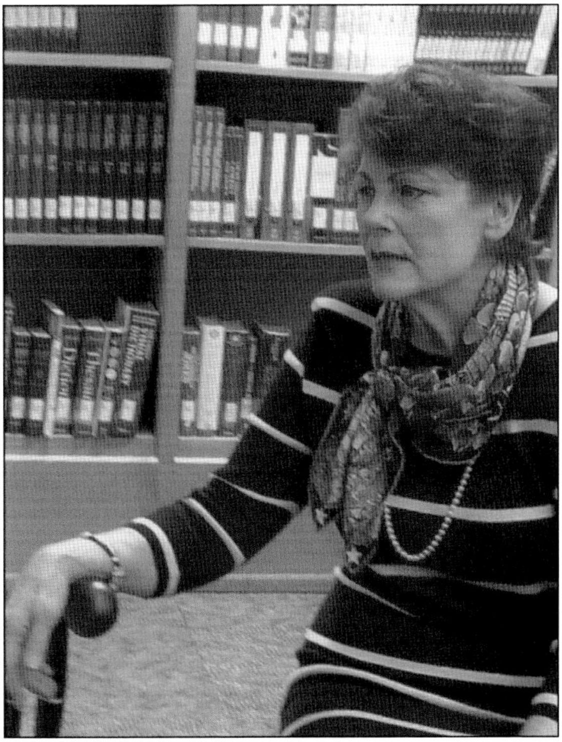

Bibliography and Further Reading

Barkley, Terry. *The Gentle Scholar: the Forgotten Story of John M. Webb and The Webb School in Bell Buckle, Tennessee.* Dickson, TN: BrayBree Publishing, 2015.

www.bellbuckleumc.org

chroniclingamerica.loc.gov

www.findagrave.com

Maury County Historical Society and Colleen Farrell. "Webb School: The Early Years in Maury County." *Historic Maury*, XXXVII, no. 4, Dec. 2001, pp. 136–145.

McMillin, Laurence. *The Schoolmaker: Sawney Webb and the Bell Buckle Story*. Chapel Hill, NC: University of North Carolina Press, 1971.

Neely, Jack. *A Splendid Instinct: Robert Webb and the Founding of The Webb School of Knoxville*. Oak Ridge, TN: Tellico Books, 2006.

Rice, John Andrew. *I Came Out of the Eighteenth Century*. Chapel Hill, NC: University of South Carolina Press, 1946.

Webb, Thompson, et al. *Thompson Webb: The Years At Webb School 1922–1975*. Self published, 2005.

Webb, W.R. "The Private High School." *Southern Association of Colleges and Schools, Journal of Proceedings and Addresses of the Sixteenth Annual Meeting Held Jointly With The Association of Colleges and Preparatory Schools of the Southern States*, 1905, pp. 121–124.